PRAISE FOR *COACH OF A LIFETIME*

"Lewis Cook is a legend. Coaching for nearly five decades, it's not just about the championships and wins but about impacting the lives of the young men and women he's in contact with. His calm demeanor and strong desire for success has been a great model for those around him to follow. A lifetime committed to developing others is what legends are made of."

—Brian Kelly, head football coach at Louisiana State University; former head coach at Notre Dame University (2010–2021), the winningest coach in the school's history

"Winning in football is about executing the game plan better than your opponent. As the stories in this book attest, Coach Cook not only provides his players with game plans to win football games but also to win at life."

—Jake Delhomme, all-time leading passer at the University of Louisiana at Lafayette; former NFL quarterback, leading the Carolina Panthers to their first Super Bowl

"This book is a must read about a man who on and off the field is the epitome of what everyone in the coaching business should strive to be. I coached 16 years at the college level and 28 years in the NFL and if Louie Cook had chosen to be a college or pro head coach, he would've been one of the best. Coach Cook is very special."

—David Culley, head coach of the Houston Texans (2021) and NFL assistant for the previous 27 years

"In my 72-year career, I've known a lot of famous football coaches. Fans measure their achievements in games won and salaries earned. Victories make reputations. Salaries get you noticed. But what makes you a coach? More than most people will ever know, it's teaching values as well as football—life skills after the scoreboard hits the final triple zeroes . . . understanding that for these kids, football will be over, but life is just beginning. I'd never heard of Lewis Cook before but now, thanks to Gaylon White's book, I won't forget him."

—Jerry Izenberg, renowned sports journalist and author who began his career at the *Newark Star-Ledger* in 1951

"I've spent a lifetime covering great coaches. In his 50 years of coaching no one has accomplished as much as Louisiana high school legend Louie Cook on the football field, in the molding of young men and the bringing together of a community in the quest to attain life's ultimate goal. Noted one longtime opposing coach: 'Louie has a lot of Jesus in him—loving, forgiving, humility, compassion, gentleness, self-control, patience, obedience, honesty and prayerful.' I will add one other, humor. None of us can go back to high school but in reading Gaylon White's masterful *Coach of a Lifetime* we can all take a knee after practice and be gifted the wise and inspirational words of Coach Louie Cook regarding faith, family, and football."

—**Kevin Kernan, sports journalist for 44 years,
the last 23 with the *New York Post***

"Guarrr-rhannn-teee you'll be cheering for Louie after reading this book."
—**Stuart Warner, Pulitzer-winning writer and editor**

"All of the awards and high praise Coach Cook has received mean nothing to the hundreds of people like me that he helped and guided. The lives we went on to live, on or off the football field, were directly related to what he did for us. He changed our lives because he coached and changed futures. That's the true measure of greatness. This book, *Coach of a Lifetime*, is a testament to that greatness."

—**Shane Garrett, outstanding receiver–running back
at Crowley High School who went on to play at Texas A&M
and for the Cincinnati Bengals in the NFL**

"Coach Cook is more than a great football coach. He's a friend and mentor."

—**Brandon Stokley, all-time University of Louisiana at Lafayette
leader in passes caught, receiving yardage, and touchdowns
who played 15 seasons in the NFL**

"An engaging and worthy read, *Coach of a Lifetime* is teeming with rich examples from Coach Louie Cook's illustrious career that can help any leader motivate and inspire others to excel and to win."

—**Myles Martel, PhD, personal debate advisor
(coach) to Ronald Reagan**

Coach of a Lifetime

The Story of Lewis Cook Jr., Legendary High School Football Coach

Gaylon H. White

Foreword by Nick Saban

ROWMAN & LITTLEFIELD
Lanham • Boulder • New York • London

Published by Rowman & Littlefield
An imprint of The Rowman & Littlefield Publishing Group, Inc.
4501 Forbes Boulevard, Suite 200, Lanham, Maryland 20706
www.rowman.com

86-90 Paul Street, London EC2A 4NE, United Kingdom

British Library Cataloguing in Publication Information Available

Library of Congress Cataloging-in-Publication Data

Names: White, Gaylon H., 1946– author.
Title: Coach of a lifetime : the story of Lewis Cook Jr., legendary high
  school football coach / Gaylon H. White ; foreword by Nick Saban.
Description: Lanham, Maryland : Rowman & Littlefield Publishing Group,
  [2023] | Includes bibliographical references and index. | Summary: "The
  inspirational true story of a high school football coach who motivates
  and encourages ordinary kids from a handful of farming communities to do
  extraordinary things on the football field and in life"— Provided by
  publisher.
Identifiers: LCCN 2023001437 (print) | LCCN 2023001438 (ebook) | ISBN
  9781538181010 (cloth) | ISBN 9781538181027 (epub)
Subjects: LCSH: Cook, Lewis, Jr. | Football coaches—Louisiana—Biography.
Classification: LCC GV939.C647 W55 2023 (print) | LCC GV939.C647 (ebook)
  | DDC 796.332092 [B]—dc23/eng/20230207
LC record available at https://lccn.loc.gov/2023001437
LC ebook record available at https://lccn.loc.gov/2023001438

To my wife, Mary; Lewis and Faye Cook; and all the athletes Coach Cook taught life lessons at the University of Southwestern Louisiana and the high schools of Rayne, Crowley, and Notre Dame in Acadia Parish, Louisiana.

Contents

Foreword

Nick Saban

You would be hard-pressed to find anyone who doesn't think the world of Coach Louie Cook. He's a great teacher who has been producing outstanding football teams and student athletes in Louisiana for decades.

All the things that we do at the University of Alabama, Louie does on a smaller scale at Notre Dame High School in Acadia Parish, Louisiana. He does his film study and game planning just like we do. His teams are always well prepared. They will run through a brick wall for him because they know how hard he's working for them. He genuinely cares about his players, and they trust him implicitly. Together they are a model of consistency and a dominant force in Louisiana high school football.

From the players, coaches, and trainers to the parents, alumni, and fans, Louie has everyone associated with Notre Dame working toward the same goal. Before every game, for example, the mothers of the players, called the Pio Moms, prepare and serve a pregame meal for the team. True to the tradition of the area, folks come together every spring for a crawfish boil that raises funds for the program. Keeping everybody focused and moving in the right direction is very difficult, so when you see it, you know a wonderful job of coaching is being done.

On and off the field, Louie is everything a football coach should aspire to be. He has a heart of gold, and he oozes with honesty, integrity, and empathy. He believes in doing the right thing and strives to get others to do the same.

When it comes to coaching philosophy, Louie and I are both old-fashioned in that we believe games are won with blocking, tackling, and execution. There are plenty of gurus out there now that think their latest spread and run-pass option offenses are the key to success, but Louie and I haven't jumped on that bandwagon.

Louie has never thought twice about reaching out to help others, so I'm delighted to be part of this book, *Coach of a Lifetime*, which shares his experiences as a high school and college coach. Hopefully, it will inspire more people to follow in his footsteps.

ABOUT NICK SABAN

Nick Saban needs no introduction, but for those who have been on another planet, he's widely considered the greatest coach in college football history with seven national championships, one at LSU and six at Alabama. Saban recruited and coached Louie Cook's, son, Jeff during the 2002 season at LSU.

Preface

Lightning could be seen and heard all around the football stadium.

Lewis Cook Jr. was standing on the sidelines waiting for his high school team, the Notre Dame Pioneers (Pios), to play their first game of the 2021 season.

Cook was seventy years old and beginning his forty-eighth year in the coaching business, twenty-fifth as the head coach at the tiny Catholic school in Crowley, Louisiana. He had been praying for God to send him a sign when it was time to retire.

The COVID pandemic marred the previous season, and the senseless killing of a talented player, Garrison Gautreaux, cast a pall over the school and forced the last week of spring practice to be canceled. When longtime secretary Karen Berken and offensive line coach Todd Gray retired at the end of the 2020–2021 school year, Cook pleaded, "All right, I've got enough signs. Stop!"

But the signs kept coming.

The Saturday before the Pios' season opener against Southside High School at Teurlings Field in nearby Lafayette, he was in his Notre Dame office considering options for the game if Hurricane Ida lived up to its Category 4 rating and wreaked havoc on the area. Three million people were in Ida's path.

"The most powerful storm in 160 years," warned Governor John Bell Edwards. "Where you go to sleep tonight is where you ride out the storm."

The shelves in area grocery stores were bare, prompting one television reporter to observe, "It's easier to make a sandbag than a sandwich."

The small TV in Cook's office was tuned to the Weather Channel.

"When Jim Cantore shows up, get out," Cook said.

Cantore soon appeared on the TV screen, standing in New Orleans's French Quarter. Heavy rain pelted the batting helmet he was wearing, and gusty winds threatened to knock him down. "Hang in there guys!" he urged viewers.

Cook echoed that message to Jimmy McCleary, the team's defensive coordinator, called Jimmy Mac: "Hang tight. Got to ride another one out."

"If it doesn't have anything to do with first-and-ten, I don't want to hear about it," Mac said.

School closings for the next week were already being announced.

"Everything nowadays is so knee-jerk and overly cautious," Mac bemoaned.

"I tell you what, they wear you out," Cook said of the hurricanes he and Jimmy Mac had to weather during their time together at Notre Dame. He rattled off Lili in 2002, Rita in 2005, Gustav in 2008, Isaac in 2012, and Harvey in 2017. Rita wiped out two contests and the others a game each.

Cook answered a phone call from another coach, Curt Ware.

"Brim!" Ware began.

"What's going on, Brim?" Cook replied.

"Sweating the storm, Brim, sweating the storm. What do you think?"

"I'm thinking we're going to get at least sixty- to sixty-five-miles-per-hour winds."

"I'll bet we have no electricity for a little while," Ware said.

"Don't look good, Brim."

Brim is a term of endearment Cook and many people around him call each other. He's the head Brimster.

"Everything is up in the air," Cook informed his coaches as they reviewed plans for the Southside game Thursday night. Depending on Ida's path, the game could be pushed back one or two days or even canceled. They would know Sunday afternoon when the storm made landfall south of New Orleans.

Ida cut a deadly swath through Louisiana with sustained winds of 150 miles per hour but missed Acadia Parish where Crowley is located. The Southside game would be played but only after the kickoff was delayed two hours by the threat of lightning.

As his players took shelter, Cook stayed on the sidelines, talking with his friend and mentor, Larry Dauterive, who coached forty-five years, his high school teams posting a record of 238–75–1. He came to watch his former student coach.

This reminded Cook of an assistant coach who requested extra tickets for his family. "They're coming to watch me coach," he explained.

"What do you do during the game?" Cook asked.

"I just stand there," the assistant said.

"Maybe they'll watch the game," Cook suggested.

Dauterive came to watch his protégé coach the Pios.

"When you play Notre Dame, you'd better hold onto your jock because you're going to get rocked," Dauterive said. "Louie's the best that's doing it right now in this state. He's the connector. He's at home with a Black kid and family as well as a prosperous white family, a crawfish farmer, or someone that works in the plants."

Dauterive was on a roll: "You can't fool kids anymore. They know if you know your shit and you care about 'em. That's the big thing. If they know you care about them, they're going to play for you. He's won state championships at two different schools in the same town. He's phenomenal."

Cook was still in college when Dauterive took him under his wing.

"He values me as one of his mentors, but the student has way passed the mentor," Dauterive said. "The biggest compliment is this: Who would you want your child to play for? Who would you want to tutor him? Who would you want to be his mentor? Who would you want to process him from childhood to adulthood? It would be Louie Cook. He's everything you'd want. I would've loved to have somebody like him to mentor me when I was coming up."

At one point Cook walked off by himself, looked up at the sky, and could be heard emulating what God was saying to him: "You were look-ing for signs? I sent COVID and you still hung in there. I retired Karen and Gray. That should've told you something. Now, I throw a lightning storm at you. It's nine o'clock on a Thursday night and your ass is still coaching. Do I need to hit you with one of those lightning bolts? It's time to go home, Dawg!"

He walked back to the sideline benches.

"Can you imagine Gray being here tonight?" trainer Jim Dorotics asked.

Not only could Cook envision what the colorful and outspoken Gray might be doing, but he also had a good idea of what he'd say. "Ahhh, he'd be under that bench beatin' and kickin' the ground," Cook said, laughing. "I can hear Gray: 'Brim, they're doin' that shit on purpose.'"

"The Ghost of Gray," Cook added. "His ghost will never leave."

Cook thought about retiring after the COVID pandemic shut down the school in the spring of 2020 and made it difficult for the players to do their summer workouts. "I was worried about the kids," he said. "They couldn't go into the locker room, and we had to stagger them in the weight room. They even had to bring their own water. By the end of the summer, I was all worn out. We didn't even know if we'd have a season."

The Pios played their first game in October, a month later than usual.

Preface

Karen was going to stay with Cook until he retired but he persuaded her to remain through the 2020 season, and then go. "She was running everything," he said.

The 2021 season came and went, but speculation continues about how much longer Cook will coach.

"Everybody is saying this and saying that," he told his coaches at the end of the season. "I don't know, so I don't know how anybody else knows. But they've been saying that for a long time. I do want to coach next year. I'd like to be back with you guys and this group coming up."

Cook coached Karen's son, David, who went on to play at Rice University and is now an orthopedic surgeon. She's hoping Cook sticks around long enough to coach her twelve-year-old grandson, Ethan Williams.

"We'll see what happens down the line," Cook said.

He's no longer praying for signs to show him the way, but he may well hear a voice from above saying, "Brim, you've always been a coach, what else you gonna do?"

AUTHOR'S NOTE

Based on a slew of newspaper articles and the preference of Coach Lewis Cook Jr. and his wife, Faye, the informal variation of Lewis is spelled *Louie* instead of *Lewie*.

Acknowledgments

I was searching for Demetra Thomas so I could get greater insight into her late husband, Orlando Sr., and the amazing relationship he had with his high school football coach, Louie Cook. She was looking online for a muscle car to give her son, Orlando Jr., on his twenty-first birthday.

Demetra spotted an ad for a 2018 Dodge Hellcat SRT and sent a text message to Robert Cook, general manager of the Sterling Automotive Group in Lafayette and Coach Cook's youngest brother: "I'm grateful for what you've done in the past and what Coach Cook did for my husband. So, if this is your dealership, I would like to purchase this vehicle. If there is another way you can think that will bless and honor Coach Cook, please let me know. Thank you!"

Demetra wound up buying the car and connecting with me.

"It wasn't so much about Orlando Jr. getting a car as it was about honoring Coach Cook," Demetra said. "It was clear to me that God wanted to pour back into Coach Cook because he was like a dad to Orlando. One of the many things I learned from caring for my husband was to honor those who paved the way."

She explained this to Robert.

"No, Demetra," he demurred, "you don't have to do that 'cause it was a mutual relationship and both parties were equally blessed."

"I get it," Demetra graciously said. "I just want to honor Coach Cook."

Orlando Sr. died in 2014 after a gallant, decade-long battle with amyotrophic lateral sclerosis (ALS)—Lou Gehrig's disease.

She was on a mission from Orlando and God, who gave her a number including the dollar amount to be gifted. "That was the exact number the car ended up costing," she said.

You can be a doubting Thomas if you want, but God also had a hand in this book.

It wasn't happenstance that Robert Cook made a loaner car available or karma that caused Tim and Christy Ledet to let me stay at their garage apartment in Rayne for nearly three months while I did interviews and attended more than half of Notre Dame's games during the 2021–2022 seasons.

It wasn't a coincidence that people donated money to help cover some of my travel expenses and committed to purchasing twelve hundred books in advance of publication. Like Demetra Thomas, they wanted to give back to Coach Cook, bless him as he has so many of them.

I'm hoping this book is as much a blessing to read as it has been to research and write. My goal is to inform and inspire coaches and others in leadership positions who can benefit from Coach Cook's wisdom.

"Winning isn't everything," he said. "Winning the right way is."

When his son, Stu, was thinking about going into coaching, he told him: "Nobody is going to know what years we won championships. They're not going to know how many games we won. But they're going to know how we made them feel."

He has advised other coaches: "Quit worrying about winning games. Just take care of the kids."

I was blessed to be around such knowledge and wisdom.

At a time when religion and traditional family values are under attack, I was blessed to see them practiced and providing comfort and strength.

I was blessed to see the love and caring in the homes I was invited to for gumbo, boiled crawfish, shrimp, boudin, bread pudding, and other Cajun delights.

I was blessed to hear many of the conversations Coach Cook has every day with his three sons, Lewis III, Jeff, and Stu. They were a wake-up call, as I don't phone my three kids enough.

Four months into the project, my family faced a major health challenge. We were blessed by frequent telephone calls from Coach Cook, showing how much he cared.

From Coach Cook and his assistant coaches to Principal Cindy Istre and Chancellor Father Brent Smith, I was treated like family at Notre Dame. Coach Cook and his wife, Faye, made me feel like a member of the Cook clan.

In interviewing 118 people ranging from current and former players to coaches and businessmen, I discovered that Coach Cook is the real deal.

Wayne Hensgens and Bryan "Buck" Leonards were visionaries in push-ing for his hiring by Notre Dame in 1997.

"He's a leader," said Ron Prejean, a lifelong pal. "He'll never be a saint. He'll never be canonized in the Church, but he has the respect of many more people than any priest I know."

That, of course, is for a higher authority to judge.

All I know is that another legendary coach, Nick Saban, once wrote in a letter to Louie, "You're one in a million."

While I'm counting my blessings, I want to thank Fritz Welter for shar-ing the transcript from his 2018 interview with Saban that is the basis for the foreword Fritz got the seven-time National Coach of the Year to approve the week after LSU upset Alabama, 32–31, in 2022. Both Welter and Coach Saban deserve a standing ovation.

Three cheers for the contributions of photographers Christell and Jason Faul, Brad Kemp, J. C. Orillion, Dwayne Petry, and Rory White, as well as artists Glen Hunter Jr. and Sydnei Smith-Jordan. Rory snapped the shot of Coach Cook on the front cover as well as the *Coach of a Lifetime* statuette on the back. He reviewed all of the photos to ensure they're as dynamic as possible.

I've known Stuart Warner since he was a columnist and Pulitzer-winning editor for the *Akron Beacon-Journal* in the 1980s. He now has a consultancy called Mr. Write Coach, so I had him pore over the manu-script and make it better. He's done just that.

Leann DeBord, my loyal assistant in all six books I've written for Row-man & Littlefield, proofread the manuscript, prepared the index, and pro-vided a valued second opinion on text, photos, and marketing matters.

Rob Kennedy, a fellow free spirit in our younger days trying to survive in the corporate jungle, read each chapter as I churned them out and kept me going with his humor and enthusiasm.

Albert John, who videotapes all of Notre Dame's games, introduced me to late-night breakfasts at the Waffle House and showed me the proper way to eat four eggs sunny-side up and a double order of hash browns. It was a sight to see.

My wife, Mary, encouraged and supported me throughout this journey that started in July 2021 and had me commuting sixteen hundred miles round trip from my home in Kingsport, Tennessee.

Christen Karniski, acquisitions editor, told me up front that Rowman & Littlefield had never published a book on a high school football coach. Not only was her candor appreciated, but it also inspired me and Coach Cook to do something nobody has done before.

Coach Cook gave me total access to his team and complete editorial freedom to interview whom I wanted and write what I thought best. I wish all of his players could be listed in the book but that's not plausible for space reasons.

After Notre Dame's last regular-season game in 2022, I got a text message from Demetra Thomas that read in part: "I definitely want you to know that I am eternally grateful for meeting you. I'm eternally grateful for all your work that you have [been] placed here on earth [to do] and all the lives that you've celebrated and honored, including my late husband. . . . I have been truly blessed and feel privileged to have spent time and broken bread with you."

I'm grateful to Demetra and everybody else who made *Coach of a Lifetime* possible. God bless all of you.

A NOTE OF GRATITUDE

Thanks to the following people for their willingness to be interviewed for this book. Not all of them are quoted but their comments were just as valuable.

Cook Family: Cathy Cook Hundley, Cecile Cook Mouton, Dave Cook, Faye Cook, Jeff Cook, Josette Cook Surratt, Lewis Cook III, Robert Cook, and Stu Cook.

Crowley High School Players: Greyson Augustus, Joe Domingeaux, Shane Garrett, Rev. Sherard Joseph, Steven Lengefeld, Walter Sampson, Joel Sinclair, Dammon Stutes, and Marcus Wilridge.

Notre Dame High School Players: Dr. Lane Anzalone, Adam Berken, Dr. David Berken, Matt Bernard, Luke Bertrand, Gavin Bourgeois, Hayden Bourgeois, Luke Bourgeois, Michael Bourgeois, Noah Bourgeois, Waylon Bourgeois, Jake Brouillette, Karson Broussard, Jackie Casanova, Johnny Casanova, Tommy Casanova, Kade Comeaux, Grady Faulk, Michaël Goss Jr., Brother John Paul (Will Fruge), Bobby Hanks, Johann Hensgens, Luke Hoffpauir, Nick Hundley Jr., Nick Hundley Sr., Steve Hundley, Glenn Hunter Jr., Zach Lamm, Hudson LeBlanc, Al Leonards, Bryan "Buck" Leonards, Ryan Leonards, Thomas Meche, Jeremy Prevost, Father Andrew Schumacher, Tyler Shelvin, Mitch Shoffiett, Lucas Simon, Wesley Simon, Alex Stevens, Hunter Stover, Nicholas Swacker, Father Nick Ware, Carson Watson, Marshall Watson, and D. J. Welter.

USL Players and Coaches: Gerald Broussard, Jake Delhomme, Mike Doherty, Troy Gisclair, Greg Hobbs, Kenny Lee, Dwight Prudhomme, Lee Rodgers, Elton Slater, Brandon Stokley, Rennick Tuck, Clarence Verdin, and Donnie Wallace.

Crowley High Coaches: Donald Adams and Bob Czarnecki.

Notre Dame High Coaches and Trainer: Dustin Albaugh, Ben Boulet, Chad Broussard, Gus Cormier, Duke Daigle (basketball), Jim Dorotics (trainer), Todd Gray (retired), Wes Jacob, Kevin Magee (also coached at Crowley), Jimmy McCleary, Jake Molbert, and Chris Stevens.

Rayne High Players and Coaches: Morris Godeaux, Hugh Roland Joseph Molbert, and Munro Rateau.

Other Coaches: Charles Baglio, Kyron Benoit, Kirk Crochet, Larry Dauterive, Kaine Guidry, Brent Indest, Corby Meekens, Bradley Dale Peveto, Julius Scott, Jeff Wainwright, and Curt Ware.

Other People: Mark Bartelstein, Karen Berken, Charlie Bordes, Jeff Bourgeois, Marty Bourgeois, Ted Cobena Jr., Mike Debaillon, Kevin Foote, Harold Gonzales Jr., Joe Guillory, Wayne Hensgens, Earl "Butch" John, Capt. Tony Olinger, Jimbo Petitjean, Richard Pizzolatto, Ron Prejean, Joel Rickert, Brad Roll, Rodney Savoy, Boo Schexnayder, Deborah Silas, Demetra Thomas, Dale Trahan, and Fritz Welter.

Introduction

Why write a book about a high school football coach?

I asked myself that question, as did others.

Pro and college football coaches get the most headlines and make millions of dollars, so they must be the best in the business.

What if there's a selfless high school football coach who puts his faith and family over everything else and chooses to teach and develop the raw talents of high school kids for life instead of for the college football powerhouses and the pros?

There's a coach like that—Lewis Cook Jr., the head football coach at Notre Dame High School of Acadia Parish in Crowley, Louisiana.

I knew enough about Cook to believe his amazing story would inspire and motivate others far beyond the coaching profession and the state of Louisiana, where he's a legend. But it wasn't until four months into the project that another coach, Julius Scott of the Geneva School of Boerne in Texas, nailed the answer I was looking for.

"You read about Mother Teresa of Calcutta," Scott told me. "They say that when you talked with her, she looked at you like you were the only human being in the world. That's the way Coach Cook makes me feel."

How many coaches are compared to Mother Teresa?

One day Scott was talking with Cook about how to handle different situations in a game when he said, "Louie, I think you coach like Jesus would've coached."

"I don't know about that," Cook replied, "but I'd like to know what he would've called on third-and-one the other night when we got stopped."

Humility is one of the qualities cited by Kirk Crochet, longtime head football coach at Loreauville High School in Southwest Louisiana: "Louie has a lot of Jesus in him—loving, forgiving, humility, compassion, gentleness, self-control, patience, obedience, honesty, and prayerful."

How many coaches are likened to Jesus?

In 2019, more than twelve hundred people showed up at the 13,500-seat Cajundome on the University of Louisiana at Lafayette campus to pay their last respects to Tony Robichaux, the school's highly popular baseball coach. Marveling at the size of the crowd, one sportswriter said, "The only other guy that I can think of that would have to have his funeral in a place like this is Louie Cook."

How many football coaching legends are also beloved?

You can count them on one hand, maybe two. But Coach Cook is both legendary and beloved in Louisiana. He is a father figure, the Dutch uncle you can count on for solid, benevolent advice, the guy students and their parents go to for answers when there are none that we can truly understand.

When one of his Notre Dame players, seventeen-year-old Garrison Gautreaux, was shot and killed in his parked pickup truck by two strangers in 2021, Coach Cook gathered the team in the school's chapel.

"You know how we always talk about achieving the ultimate goal of getting to heaven?" he asked. "Garrison just got there early. He's achieved his goal. When you want to doubt or wonder why this happened, offer a prayer for Garrison and his family. I want to question it, too. Our faith is being tested. Hang together. Be there for one another."

He was there for his youngest sister, Cathy Cook Hundley, the night before she had her left leg amputated above the knee. The leg was mangled in a boating accident and gangrene had developed, requiring amputation. Cathy was fifteen at the time.

On learning she was going to lose the leg, Cathy had everyone leave her hospital room except for Louie, then twenty-three. He spent the night at her side.

"You'd think I would've wanted Mama, but I wanted him with me that night," Cathy recalled. "Mama would always try to make things better by talking. I didn't want that. I just wanted a calming presence."

That was Louie demonstrating one of the Jesus-like qualities that have made him a Hall of Fame coach. He's enshrined in the Louisiana Sports Hall of Fame as well as the state's High School Coaches Hall of Fame. In 2019, the New Orleans Saints of the National Football League (NFL) honored him as the state's high school coach of the year.

At the end of the 2022 season, his thirty-ninth as a head coach, he ranked third among active Louisiana high school football coaches and in the top twenty-five nationally with 392 wins. Thirteen of his teams at

Notre Dame and nearby Crowley High made it to the state finals, Notre Dame winning the championship four times and Crowley once.

But the number of wins and state titles don't fully reflect Coach Cook's accomplishments as a coach and his impact on those around him.

"It's priceless the lives of the people he's touched and influenced with what he's done," said Bradley Dale Peveto, a former assistant coach at Louisiana State University, Ole Miss, and Kentucky. "He's got a magic and a love to him that is second to none. And he leads with love."

In 1988, Julius Scott set out to interview as many successful coaches as possible to learn about their leadership skills.

It's an impressive list of college football coaches ranging from Bobby Bowden of Florida State to Will Muschamp of Florida and South Carolina to Gene Stallings of Texas A&M, Alabama, and the St. Louis/Arizona Cardinals in the NFL.

Scott also visited such high school coaching icons as J. T. Curtis of John Curtis Christian in River Ridge, Louisiana, near New Orleans, the winningest active prep football coach in America with 615 career victories, and Bob Ladouceur, who led De La Salle High School in Concord, California, to a record-shattering 151-game winning streak.

"Coach Cook is up there at the top," Scott said. "Year after year, decade after decade, there's something that he's got that keeps folks going. And I believe that's love. There's no doubt he has a genuine love for his players, coaches, and people that surround him. That's what gets them to respond."

That "genuine love" is what makes Coach Cook so effective as a leader, Scott said.

"Love is the greatest motivating force on the face of the earth," he explained. "When you're driving your teams by either fear or rewards, they're going to get tired of both. The fear of punishment is going to fade away and the reward that you're giving them or the carrot that you're hanging out there, that's going to fade away, too."

Of the 313 students enrolled at Notre Dame during the 2022–2023 school year, 166 were boys and 117 or 70.5 percent of them were on the football team. "Get 'em out, get 'em involved," Scott said. "That's what Coach Cook is doing. He has created an environment at Notre Dame that should be emulated all over—every community and every school."

One of the coaches Scott interviewed was Gerry Faust, the Ohio high school coaching legend hired by Notre Dame University in 1980 to run its storied program. Faust resigned after posting a record of 30–26–1 in five years, causing colleges to shy away from high school coaches because of what the *Los Angeles Times* termed "The Gerry Faust Syndrome."[1]

In 2001, Cook was offered the top job at his alma mater, the University of Southwestern Louisiana (USL), now known as the University of

Louisiana at Lafayette. The previous coach was fired after losing twenty-seven of thirty-three games.

Cook already had eight years of experience as an assistant at USL and was considered the frontrunner when he withdrew his name from consideration.

"I was never convinced that I should be the head coach at USL," he said. "No matter how much money you make, it doesn't make up for that feeling on Sunday morning if you got your butt kicked Saturday night."

Cook has no regrets.

"Saban is more comfortable in college than the pros and I'm more comfortable in high school than college," he said, referring to Nick Saban, who had a 15–17 record in the NFL, sandwiched between a national championship at LSU in 2003 and six more at Alabama.

"Louie is exactly where he needs to be—in high school," said Mike Doherty, who coached with him at USL. "If you are an artist, you have a clean slate in high school. In college, you have one that's been scribbled all over. Louie likes the idea of starting kids off from the beginning and carrying them up."

High school coaches "have to play with what the Lord shines on you," according to Crochet.

Nobody does that better than Cook.

"He takes five-foot-six guys from the crawfish farms and turns them into successful football players and people," said Dale Trahan, a businessman and one of Cook's closest friends. "The process is about the kids, but it goes much further than just the kids. He affects the people all around them. He pulls people together, taking all these kids from across the parish and turning them into winners."

Cook was offensive coordinator and quarterback coach at USL in 1993 when a skinny eighteen-year-old kid named Jake Delhomme arrived on campus. Instead of redshirting Delhomme during his freshman year as planned, Cook made him the starting quarterback, and he went on to become the school's all-time leading passer and to play eleven years in the NFL, leading the Carolina Panthers to three playoff appearances and the 2004 Super Bowl.

"Louie's greatest strength is making a young kid a man and believe he's better than he could possibly be and not letting him down while he achieves that along the way," Delhomme said. "To me, that was always the definition of Louie Cook. There was never a panic in a situation. In football and in life, never get too high or too low . . . keep a level playing field. I got that from him."

Just as the best CEOs are not necessarily at the biggest companies or the most capable people at the highest levels of government, the pros and major colleges don't have all the great coaches.

"Everybody thinks NFL coaches are the smartest guys, but that's not fact and it's not true," Delhomme said. "There are a lot of great coaches in the NFL, but there are some great coaches in high school, junior high, and college, and I'm a prime example of following two great coaches who are better men—Coach Cook and Sonny Charpentier, my coach in high school."

Brandon Stokley, a wide receiver, teamed with Delhomme in 1995, Coach Cook's last year at USL, to catch 75 passes for 1,121 yards and nine touchdowns. In fifteen NFL seasons, Stokley totaled 397 receptions for 5,339 yards and thirty-nine touchdowns while earning two Super Bowl rings.

"When you can check all those boxes as a coach, you end up being Louie Cook," Stokley said. "He has this charisma, he knows what he's doing, people trust him. He would've been a great head coach in college or the NFL."

So why write a book about a high school football coach?

Kirk Crochet retired in 2009 and spent the next year at Notre Dame assisting Coach Cook.

In twenty-eight years at Loreauville, Crochet's teams won 201 games but never made it to the state finals at the Superdome in New Orleans. Notre Dame won 13 straight games in 2010 before a loss in the semifinals foiled a trip to the Dome.

"When the final horn sounded," Crochet recalled, "Louie took his headset off and walked straight up to me and said, 'I'm sorry, man, I was trying to get you one.' What a guy! Who else does that?"

As Bradley Dale Peveto put it: "When the Good Lord made the perfect coach, he made Louie Cook."

Julius Scott said: "He's everything that's right for what a human being should be, not just a coach."

David Martin, one of Coach Cook's players at Crowley High, summed it up nicely: "He's the closest thing to God with a whistle."

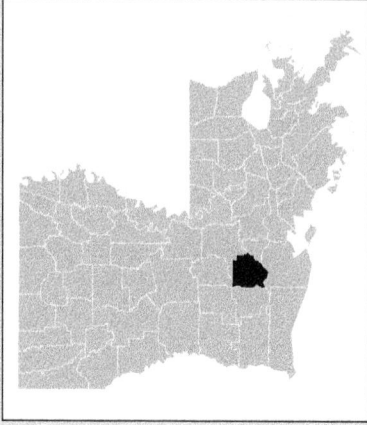

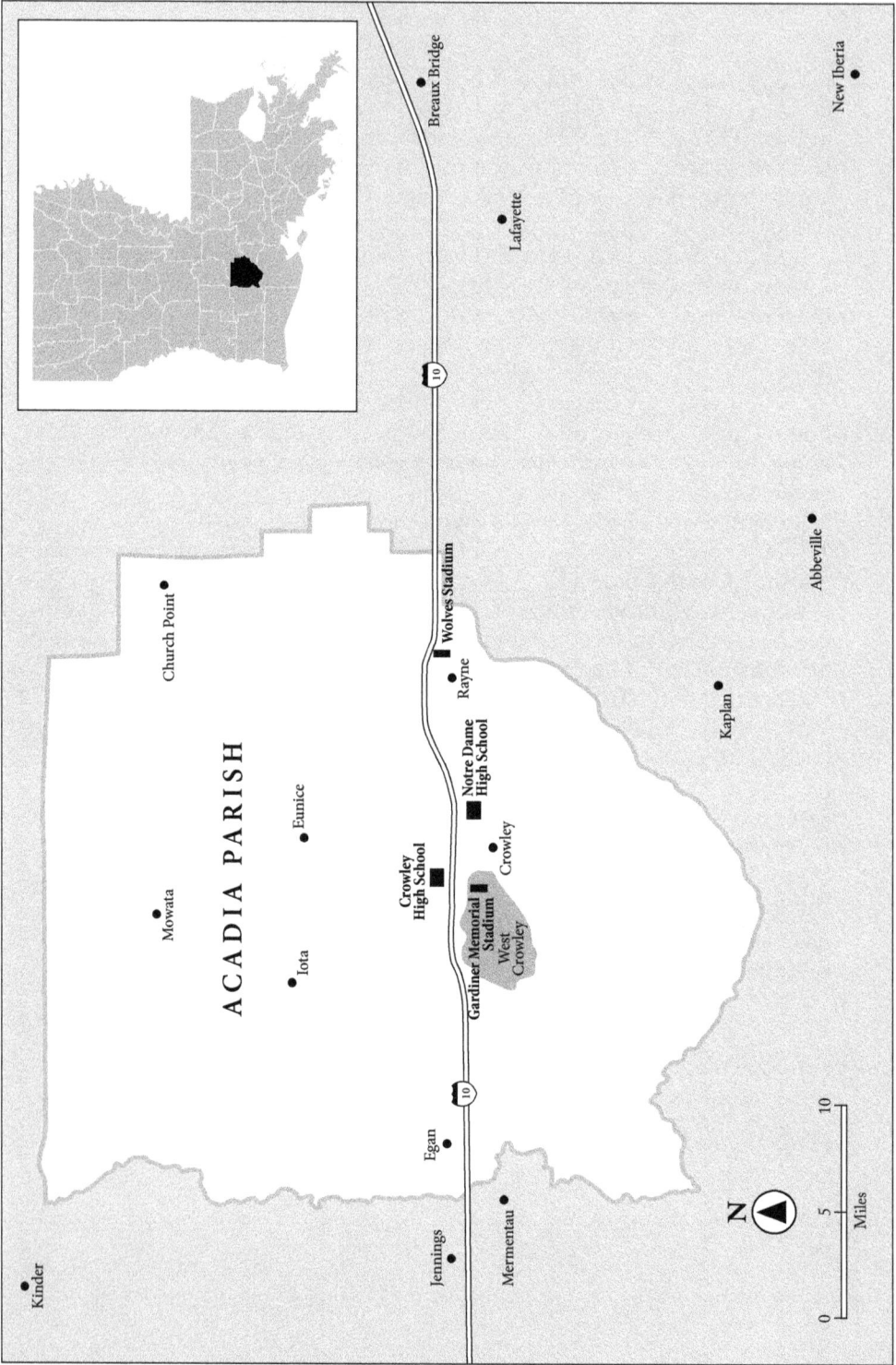

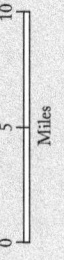

1

♦

The Birth of a Legend

Tucked in the corner of the cluttered office is a Heisman-like trophy of a football player catching a pass, his outstretched arms hidden under a Minnesota Vikings cap signed by Orlando Thomas, a bone-crushing free safety for the Minnesota Vikings from 1995–2001(see photo on back cover). Inscribed on the base of the seventeen-inch-high bronzed statuette is:

COACH OF A LIFETIME
LEWIS COOK
Thanks For Your Support, Love, Honesty and Friendship

Lewis Cook Jr. is the legendary and beloved head football coach at Notre Dame High School of Acadia Parish in Crowley, Louisiana. Before going to Notre Dame in 1997, Cook coached Orlando across town at Crowley High School. He was the offensive coordinator at the University of Southwestern Louisiana (USL) in Lafayette, when Orlando topped the nation's major colleges in interceptions as a junior and was named to the Associated Press All-American team his senior year. After the Vikings selected Orlando in the second round of the 1995 NFL draft, Cook helped him find an agent he could trust. Orlando signed a $2 million contract with the Vikings initially, and then $11 million.

"Coach, I want to do something for you," Orlando said. "I want to get you something."

Cook pushed back. "I told you from the very beginning, all I ever wanted was for when you finished playing that anything you do after that was a hobby—you don't need to do it for money because you took care of your money."

1

Orlando ended up giving Cook the statuette, which reflects the father-son bond that connected them and symbolizes his career as a high school football coach who has shaped the lives of a legion of players over the last half-century.

The greatest college football coach of them all, Nick Saban of the University of Alabama, said as much in a letter to Cook on his induction into the Louisiana Sports Hall of Fame in 2018. "You're one in a million," Saban wrote. "They broke the mold when they made Coach Louie Cook. Not only are you a master of X's and O's, but, more importantly, you've been a great mentor and teacher of life skills."

Cook is a legend throughout Louisiana, especially the Acadiana region of the state known for football, drive-thru daiquiri shops, crawfish boils, and authentic Cajun food and music.

The *Lafayette Daily Advertiser* once asked readers in a poll, "If there was a Mount Rushmore for Acadiana area prep football, who would be carved on it?"[1]

Cook was the people's choice, along with former NFL stars Kevin Faulk of the New England Patriots, Johnny Hector of the New York Jets, and Jake Delhomme of the Carolina Panthers.

The greatness of a high school football coach is usually measured by the win-loss record of his teams, the number of state championships, and the players that advance to major colleges and the NFL.

"So many people associate success with winning, but it's not just about wins," Cook said. "State championships don't tell how good a coach is. There are a lot of places that a really good coach can go, and it doesn't matter how good he is, that school is not winning a state championship. There are coaches that like to say, 'I coached this kid—he played in the NFL,' but the coach didn't put him there."

He cites as an example Tracy Boyd, a hulking tight end at Crowley High in 1985 selected by the New England Patriots in the sixth round of the 1992 NFL draft. "Tracy got in the NFL," Cook said. "We had a little bit to do with that because he wasn't even going to play football. We got him interested in football. If he doesn't play high school football, obviously he would've never got in the NFL. God got him in the NFL because he had the talent."

For Cook, it's all about consistency. Over the last twenty-six years at Notre Dame, his teams compiled a 292–47 record, appearing in ten state championship games and winning four of them.

"In twenty-six years, we've lost twenty-five regular-season games," he pointed out. "We don't average a loss a year. Who has that kind of consistency? It's a testimony to the system that we've set up but more so the work ethic of our kids and how they bought in."

Most of the kids that wear Notre Dame's red helmet are unlikely to play a single down after graduation because they are in the pipeline to life, not college and pro football. They go on to become priests, doctors, lawyers, accountants, engineers, soldiers, rice and crawfish farmers—everyday people. Football is a tool Cook uses to prepare his players for the rest of their lives.

"He's put some people in the NFL, but he's put a lot more people in heaven," said Rodney Savoy, a retired certified public accountant and real estate developer and lifelong friend.

"There are two professions that you can see the heart of a person," Cook tells his players. "Cardiologists see it when they do open-heart surgery. Every day on the practice field, every day in the weight room, every day when you're tired and hurting, I see your heart. I see the kind of heart you have when you play this game. But you learn about yourself, too. You find out what kind of heart you got."

Cook guided the Crowley High Gents to a state title in 1989, five years after suffering through back-to-back winless seasons. In eight years under Cook's tutelage, the Gents had a 76–24 mark, making it to the playoffs every year and the championship game at the Superdome in New Orleans three times—1989, 1991, and 1996.

He was an assistant coach at USL on two separate occasions—1981–1984 and 1992–1995. Friends joked, "Coach, you're the only guy with two stints in college, three different high school head coaching jobs, and you haven't moved out of your house yet."

Cook has always lived in Rayne, Louisiana, a town of eight thousand people, about ten minutes by car from Crowley and twenty-five from Lafayette. He coached at Rayne High from 1974 to 1980, the last four years as head coach. "The one thing I feel really good about is when my boys refer to home, they know where that home is," he said, citing the house address.

"People don't leave Southwest Louisiana unless their job requires it," said Savoy, who also grew up in Rayne. "It's about family. People stay within driving distance of their parents and grandparents."

"It's Louisiana—laid back and easygoing," added Shane Garrett, a superstar at Crowley High who went on to play for the Cincinnati Bengals in the NFL. "We're country folks down this way. We're used to country roads, a couple of red lights, one lane highways, gravel roads, and, yeah, good food—good southern eatin'."

Cook took one of those country roads back to Crowley High in 1996 and then went cross-town to Notre Dame the next year so he could coach his three sons—Lewis III, Jeff, and Stu.

In a profession where moving up usually means moving around and repeatedly uprooting your family, Cook stayed put and true to his priorities of the Three Fs—Faith, Family, and Football, in that order.

Clasping hands with Teddy Menard, a senior wide receiver on the 2022 Notre Dame team, Coach Louie Cook led his players in saying the Lord's Prayer after a game. For nearly a half-century of coaching, Cook has been steadfast in his commitment to the Three Fs—Faith, Family, and Football, in that order. The entire team attends a morning mass on game days. *Photo by author.*

"What I admire so much about Dad is he came back to high school to coach us," Stu said. "He turned down job offers at some big-time schools, so we didn't have to move. Mom never wanted to move, and he wasn't going to make her move."

Cook had an opportunity to go to Texas A&M as an assistant. He topped the list of candidates for USL's head coaching job in 2001 and walked away. Ten years later the Ragin' Cajuns were wooing him again.

Around the same time, his wife, Faye, was diagnosed with breast cancer. "Deep down, I think he wanted it," Stu explained. "Selfishly, I wanted him to take the job."

Stu prodded his father: "Dad, you need to go in there and put your name in. Just go get it."

"What kind of man would I be now if I left your mom when she needed me most?" he said to Stu. "I'm not going anywhere."

It was more important for Cook to be at his wife's side than on the sidelines as a head coach at a major college.

"Me and Miss Faye, we don't need that," Cook told Gerald Broussard, another coach at USL.

"Coach has never been a grass-is-greener guy," Broussard said. "He's substance, not image. He's the best football coach I've ever been around, and that's regardless of the level. He can coach in the NFL, but he's not going to compromise being Louie Cook."

"He could've coached at any level," added Bradley Dale Peveto, a widely traveled assistant coach now at the University of Texas–El Paso. "He just chose to go the high school route because he put his family first."

Peveto considers Cook the best high school football coach in America. "One Friday night he'll beat you with his kids. If you swap schools, the next Friday night, he'll beat you with yours."

Cook coaches by love, not fear or intimidation.

"Louie's key to winning is he loves the kids, and they love him," said Mike Doherty, who also coached with him at USL. "You could put Louie in the worst high school program in the nation and he'd turn it around. He's going to get the kids out and they're going to love him and play as hard as they can for him. That's a gift that very few people have."

That's what happened in 1985 at Crowley High where the legend of Louie Cook was born.

"Everybody thought I had lost my mind," Cook said. "I went from being a Division I quarterback coach to taking a high school team that hadn't won a game in two years."

The losing streak peaked at twenty-two after Cook lost his first game at Crowley.

"Here we go again," one teary-eyed fan moaned in the stands.

"You don't know my husband," Faye said. "We might've lost this game, but we're not going to lose many more."

"She had more faith than I did," Cook quipped.

Things got better, just like Faye said they would.

The Gents had a 6–5 win-loss record in '85 and 10–2 in '86.

"Coach Cook has a knack for getting the best out of people," said Dammon Stutes, the Gents' starting quarterback from 1984 to 1986. "We achieved more than we ever thought we could."

One of the players that kicked it up a notch was Shane Garrett, a speedy all-purpose back who, as Cook puts it, "is one of those guys that can make you miss in a phone booth." In 1986, his senior year, he scored twenty touchdowns on 1,834 yards rushing, receiving, and returning punts and kickoffs.

"You gave a little extra all the time because you didn't want to disappoint him," Garrett said.

Garrett played at Texas A&M and for the Bengals in the NFL. "When I got to college, I was prepared. Coach Cook taught me everything about football and life, being good on and off the field."

Orlando Thomas, *left*, conferred with Coach Louie Cook during a Crowley High game in 1989. "He was the spiritual leader," Cook described Orlando, who played both defense and offense. "He had such a strong will to succeed that he willed us to the state title." ***Photo by Brad Kemp.***

The Gents were a model of the consistency Cook extols, posting records of 9–3 in 1987; 10–2 in 1988; and 13–2 in 1989 when they won the state 3A title with Orlando Thomas leading the way.

"Orlando willed our team to the championship," Cook said. "He made play after play. He expected everybody else to do what he did."

And they did on and off the field.

Earlier in the year, Orlando teamed with four other Black players to ease tensions at the school over a controversial new rule that required cheerleaders to be in the marching corps and attend home basketball games. A bunch of the girls, both Black and white, didn't show up at the games and quit.

Cook huddled with the players. "Y'all know what's going on—no Black cheerleaders for our team this year."

"Coach," Orlando said, "if we don't come to practice, we don't get to play in the game, right? If they wanted to cheer, they should've kept their ass in the marching corps. They quit because they didn't want to come cheer for us during basketball. I have no problem with having no Black cheerleaders. Any y'all have a problem?"

Orlando had spoken.

Coach Louie Cook got a joy ride from Jason LeJeune, *left*, and Warren Boyd, no. 42, after his Crowley High Gents beat Broadmoor, 34–26, in the semifinals of the 1989 state playoffs to advance to the Class 3A championship game in the Superdome in New Orleans. At the Dome, the Gents nipped Wossman High, 17–15, to earn the school's first and only state football title. *Photo by Brad Kemp.*

He spoke out again near the end of spring practice as the team was kneeling around Cook, listening to him talk about the importance of the upcoming summer workouts. Orlando raised his hand and asked to speak.

He stood up to face his teammates. "All of us seniors got together. We want to win the state championship. If you're not intending to come work out this summer, turn your shit into Coach when we get back 'cause you don't need to be on the team. We're going to be there. We all got to get ready."

That's how Orlando was.

The Gents were 2–2 after four games before reeling off eleven straight wins to capture the school's only state football title.

In one game, Orlando intercepted a pass on Crowley's nineteen-yard line and then, on the next play, caught an eighty-one-yard touchdown pass. He starred in the semifinals, making two clutch interceptions in the end zone. He picked off a pass on the second play of the championship game against Wossman to set up the Gents' first touchdown in their 17–15 victory.

On one play, Orlando teamed with fellow safety David Martin to stop Wossman's star running back, Antonio Moffet, from getting a first down. Moffet taunted Martin: "If your football career don't take you nowhere, baby, we need a gardener."

Orlando helped Martin to his feet, slapped him on the side of the helmet and said, "Don't worry about it. I'll get him for you."

Orlando was a fierce competitor who would go on to become one of the NFL's most punishing tacklers.

"He was going to hit you as hard as he could during the game but very respectful afterward," Cook said. "He was going to do what it took to be the best he could be and take care of other people along the way. It was never about Orlando. He cared about others first."

Orlando wound up at USL where he was reunited with Cook three years later.

"I had him in high school and then, I had him again in college," Cook said. "I had him when he was thirteen years old and I'm on a plane with him when he was twenty-two years old going to sign with an agent. And I was there at the end."

The end came far too soon.

Orlando was forty-two when he died in 2014 after a ten-year battle with amyotrophic lateral sclerosis (ALS), or Lou Gehrig's disease. ALS attacks the nerve cells in the brain and spinal cord, ultimately leading to complete paralysis and the inability to talk. Eventually he had to communicate through his wife, Demetra, raising his eyebrows when she came to the letter of the alphabet needed to spell the words he wanted to say.

On one of Cook's last visits, Orlando's eyebrows spoke for his heart. "Orlando wants you to know," Demetra said, "there would be no Orlando Thomas without Coach Cook."

Wes Jacob feels the same way. He calls Coach Cook "Pop" and credits him with saving his life.

"Closest thing I have to a father," he said. "My mom was on her own. My sister was away at college. Was I bad? Yes. Was I rebelling? Yes. Was I mad at the world? Yes."

Wes got suspended in kindergarten. "You know those little rings you get out of a bubble gum machine? I put one on a girl's finger and it got stuck."

It took Wes three years to get through junior high school, and it wasn't because he was dumb. "I was always smart," he said. "For the most part, I was a shithead. I did most of the things they say I did."

Twice he was kicked out for fighting, the second time for punching a coach. His mother, Rose, couldn't take any more. "You're going to Houston to live with your sister."

Wes's reputation preceded him at Crowley High, Cook's first year in 1985. A junior high school coach warned him, "Coach, if you don't want your program wrecked, don't let Wes Jacob anywhere near it."

Most summer mornings Wes slept while his football-playing buddies worked out. One day he drove them to practice and was leaning against a wall in the Crowley High gym when Coach Cook walked up and introduced himself.

"Wes Jacob?" Cook mused. "I know that name from somewhere. You go to school here?"

Wes said he was moving to Houston.

"Wes Jacob . . . Wes Jacob. How do I know that name?"

"I don't know," Wes said. "I never met you."

Cook started walking away and then stopped. "Hold on. Now I got it . . . the coach at the junior high school told me that if I wanted to have a good program, NOT to let you in it."

Wes bristled. "You don't have to worry about that. I'm going to Houston."

The next words that came out of Cook's mouth were life-changing for Wes.

"I don't know you," Cook said. "You haven't done anything to me. You can come here if you want as long as you do things the right way."

Wes was stunned. "It was like a light switch. It was the first time a man, let alone a white man, had ever talked to me like I was somebody."

He rushed home to tell his mother he was staying in Crowley.

"Uh-uh," she said, "I ain't falling for this again."

Wes promised to behave. "I kept on beggin'-beggin'-beggin'. All I can say is that the Lord must've pinched her or something. And boom! I was in."

The only trouble Cook had with Wes was his senior year when he got on the bus going to a game wearing short socks instead of the required baseball leggings socks. He sat next to Cook who looked down and said, "It's going to be a long game if you don't have them socks on. You ain't going to be in the game."

By the time they got to the game site, Wes had the right socks on.

"I was praying he'd find some," Cook said.

"I was already on the bus," Wes said, "so I stole them from somebody—a freshman or sophomore."

Wes caused plenty of trouble for opponents. The six-foot-two, 190-pound wide receiver piled up 2,033 yards on 109 catches and scored twenty-seven touchdowns his last two seasons (1987–1988), earning high school All-American and state Most Valuable Player honors his senior year and attracting scholarship offers from LSU, Florida, Texas A&M, Nebraska, and the University of Southern California.

"Wes could catch everything," Cook said. "One time the ball got tipped and just before it hit the ground, Wes grabbed it at full speed, tucked it, and kept running. He caught the tip of the ball."

Wes ended up at LSU, starting all four years and amassing 1,061 yards on seventy-one receptions.

Since 2012, Wes has coached receivers for Cook at Notre Dame. "I'm going to write a book one day," he said. "The title is: 'The Wonder Years.' It all starts with Coach Cook."

Just before David Martin began his freshman year at Crowley High in 1986, Cook got another phone call from the same junior high school coach: "You know what I told you about Wes? Well, I've got one that's way worse than Wes—David Martin. I'd keep him away, too."

David was the youngest of seven kids. His mom, a single parent, worked two jobs and had little time at home. "I was pretty much raising myself," David said. "I was a troubled kid. I liked a lot of attention, and I went about getting it all the wrong way."

David and some of his buddies once rode their bicycles in and out of a department store, cleaning off a rack of expensive Panama Jack and Bahama Mama shirts along the way.

Cook went to see David while he was still in eighth grade and made a deal with him. "If I can stay out of trouble, he'll give me the opportunity to change my life," David recalled. "Nobody ever told me that before."

"I knew he could be a good player," Cook said. "And he needed to be with us. That was the only shot he had."

Wes Jacob, *left*, and Shane Garrett, nicknamed "Salt" and "Pepper," went from playing for Coach Louie Cook at Crowley High to starring roles as wide receivers at LSU and Texas A&M. Jacob, a.k.a. Salt, caught seventy-one passes for seven touchdowns and 1,061 yards at LSU from 1989 to 1992. Garrett, a.k.a. Pepper, was at Texas A&M from 1988 to 1990, totaling 696 yards and five touchdowns on thirty-five catches. He also carried the ball six times for 85 yards and a TD, and as a punt and kick return specialist, he averaged 7.6 yards on punts and 18.1 yards on kickoffs. *Photo courtesy of Lewis Cook Jr.*

David almost blew it his freshman year, missing a game and skipping out on a spring practice with another player. Cook ordered their lockers cleaned out.

The next morning David was standing outside Cook's office, waiting to talk to him.

"We go in and we're sittin' there," Cook said. "I'm not saying anything. I'm just staring at him. I guess he was waiting for me to say something."

Finally, Cook said, "You wanted to talk . . . talk."

David blurted out: "I don't know what Trimble (Curt Trimble) is going to tell you but it's a lie. Coach, we just skipped, I don't know why."

"Y'all are riding around in air conditioning, cruising all afternoon while we're out in the hot sun working our ass off," Cook said calmly. "David, let me ask you something: Who at this school really cares about David Martin? The teachers?"

"No, sir."

"The principal . . . the assistant principal?"

"No, sir."

"How about the janitor or the cafeteria ladies? Do they know who you are?"

"No, sir."

"Do you think the coaches care about you?"

"Yes, sir."

"So, the only people in this whole school that care about you are the ones you shit on yesterday when you hauled ass," Cook said.

"You can be on the team, but I'm not giving your equipment back. Maybe you can talk one of the other coaches into giving it to you."

Cook had already arranged for the coaches to return his gear.

David wanted to wear jersey no. 5 worn by his idol, Shane Garrett, but Cook told him he was going to get a white jersey with no number on it. "You're going to have to earn a number."

Wearing no. 5, the swift and shifty Martin averaged nearly nine yards every time he carried the ball his junior year in 1988. The next year he spearheaded the Gents' offense with 1,037 yards rushing and receiving combined and nineteen touchdowns, five on punt and kickoff returns.

"You knew when Coach wasn't happy with you," Dammon Stutes said. "He didn't have to yell at you. He'd just look into your soul."

Cook once looked inside the helmet of Sherard Joseph at practice after the tight end didn't come out of his three-point stance on a running play. "Is that you in there, Sherard?" he asked.

"It was definitely not me," Joseph said.

Joseph didn't feel like being bothered by football or anything else that day. Instead of confronting Joseph on the spot, he pulled him aside after practice to find out what was going on.

"He was fragile at that point," Cook explained. "He was a classy kid, and I didn't want to lose him."

Looking back on the incident that took place late in the '91 season, Joseph, now the pastor of two historic Black Baptist churches in Crowley, said: "Coach Cook knows every one of his players. It's like a shepherd knows his sheep. You've got to know the people, know the players."

Jerome Robinson was a seldom-used player on the 1991 team that advanced to the state championship finals at the Superdome in New Orleans. When it was time for the Gent buses to leave Crowley, Robinson wasn't around. Most coaches would've gone by the book and left without Jerome. Cook went by his heart. "This bus is not leaving until Jerome Robinson gets here. We're not leaving Jerome."

Robinson appeared a few minutes later and got on the bus. Going to the Dome was the highlight of his high school years and perhaps his entire life.

"It's about people," Cook said. "That's how it's supposed to be."

"The football field is Louie's pulpit," said Bob Czarnecki, one of the assistants that Cook kept when he took over at Crowley. "He uses it not only to teach football but to teach life."

During Cook's eight years at Crowley, Black players made up anywhere from 30 to 50 percent of the roster.

"Louie gave them hope," Czarnecki said. "He convinced them that you had to work in order to succeed at anything. It wasn't just football. You had to learn how to roll with the punches, and you had to learn to sweat and even to work when you didn't want to. And the kids bought into that because so many of them did not have a father growing up. He created a stable situation for them."

David Martin is a living example.

"If it wasn't for Coach Cook, I'd probably be dead or in prison," David said.

Orlando, Wes, David, Sherard, and Jerome have one thing in common. They're African Americans. Cook is of Syrian descent and has dark skin, too.

"We knew he was not 100 percent white, as ignorant at that sounds now," said Greyson Augustus," an African American who was a powerful force on the offensive line for the Crowley team Cook took to the Superdome in 1996. "But back then it was like he's white but he's not really white. In our heads, that's what we thought. He's not really white so maybe it's OK."

Growing up in the 1950s and 1960s when segregation laws in the South were in full force, Cook often played with Black kids and saw the mutual respect his father, Lewis Sr., and the Black workers at his car dealership had for each other.

At one time Louie and Faye went to mass at an all-Black Catholic church in Rayne and when their youngest son, Stu, coached at Crowley, they sometimes showed up at a Gents' game.

"He didn't go sit with the white folks," said Michael Thomas, one of Orlando's younger brothers. "He'd come sit with the Black athletes he coached at Crowley—dead in the heart of 'em. You could feel the love and the attention from people all over the stands, yelling 'That's Coach Cook! That's Coach Cook!' It was as if Orlando Thomas was still living."

Cook affectionately refers to his Black players at Crowley as "the brothers."

"I loved coaching the brothers," he said.

Several of them had nicknames. Orlando was "Poosie"; Shane was "Five," his jersey number; Wes was "Quick"; strong safety Marcus Senegal was "Cheese." There also was Danny "Yuk" Castille and Howard "The Refrigerator" Claiborne, both defensive linemen, and running backs Marlon "Baby D" Williams and Tony "Ninja Turtle" Washington.

At one practice Ninja Turtle got hurt and was being carried off the field. "Hey," one of the brothers hollered, "y'all move out of the way . . . we got a turtle crossing."

Sometimes they trash talked each other: "Ya mama's so dumb she sold her car to buy gas."

"They make you laugh," Cook said.

Cook had the brothers laughing, too.

"They don't think very highly of us," he said going into a game against St. Thomas More (STM), an exclusive private high school in Lafayette. "They got us for homecoming. That's disrespect right there. Look at the teams on their schedule—none of them have brothers. They don't want nothin' to do with y'all."

He turned to The Refrigerator, as good-natured as he was large: "Fridge, they have so little respect for us, they asked me if I could talk to you about washing their cars before the game."

"Ah, Coach, that's low!" Fridge said.

"They've got no respect for y'all," Cook continued. "The biggest decision they've got to make is whether they're going to drive the homecoming court girls around in a Mercedes-Benz or a BMW. That's all they're worried about."

Running off the field after warmups, one of the brothers said, "Coach, I guess the Mercedes won out. I don't see nothin' but Benz."

In the locker room, Cook said, "Y'all better make sure we've got the lead at the half. I don't want to go out there with all those people and hear their noise."

With the Gents leading 21–7 at halftime, Cook slipped behind a concession stand and put on a shirt, tie, and coat to escort one of the homecoming court princesses, his godchild and niece, Katherine Surratt. "Faye had everything ready for me," he said. "Slipped it on and went on the field."

The Gents treated their hosts like a Yugo, rolling to a 35–14 victory.

"You have to be compassionate or at least considerate of their situation," he said of coaching the brothers. "We all want them to conform to our way. They're looking at it like, 'Why can't you conform to my way a little bit?' Sometimes it can be two different worlds sharing the same space. We've got to make it work."

Cook makes it work by being fair and compassionate to everybody.

"The way he treated us allowed us as players, Black and white, to come together and just play ball with each other, have a good time," said Joel Sinclair, an offensive tackle at Crowley High from 1989 to 1991 who also played at Michigan State. "We had a bond that supersedes race despite how our families might be different."

One morning at Crowley High, Cook noticed a suspicious-looking character hanging out in the hallway with a small posse of Black kids. He didn't recognize the guy, so he asked one of the brothers, "Who is that dude?"

"Oh, man, that's Johnny. He's a thug. We don't fool with Johnny."

The next morning Cook saw him again and said, "Hey, Johnny, how ya doin', buddy?"

Johnny froze. Cook kept walking but he could hear Johnny say, "How did that man know my name?"

Before Cook could say anything the following day, Johnny said, "Hey, Coach, how ya' doin'?"

The wall that previously existed was gone. Every time Cook saw Johnny, they talked because he took time to find out his name.

The moral of the story for coaches is to know the names of your players and talk to them. Listen to what they say. Show them you care.

"It really is the sincerity of everything about Coach Cook," Gerald Broussard said. "You talk about him coaching with love, but it's the sincerity of that. It's his ability to communicate, but it's the sincerity in which he communicates. It's his knowledge of the game, but it's his sincere knowledge of the game. He's sincere in how he lives his life and how he treats others."

It's not rocket science.

"Kids will play harder when they know you care," Cook said. "To me, the biggest part of coaching is can you get 'em to compete for you? Will they go to the wall and have your back like you have their back?"

The answer has never been in doubt either at Crowley High or Notre Dame.

"If you can get someone to believe in himself and you motivate them, they'll try to knock down a wall if you ask them to," Sherard Joseph said. "That's what he did. He woke up inside of you what you never knew was inside of you. Coach Cook knows how to bring out the best in everyone."

On the sidelines he's known as Cool Hand Louie, never slamming his headset on the ground or yelling at his coaches. "I want our kids to think that the guys coaching them are the best in Louisiana."

He treats his quarterbacks with the same respect. "If I call him a dumbass or something in front of the team, they think, 'We got a dumbass for a quarterback.' I want them to think this guy is the one who's going to get them in the end zone when the game is on the line."

Long after he became the first Black to quarterback for Cook in 1988, Edward "Tiger" Hollier sent him a text message reading: "Happy Father's Day."

"Coach Cook was a dad, mentor, counselor, doctor, and lawyer to many of the African American kids that came up in West Crowley," Rev. Sherard Joseph said. "I was fortunate enough to have a stable family with two parents in the house. But a lot my friends—my classmates—probably would not have graduated if it hadn't been for Coach Cook."

The high school is located on the outskirts of town, about three miles from West Crowley where most Blacks reside. Cook wrangled a used fifteen-seat van to transport players to and from school. Donald Adams, a Black coach the brothers called "Love," usually drove the van, but sometimes Cook was at the wheel.

"If you wanted to be on his football team, you had to live to a certain standard," Rev. Joseph added. "You had to get your work done in the classroom. He knew what the problems were outside, the trouble you get into. So, guess what? Of the twenty-four hours in a day, we spent probably nineteen of them at Crowley High. He kept us together at school during the summer workouts, going to camps, just to keep people out of the streets and getting into trouble."

Bob Czarnecki was there to see the maturation of Orlando Thomas and the transformation of Wes Jacob and David Martin.

"Coach Cook was what they needed in their life in terms of a male role model," Czarnecki said. "No one would ever call him perfect. But that's not what people are looking for. They're looking for somebody that loved them and cared about them and would give them their time and be honest with them."

At Notre Dame, he has worn as many as three hats—school administrator, athletic director, and head football coach. He's down to one now—coaching kids.

"In his heart, he has always been a high school coach," Gerald Broussard said. "He wears that as a badge of honor."

One of Cook's favorite scenes from the movie *The Man Who Shot Liberty Valance* is the introduction of Dutton Peabody of the *Shinbone Star* at the territorial convention. "Thank you, Mr. Chairman, for those kind words," Peabody bellowed, "but why don't you tell them the whole truth: founder, owner, editor, and I also sweep out the place."

Cook washed the uniforms, cut the grass, put out the pylons and, of course, swept out the place. "Now we're coaching," he joked.

"He doesn't see himself above or below doing anything," Broussard said. "He's whatever you need me to be today, and at this moment."

"You always want to stay grounded," Cook said. "Don't take yourself too seriously."

He reminds himself and other prep coaches: "We're not doing heart surgery or brain surgery. And we ain't building a rocket ship to go to the moon. We're just a high school coach. Now, we can probably change more lives than the guy building that rocket."

The legend that was born at Crowley High has grown so large that Coach Cook often winds up quoting the classic Liberty Valance line, "When the legend becomes fact, print the legend."

He was introduced at a reunion of his college fraternity "as the only known living Kappa Sig to have never taken a drink."

It's true.

"I lived in the frat house at USL for three years and never took a drink of alcohol," he said, adding, "and I swept out the place."

He was once asked, "Are you a Baptist?"

"No," he replied. "I'm Catholic."

On some things, religious affiliation doesn't matter.

"I'm a Baptist preacher," said the Rev. Sherard Joseph. "My son, Christian, is in the fifth grade now. If Coach Cook is still coaching when he gets to high school, Notre Dame is where he'll be coming. Playing for Coach Cook was special—a gift from God. I want my son to play for him, too."

2

No Golden Dome at This Notre Dame

The first thing a visitor notices at Notre Dame High School in Crowley, Louisiana, is there's no golden dome like there is at the famous university with the same name.

There's no "Touchdown Jesus" mural overlooking the football field either. The school's football team, the Pios, short for Pioneers, play their home games across town at Gardiner Memorial Stadium, which belongs to Crowley High School.

But the Pios have "Little Jesus"—Louie Cook, the school's revered head football coach.

The story goes that Cook was attending a baseball game at Crowley's Miller Stadium when he learned an electrical problem at the ballpark hadn't been fixed yet.

"I've been calling Fat-Ass Audie for two months and I can't get his Fat-Ass to come fix it," complained Richard Pizzolatto, the city's parks and recreation director.

"Let me call Audie," Louie said, referring to Audie Hanks, the go-to electrician in Crowley. He phoned Audie and, by coincidence, he was one block away.

"Audie says he's coming," Louie informed Pizzolatto.

"Ah-h-h, I'll believe it when I see it," he grumbled.

One minute later in walks Audie.

"That's about right," Pizzolatto groused. "I called his fat ass for two months; Little Jesus calls him, and he comes in one minute."

To other coaches, family, and friends, Cook is known as Brim, a moniker that's a shared password to a close-knit brotherhood that revolves around him. It's a term of endearment similar to "Bro" and "Dude."

"Brim!" They greet each other and then sprinkle it throughout a conversation.

"Louie imparted that on everybody," said Jimbo Petitjean, a cousin. "I text my son, 'Good night, Brim, love you.'"

Cook's son, Jeff, also answers to Brim.

The nickname can be traced to 1971, when Louie played on the University of Southwestern Louisiana (USL) baseball team. "What's up, Bro?" was a common greeting at the time.

At practice one day Cook walked up to second baseman Mike Debaillon and said, "What's up, Brim?"

And that's how Debaillon became the original Brim. "It just stuck with all my friends," he said. "Whenever I see anybody from my college days, that's who I am—Brim."

Around the same time, one of Cook's coaching buddies, Charles "Bags" Baglio, was doing a lot of fly-fishing for bream and bringing home so many of them that folks around Independence, Louisiana, started calling him Brim. "Matter of fact, a friend of mine got me into some real estate deals, buying a couple of houses," Baglio said. "So, we named our little checking account Brim Realty."

Whatever the origin of Brim, the term has come to personify Cook and the down-to-earth qualities he radiates around Notre Dame, which could be called "Brimsville."

Irving "Boo" Schexnayder, a sports performance consultant, compares Cook to Andy Taylor, the affable sheriff of the fictional town, Mayberry RFD, played by actor Andy Griffith on his popular television show in the 1960s.

"Like Andy, he's on top of everything, never gets bent out of shape, has a deep understanding of everybody, and knows how to deal with all different kinds of people," Schexnayder said. "He can see the good in every single person."

In one episode, Mayberry Deputy Sheriff Barney Fife (actor Don Knotts) defended his boss's genial ways by explaining, "When you're a lawman and dealing with people, you do a whole lot better if you go not so much by the book, but the heart."[1]

Cook is speaking from his heart, not the book, when he says to other coaches, "Quit worrying about winning games. Just take care of the kids."

There's no mistaking what Andy Taylor does in Mayberry, but that's not the case with Cook at Notre Dame.

"If you put Louie in a room with several others and said pick out the coach and pick out the janitor, you're going to pick him as the janitor," said Gerald Broussard, who coached alongside Cook at USL.

Bradley Dale Peveto recalled the time he was an assistant coach at LSU and visiting Notre Dame when a coach from out-of-state walked up and asked, "Can you help me find Louie Cook?"

"Coach's office is right there," he pointed to it.

"Yeah, I peeked in the office and there was a guy sittin' in there but he ain't no football coach," the visitor said.

"What did he look like?" Peveto asked.

He described him.

"That's Louie Cook."

"That can't be," the coach said. "I thought he was a maintenance man or janitor."

"Don't let his looks fool you," Peveto cautioned. "That's the best football coach in the country."

Broussard's description of Cook is befitting their father-son relationship: "He's dark complexioned, he's undersized, he's overweight, he's got droopy eyes, he looks more like an unmade bed. And he don't care. He's not there to impress you with his looks."

The Notre Dame campus is not all that impressive, either. Sitting amid approximately ten acres on the eastern edge of Crowley, the classroom buildings are nondescript, and the football field is used only for practices and junior varsity and freshman games. A statue of Mary in the center of the campus and a chapel at the north end are intertwined with the school's proud football tradition.

The entire team attends mass in the chapel on game days, Cook and his oldest son, Lew, sitting together in the front. "Most head coaches would sit in the back row to make sure the kids did not talk or misbehave," Coach Kirk Crochet said. "Louie sits in the front pew. And he leads from the front."

After every game the players gather in their uniforms around the statue of Mary to offer a prayer.

Now and then Cook escapes to a small office in the chapel for quiet that's hard to find in his main office in the athletic fieldhouse, the school's newest building. This office is more like a railway station, with people walking through or sitting around Cook's desk, making small talk. "You think Saban has got guys sittin' around his office?" Cook asked one day.

There are several similarities between Cook and Nick Saban, the great University of Alabama football coach.

"We were born the same year [1951]," Cook said. "We married a girl a year behind us in school that were both majorettes. His dad ran a gas station and repair shop, and my dad had the same thing but sold cars. We were quarterbacks on our high school teams. Obviously, we went a little bit different direction as coaches but we've both been coaching a long time."

Of course, there's one big difference, and he was reminded of that the morning he turned on his office computer and read about Saban signing a new eight-year contract worth $84.8 million.

"I'm the clown that took a $6,000 cut in pay to leave college ball," he said, laughing. "I could probably still be in college today if I had wanted to move all these different places. That just wasn't for me."

Cook and Notre Dame are made for each other. One is a staunch traditionalist and the other rich in football tradition.

The school has had only four head coaches in its fifty-five-year history: Gerald Dill, 1967–1973; Ashton Cassedy, 1974–1988; Donnie Gaspard, 1989–1996; and Cook, 1997 to the present.

In the thirty years before Cook's arrival, the Pios won two state championships (1973 and 1976) and averaged nearly nine wins per season. The best of them all was probably the first Pios team in 1967, described by one reporter as so powerful it could "do just about anything with a football except make it talk."[2]

Paced by running back Tommy Casanova, who averaged 7.5 yards per carry and went on to become a three-time All-American at LSU, the Pios outscored nine opponents, 298–6, before losing in the state playoffs on the tiebreaker, which was the number of first downs.

At first, Gerald Broussard had doubts about Cook going to Notre Dame. "I'm thinking, 'That don't fit you. You're not the private school kind of guy.'"

He didn't realize Notre Dame is a private school with a public school mentality—the perfect situation for Cook.

One day USL quarterback Brian Soignier visited Notre Dame. When he was offensive coordinator and quarterback coach for the Ragin' Cajuns, Cook recruited Brian out of Cecilia High, a public school.

"Coach, this doesn't seem like a private school," Soignier said. "The kids, they're not uppity."

"Look at the parking lot," Cook said.

"Yeah, there's nothing but old, beat-up farm trucks," Soignier replied.

"That's our kids," Cook said. "There aren't many of them driving fancy automobiles. Their parents are slavin' every day to put their kids through Notre Dame."

Tuition at the school for the 2022–2023 school year was $7,440.

Cook has honed Notre Dame's blue-collar mentality into something tougher and better.

"This is a tough place with tough, gritty people," defensive coordinator Jimmy McCleary said of the surrounding communities. He came to Notre Dame in 1998. "They're gritty, hardworking people."

Even Babe Ruth commented on this grittiness in 1921, when the home run king and his New York Yankees teammates played an exhibition game in Crowley.

"I noticed your skyscraper," Babe said, referring to a new seven-story bank building and the prosperity it represented. "Grit like that makes cities. Keep it up, snap your finger at failure and hit the ball hard."[3]

"Out of the mouth of the Babe," McCleary said with a grin. "This community handles adversity well. You're looking at people with the same last names over and over. They're all tied together so the sense of community and togetherness is extremely special. They understand what it takes and the sacrifice that must be made physically, mentally, and in a lot of ways emotionally, to be successful."

Kaine Guidry was an assistant coach at Notre Dame before taking over the head job at nearby Rayne High School.

"The family aspect of the football program just kind of blossoms and it grows, and it radiates and it's contagious," he said. "There's no secret as to why those guys are always successful. It's a real family-oriented atmosphere and Coach Cook is the head of it. Whenever he speaks, everybody listens."

Said Boo Schexnayder: "It's kind of the perfect storm when you get a special coach in a special place."

Charles Baglio has a slightly different view: "I don't think it's the perfect storm. I think it's the perfect guy—Louie Cook."

The results speak for themselves:

- Four perfect seasons—15–0 in 2000 and 2009; 14–0 in 2015; and 13–0 in 2018, all ending in championships.
- Ten appearances in the state finals, five in a decade (2000–2009) and three in consecutive years (2003–2005).
- Overall win-loss record of 292–47 for an .861-winning percentage at Notre Dame, with no more than four losses in a single season (8–4 in 2011). In thirty-eight years as a head coach, Cook's teams have won 392 games and lost 92, a winning percentage of .810.

"It not about the 392 wins as much as it's about the 392-plus lives that we may have helped form to be successful people," Cook said. "If you asked our kids how often I talk about winning, they're going to say, 'We hardly ever hear that.' What we preach is that if you work hard and do things the right way, the winning is going to take care of itself."

Cook emphasizes "there's no substitute for hard work" and "good things happen to good people." They're clichés but they still ring true.

"We're trying to learn how to become a man and be prepared for adversity and struggles and how you fight through that," he said. "We have a fundamental, sound approach to the game. We're going to compete really hard."

Cook doesn't stop working when he leaves the practice field. He's constantly studying, planning, and building relationships with his players. "I've been around and played for head coaches who probably had more knowledge than me," he said, "but they weren't very successful because they couldn't get the guys to play hard for them. To me, a good coach is one that can take average players and get 'em to play a little bit better."

That means working harder than the other guy.

"We don't have talented guys, we just have hardworking guys," McCleary said.

The hard work that unleashes the talent begins in the weight room, the epicenter of everything Notre Dame does.

"Games are won in January, February, and in through the summertime," Cook said. "If you don't get it done there, you don't have a chance."

The weight room at Notre Dame is even busy on Friday afternoons in January and February. "Go find me another high school that has guys in there with coaches on Friday after school," Cook said. "They might have kids, but the coaches won't be there with them."

McCleary handles the strength and conditioning program in addition to his duties as defensive coordinator.

"He trusts his coaches," McCleary said. "Since I've been coordinator [2007], he's never sat in one meeting or looked over my shoulder. If you asked him what Mac does, he'd probably say, 'I don't know but whatever it is, it's working.'"

Cook gives McCleary free rein as well as the top athletes.

"He puts the best players on defense," McCleary said, "and we're going to play tough, sound football. We're going to run the football, take time off the clock, play field position, and try and play great defense. And we're going to win a lot of close games because of that."

In a quarterfinal game against Richwood in 2008, the Pios were leading 16–0 when star quarterback Ryan Leonards broke his collarbone just before half-time. As they walked off the field, Cook put his arm around McCleary and said, "I'm just going to let you know, we will not get a first down in the second half."

The offense managed one first down, but Richwood could only score on a fumble return and a short drive enabled by a botched punt. The Pios won 16–12.

"Every snap that was taken in the second half by them was on our side of the field," Cook said. "How we won that game I'll never know."

In 2015, both the defense and offense were dominating, steamrolling foes 507–52 to post a 14–0 record and capture the state title.

Kevin Foote is the sports editor of *The Acadian Advocate*, based in Baton Rouge, and a talk show host for a Lafayette radio station. He followed Cook throughout his twenty-six years at Notre Dame.

"I never have any hesitation saying he's the greatest high school football coach in the history of our area and maybe in the history of our state," Foote said. "That's not because he has the most wins but what he's done, how he's done it and what he's done it with. He hasn't won because he has all this talent. He's won because he has a great system and he's a great football coach and a great communicator."

Charles Baglio agreed: "Notre Dame doesn't have the athletes that everybody else has, but Louie wins because of who he is and the way he runs his program."

Baglio was head coach at Independence High School for twenty-two years before serving as coordinator of football relations at LSU for two decades.

"Louie doesn't have great athletes, so he has to make great athletes out of what he has," Baglio added. "His approach to the off-season program is to make those kids better."

Baglio was at one of the January workouts, standing beside a building to block a strong north wind that made the freezing temperature even colder. "The kids ran barefooted through puddles of water, laid on the ground and did those crunches and stomach exercises. Nothing bothered them because they knew that's what they had to do to win."

Summer workouts begin at 5:30 in the morning. "When your ass is still sleeping," said Coach Larry Dauterive, "those boys at Notre Dame are out running in the sand pit."

The sand pit has been replaced with artificial turf, but the workouts are just as gut-wrenching.

"If you work, you win," Baglio said. "Do what Louie asks you to do, you're going to win. Whatever he tells a kid, it's always for the kid's benefit. They'll run through a wall for him. I saw it that day I went there."

When Cook moved across town from Crowley High to Notre Dame, he vowed to himself that he wouldn't recruit players as some private schools do in Louisiana. The animosity between public and private schools has divided football in the state. Public schools are designated "non-select" and private schools are "select" with separate playoffs.

In 2022, the Louisiana High School Athletic Association (LHSAA) changed its definition of select schools to include open-enrollment schools, charter schools, and others with students from outside of zoning boundaries.

Schools are now organized into four groups, Divisions I–IV, with the largest schools in Division I. Notre Dame is in Division III. Previously, schools were classified 1A through 5A, Notre Dame falling in either 2A or 3A over the years.

"I'm anti-split, I want it the way it used to be," Foote said. "I wrote a lot of columns with very strong opinions anti-split. Even in the most bitter public-versus-private days when things were really bad and they all hated each other, I never once talked to a coach that said anything bad about Coach Cook."

Cook has won championships at both public and private schools. He understands the split is about more schools winning. But he liked it better before the split in 2013, when the Pios had to win as many as five games to be state champs and there were five state titles instead of the current nine. Of the 302 teams in Louisiana in 2021, a whopping 204 or 67.8 percent made the playoffs, 40 of them with losing records. "It's a flawed, watered-down, bloated playoff system," according to Ken Trahan of CrescentCitySports.com.[4]

Cook is more diplomatic. "We've become a select society," he said. "I lived across the street from the high school growing up and if they hadn't won a game in umpteen years, it didn't matter to my dad—'That's where you're going to school.' It wasn't about finding a place where I could showcase whatever talent I might have."

His personal pledge not to recruit was put to an immediate test when he came to Notre Dame from Crowley High in 1997. Nick Dugas, a multitalented, Black sophomore quarterback who led Crowley to the state finals in 1996, wanted to follow his mentor. He went to see Cook with his father, Horace.

"Coach," Horace said, "Nick is going to transfer to Notre Dame. He'll sit out his junior year."

"There's nothing I'd love more than having Nick playing for me, but we're not doing that," Cook replied. "Suppose he gets hurt his senior year. That means he wouldn't play his last two years of high school. It's not fair to Nick, and it's not fair to Crowley High. I'll help Nick but y'all need to stay at Crowley."

Dugas remained with the Gents and took them to the Division 4A playoff semifinals as a senior in 1998.

Several of Crowley's other Black players also wanted to continue playing for Cook at Notre Dame. They called him "Little Jesus" and assistant Donald Adams "Black Jesus." Many of them cried when Cook told them he was leaving.

"We gonna be all right," Adams reassured them. "Black Jesus is still here."

"You ain't Coach Cook!" snapped Walter Sampson, an outstanding running back who went on to play at USL.

"He was more than a coach," Sampson said. "He was a dad for all of us. I call him my grandfather now."

Cook doesn't want to do anything to siphon Black athletes from his former school.

But the biggest reason he has coached only sixteen Blacks in twenty-six years at Notre Dame is the tuition is well beyond what most Black families in Crowley can afford.

David Martin, a running back at Crowley High from 1986 to 1989, summed it up with a saying they had at Crowley High when he was there: "People at Crowley High eat Church's chicken; people at Notre Dame eat Popeyes chicken." In other words, if you've got the money, you go to Notre Dame. If not, you go to Crowley High.

Bob Czarnecki was one of Cook's assistant coaches at Crowley.

"If a kid came and he's qualified to be there, Louie would take him," Czarnecki said. "But he would never ever go to a kid and try to convince him to come to Notre Dame. It wouldn't be worth winning for him to do that. He has a moral compass that never wavers. Right is right and wrong is wrong. It's in his DNA."

Bryan "Buck" Leonards is a rice, soybean, and crawfish farmer and publishes a monthly farm magazine. He started at defensive tackle on the Pios' state championship team in 1976 and his son, Bryan, was on Cook's first club at Notre Dame.

"We're just average white boys," Buck Leonards said. "We don't recruit. We don't go grocery shopping. When we're missing a spot, Louie just coaches up a kid to play. Our goal as a family and multigenerational school is that we want Louie to coach our kids. How unfair would it be if a kid comes in and just because he's a good athlete, pays no tuition and plays while another kid who pays tuition and wanted to play here his whole life, sits on the bench? Our goal is for Louie to coach what we've got."

Shortly after Cook got to Notre Dame, he had a team meeting to discuss the N-word.

"Guys, I've been here long enough to realize one thing that I don't like," he said. "Y'all call me whatever you want, but I don't want to hear the N-word. Before you say it, you'd better look and make sure I'm not around because if I hear it, I'm going to be on your ass. Ain't nobody in this group any better than anybody else. I'm not talking as a player. I'm talking as a person. I'm not better than nobody. Y'all not better than nobody. In fact, the Black guys y'all talking about, they put a ring on my finger. Y'all got any rings?"

Tolerance. Respect. Humility. This is what Cook teaches along with blocking and tackling, throwing, and catching the ball.

"I'm going to stand up for what's right," he said. "That's all we try to convey to the kids. It's moral courage. Just be a man. Stand up. Don't let nobody push nobody else around if you can help it."

Tradition is important, too.

Cook was coaching at USL and Gerald Dill was working at the Catholic diocese in Lafayette when they met.

Dill was Notre Dame's first coach, guiding the Pios to a state title and 65–13–3 record the seven years he was there. Before that he coached at St. Michael High in Crowley, one of three small private high schools that were consolidated to form Notre Dame. The other two were St. Joseph of Rayne and St. Francis of Iota.

Cook asked Dill if he was still helping at Notre Dame.

"No, Louie," he said, "I've offered to help but I don't think they want me around."

Dill was told that he could come to watch practices but to stay off the field.

When he took the job at Notre Dame a few years later, Cook remembered the conversation and reached out to Dill. In his mind, Coach Dill was Notre Dame.

"Coach, I know you probably had something to do with me getting the job," Cook said. "If you're still interested in helping, I'll take whatever time and help you can give."

Dill was sixty-six years old at the time. Every year for nineteen years Dill's wife, Norma, called Cook to ask, "Is he getting in the way?"

The answer is obvious when you look at a photo on Cook's office wall. It shows Dill, then eighty-five, standing on the Superdome turf, holding onto a walking cane. The scoreboard behind him explains the content look on his face: Notre Dame 13, Riverside Academy 3.

"We had just beat Riverside for the championship," Cook said. "Two weeks later he had open heart surgery and there were complications. He passed away. To have him here was a blessing."

Buck Leonards feels the same way about Cook.

"Everybody looks up to Louie," Leonards said. "People relate to him. He can neutralize a bomb better than anybody I know of—in a very peaceful way. He doesn't beat around the bush."

The principal of a public school found this out when he claimed Notre Dame had a big advantage over his school because its students came from a larger area. To make his point, the principal drew two circles, a big one for Notre Dame and a small one for his school.

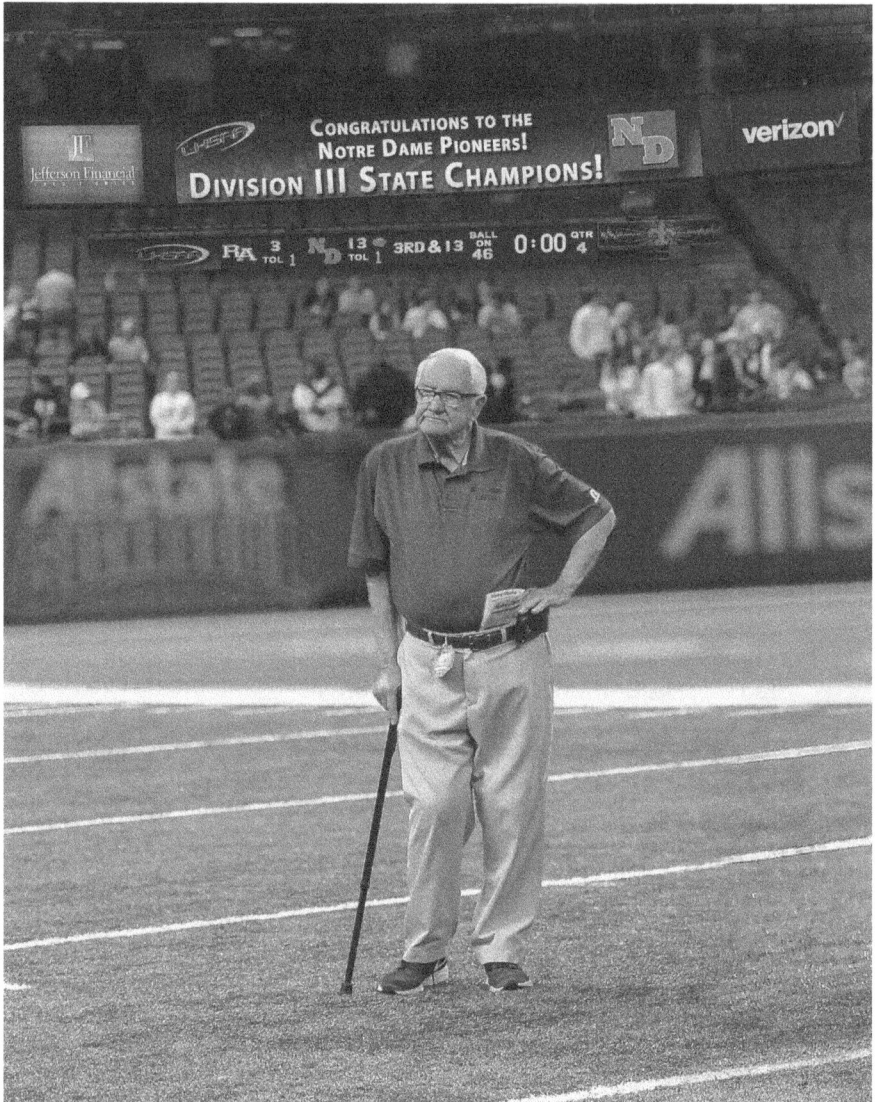

Notre Dame's first head football coach, Gerald Dill, lived to be eighty-five, long enough to see the Pios win their first state title under Louie Cook in 2000. Standing on the Superdome turf, Dill basked in Notre Dame's 13–3 victory over the Riverside Academy. Dill coached the school to a state championship in 1973 and assisted Cook in later years. *Photo by Dwayne Petry.*

"How many kids do you have in that little circle that's your school?" Cook asked.

"I've got 699," the principal said.

"We've got 425 in that big ol' circle," Cook said. "You got nearly 300 more than I've got."

"But they can't pass," the principal said, referring to the grade point average of his students.

"That's the big circle's fault?" Cook replied.

He drew another small circle for Crowley High.

"From 1977 to 1999, the big circle [Notre Dame] never went to the Dome," Cook continued. "But the little circle [Crowley] went three times. Why's that?"

"Because you were coaching at Crowley High," the principal said.

"So, is it the coach or is it the big circle?" Cook said. "Make up your mind."

By the way, the principal wound up at a private school in a nearby parish.

"Whether he's in the boardroom or locker room, he's able to communicate at that level," said Bobby Hanks, chief executive officer and owner of Crowley-based Supreme Rice. "He knows how to speak the language of whoever he's with. He's captivating. Everyone pays attention."

Leonards described the current situation in prep football. "We're in an era of Daddy-ball and Mommy-ball. Everybody wants their way. Everybody wants to be state champions NOW! It's a tough era for high schools. There's a lot of athletics in turmoil, but here we have 166 boys at school and 117 on the football team. It's amazing."

Cook had the title of administrator for eighteen years until he willingly gave it up in 2021 to focus on coaching. At one point, the chancellor-priest assigned to oversee the school wanted to remove him from the position.

Leonards protested loudly: "Louie is the heart and soul of Notre Dame. You can take the title away and name him janitor, and when a family has an issue at this school, they're going to want to see the janitor."

3

The Ultimate Goal Is Heaven

At the end of every practice, the Notre Dame players kneel in a circle around head football coach Louie Cook.

"Guys, let's talk about what our goals are going to be," he said following the first practice of the 2005 season.

One of the players was sixteen-year-old sophomore Andrew Schumacher. It was his first day on the varsity team.

"What is our ultimate goal?" Cook asked.

The year before, Notre Dame made it to the Class 3A finals at the Superdome in New Orleans. As Cook paused to let the question sink in, Schumacher was thinking the ultimate goal had to be going to the Dome and winning the state championship.

"Guys, if you answered anything other than to get to heaven, we need to change that," Cook said.

That not only set the tone for the next three years Schumacher played at Notre Dame but also for the rest of his life. He told the story in his first homily after being ordained as a Catholic priest in 2018.

"My vocation came a lot from that one comment he made about the goal of life—getting to heaven," he said. "That changed everything. It really hit me. I kind of felt this tug in my heart to go to the seminary."

Cook has a gift for motivating people and transforming lives.

"Here's a bucket of golf balls and a club," he'll say, "go hit 'em and see how close you can come to the hole."

"But, Coach, where's the hole?"

"I don't know," he'll reply. "It's out there somewhere."

The moral of the story is you've got to have a target.

"We're going to set goals and we're going to see if we can hit our target," he'll say as he reviews the team's short- to long-term goals. "Our immediate goal is obviously to get to the championship game. You can't win a championship without getting to the championship game."

The ultimate goal, of course, is getting to heaven.

On the way there, Cook wants to stop at the Dome every year.

"I have two kids that played football for me that are now priests," Cook said. "And there's another one who will soon become a priest. What other job could you have that you get to meet and work with these kinds of people?"

The trio Cook refers to are Schumacher, a wide receiver; Nick Ware, a cornerback; and Will Fruge, a linebacker who now goes by the name John Paul. Schumacher graduated in 2008; Ware in 2009; and Fruge in 2011.

Cook seems more like a priest than a football coach. That's understandable because his coaching career has become a ministry, the football field his pulpit, and his players the congregation. He's a teacher, not a Bible-thumping preacher, who frequently bases his messages on personal experiences such as his abstinence from drinking alcoholic beverages and smoking.

"I got called 'chicken' in high school so many times because I wouldn't drink or smoke," he said. "I had to look in the mirror to see if I was growing feathers. But nobody was going to get me to do something I didn't want to do."

Father Schumacher, nicknamed Schu, described Cook's post-practice speeches as *fervorinos*—Italian for a quick religious exhortation or pep talk.

"Coach Cook's lessons naturally flow out of me," Father Schu said. "They became part of who I am and how I preach, particularly when I preach to athletes. He embedded a lot of life lessons—a good foundation—to speak to athletes and it just naturally flows out of those guys that were listening to him. I was one of the guys listening."

So was Lane Anzalone, the starting quarterback for the Pios in 2006. He's now a doctor, specializing in ear, nose, and throat surgery.

"When I think back to all of the speeches that we had after practice, I don't remember a lot of football talk," he said. "But I remember a lot of the background talk: 'This is what men do . . . this is what we're trying to create.'"

It was the non-football stuff on success, failure, and the day-to-day grind of life that got Lane through medical school, five years at the Mayo Clinic, and now his private practice in the Crowley-Lafayette area. "I take the lessons with me each day in the clinic, in the operating room, caring for patients," Lane said.

Notre Dame High is more of a pipeline to the priesthood than college football. Here, Coach Louie Cook, *third from left*, is pictured with three former players, *left to right*, Father Andrew Schumacher; Father Nick Ware; and, *far right*, Brother John Paul, previously known as Will Fruge. *Photo courtesy of Lewis Cook Jr.*

He learned that success is about consistency—setting a high standard and aiming to achieve that daily.

"You learn to do the hard things others won't in a relentless manner," Lane said, "and success is sure to follow, particularly when that message is tempered with other messages of acting with character, integrity, humility, and the overarching mindset of 'the ultimate goal is to get to heaven.'"

He recalls Cook talking about the proud tradition at Notre Dame as a chain connecting one team to the next. "The bar had been set and no team wanted to be the weak link," Lane said. "I wasn't going to break the chain. And I knew the guys that came after me would carry on the legacy."

Lane quarterbacked the Pios to a 12–2 record in 2006, losing 20–14 to Lutcher High School, a perennial powerhouse, in the Class 3A semifinals. Lane completed seventeen of twenty-nine passes for 232 yards and a touchdown, and Schumacher had three receptions for thirty-nine yards.

"The receiver is a priest and the quarterback a doctor," Cook chuckled as he and Lane reminisced about the game.

"I can remember Schu being in the receiving line, probably around the time he was hearing the call to heaven," Lane said. "Every time he'd run his routes, Coach would holler, 'Schu has gotta a chance.' And I thought, 'This guy doesn't have a chance.'"

Tall and gangly, Schu didn't see much action until the semifinal game of his junior year.

"One of the first plays I called, he never breaks the huddle," Lane said. "He's just standing there."

"Schu, what's going on?" Lane said.

"I don't know what I'm doing," Schu said. "Which way do I go?"

"Schu, go over there and run this route."

Schu caught Lane's pass for a twenty-one-yard gain, a preview of the next season when he was the team's top receiver.

In his first sermon as a priest, Father Schu recalled that first practice with Coach Cook.

"Just as he set the tone at practice from day one, I wanted to do the same as a priest," he said. "So that story came back. Let's not get distracted by all these other things that seem so appeasing or difficult now. Our goal is to get to heaven."

Growing up in Crowley, three blocks from Notre Dame, Father Schu's goal was to play football for the Pios like his oldest brother, Chase, a defensive end who is now an orthopedic surgeon. He went to all the Pios' games and pep rallies and dreamed of wearing their signature red helmets.

Father Schu's parents divorced when he was in fifth grade, and he credits Cook with helping him and his three brothers deal with it. "When I got to high school, I had a solid coach who cared about me," he said. "Man, that really made a difference."

Cook has the uncanny ability to communicate with people where they are at any given moment. "He kind of knows the bigger picture of their own life as well," Father Schu said. "He's going to know what's going on at the house, what's going on with mom and dad, whether they've been through a divorce or lost someone in the family, if the youngest boy is going to act differently than the oldest boy in the family. When you know all that, you can look at a boy who's struggling and go to him and say, 'Hey, Brim, let's talk about this.'"

Cook never writes off a kid because he knows his background and story. "If we know people's stories, we can relate with them a lot better," Father Schu said.

All this Brim stuff has nothing to do with Cook's ability to remember people's names. If his memory isn't photographic, it's encyclopedic. He can rattle off the details of games, plays, and conversations from decades

Andrew Schumacher was a sophomore wide receiver for Notre Dame when Coach Louie Cook surprised him by saying the team's ultimate goal was to get to heaven, not the Superdome in New Orleans where the state championship game is played every year. The message had a lasting impact with Schumacher, who was ordained as a Catholic priest in 2018. "My vocation came a lot from that one comment he made about the goal of life—getting to heaven," he says. *Photo by Dwayne Petry.*

earlier, and he can vividly describe what it was like playing "in the middle of nowhere" against East Feliciana in the 2012 state 3A semifinals. That's what he did in a post-practice talk in August 2021.

"The only thing lit was the field," he told the team. "And I thought to myself: 'If I was to Google *home-field advantage,* this is the picture I would see.' It was a goat ranch. You could hardly see the lights."

The quarterback for East Feliciana was Kendell Beckwith, who became a star linebacker at LSU and the Tampa Bay Buccaneers in the NFL.

"And they came running out," Coach Cook continued. "They didn't come from the goal posts. They came from between the stands when they ran onto the field because the locker room was behind them. They ran all the way out past the hash mark. And they're giving us this look. I'm looking for a place to hide. The Pios start walking toward them."

Notre Dame won, 16–14, to advance to the championship game in the Dome, reinforcing his message that the Pios never back down.

"We've got to find the guys that will walk forward in the dark in hostile territory and just battle," he said. "We'll worry about the outcome later. The outcomes don't say who you are."

It was the kind of teaching moment that Cook relishes, taking a page from the past and applying it to the present. He moved seamlessly from a game in 2012 to his first year as a head coach at Rayne High School in 1977 when his team won only two games.

"We shouldn't have won any games that year," he told the young Pios. "Two years later I coached a team that won eight games. They should've won ten. I had more winners on the team that was 2 and 8 than the one that went 8 and 3. The record doesn't make you a winner or loser. It's the process that you put yourself through and how you handle it, and you perform. That's what determines who you're going to be."

By his senior year at Notre Dame, Father Schu was determined to enter the priesthood, even calling the vocation director at one seminary to begin the process. "He didn't answer the phone, praise the Lord, so I ended up going to UL (University of Louisiana at Lafayette)."

At UL, he joined the same fraternity Cook belonged to in the 1970s— Kappa Sigma. "The legend lives on in that fraternity of the man he was," Father Schu said.

In a fraternity known for wild parties right out of the movie *Animal House,* Cook never took a sip of alcohol in the three years he lived in the Kappa Sigma house.

Cook was a designated driver before the term existed. He'd jump out of bed in the middle of the night, get dressed, and rescue a fraternity brother too drunk to find his car in a parking lot.

On one occasion Cook and other pledges were locked in a closet and ordered to smoke cigars they were given. He refused to smoke, just as in another incident he resisted attempts to remove a religious scapular medal he wore around his neck.

"Louie, why are you there?" his older sister, Josette Cook Surratt, asked.

"I got to take care of the people who come in drunk," he said.

When those around him were irresponsible, Cook was responsible.

"That was our dad," Josette said. "Make sure all the doors are locked in the house."

Besides, the Kappa Sigma house was directly across the street from the UL campus and had the best parking around.

"I knew my coach made it through and didn't do anything silly or mess up his future career choices," Father Schu added. "He lived out what the best of the fraternity offers, and he was able to stay true to who he was."

Once Father Schu got a taste of college life, thoughts of the seminary faded away.

In addition to his classes as a business-finance major, he played intramural football, partied with his pals, and ran a business, renting a couple of houses and a duplex he owned to college buddies.

As the demon Screwtape observed in C. S. Lewis's classic novel, *The Screwtape Letters*, "The safest road to Hell is the gradual one—the gentle slope, soft underfoot, without sudden turnings, without milestones, without signposts."[1]

The role of the demons, Father Schu said, "is to keep us so busy, the noise so loud that we can't hear the voice of God."

That's what happened in his first three years at UL. "I didn't want to hear the whispers of God inviting me to the seminary," he said.

In 2011, Father Schu's junior year, the Ragin' Cajuns notched a 9–4 record, including a New Orleans Bowl win that was the school's first postseason football victory in sixty-seven years. "It was the most amazing football season," he said. "The fraternity was at an all-time high. We were just having a blast. I sure wasn't going to listen to him [God] at that point."

Soon after graduating in 2012, he went on a pilgrimage to Rome. "I prayed a lot leading up to that pilgrimage: '"Lord, if you want me to be a priest, make it clear to me while I'm in Rome in this holy land, this holy spot.'"

He was facing the biggest decisions of his life. He was in love with a girl he was thinking about marrying and he had an upcoming interview for a job he wanted. But every church he walked into, there was this tugging on his heart like he first felt on the practice field at Notre Dame.

One night after returning to the United States from Rome, he headed to Haiti. What he saw there stopped him: "Man," he thought to himself, "if they can remain that faithful in that type of poverty, I can't keep running from the will of God. I've got to surrender."

It was time to go into the seminary. The first person he told was his brother, Chase. "If you feel this on your heart, you've got to stay true to it and at least give it a try," Chase said. "You'll always wonder what could've been."

He informed his fraternity brothers the night before he went into the seminary. They were confused and threw him a bachelor's party. "They thought I was leaving forever," he said.

Coach Cook echoed what Chase said: "You'll never know unless you try."

In the summer of 2021, Father Schu became pastor of St. John the Evangelist Catholic Church in Mermentau, a village of about seven hundred people located fifteen miles west of Crowley.

"Coach Cook is a man who loves what he does and he's OK being where he's at now," Father Schu said. "I'm in Mermentau, with a smile on my face and I love what I do. I thought I wanted my own family, my own children, my own business, and all that. I wake up every day and say, 'Lord, you're so great because I am fulfilled.'"

Father Schu never made it to the Dome. Nick Ware got there twice, losing both times.

Nick began at Notre Dame as a ball boy, played four years (2005–2008), and coached for six years (2010–2015).

"I saw being a ball boy as something that was integral to the team," Nick said. "We got to be on the sidelines at every game. The players would talk to us during the games. We just had this connection to something greater than ourselves."

One of the players was Nick's brother, Adam, the Pios' starting tailback in 2002.

Nick ended up at cornerback and, at five feet seven, 155 pounds, personified the undersized overachievers that Cook is a master at producing.

"I'm a product of the program," Nick said. "Notre Dame specializes in taking players with average athletic ability and moving the needle slightly to above average. When you can get a group of guys to move in that direction, it doesn't matter who your outliers are. You're going to be successful."

Notre Dame had a 47–6 record and was state runner-up twice while Nick was there.

"Nick was a student of the game," Cook said. "He really studied his position and learned how to play it well because he was an attention-to-detail guy. He was always prepared."

Those qualities prompted Jimmy McCleary, the Pios' defensive coordinator, to invite Nick to help coach the defensive backs at spring practice in 2009. He had yet to graduate.

Nick Ware was looking heavenward even when he started at cornerback for Notre Dame in 2008. Ware was coaching defensive backs at his alma mater in 2015 when he got the "call" to be a Catholic priest. "The call ain't coming from no cell phone," Coach Louie Cook told another assistant. "He ain't getting a text. That's the Big Guy calling." Father Nick was ordained in 2022. "The souls that the Lord saves through me and his priesthood will also be because of Coach Cook, who took the time to form a young man," Father Nick says. *Photo by Dwayne Petry.*

Nick's ears were numb. "Coach, I played with these guys. They won't listen to me."

"Trust me," McCleary said. "Go out there and see what happens."

Nick liked coaching so much that he continued at Notre Dame while he attended UL, graduating in 2014 and then pursuing a master's degree in kinesiology the next year.

"There was a time where I was kind of straying away from my faith, living a lifestyle that was contrary to the Gospel," he said. "As I was coming back into the faith and I was coaching, I devoted more time to prayer and conversing with the Lord."

"Is this really what I want to do?" he would ask.

He soon realized that was the wrong question and rephrased it: "Lord, what do *you* want me to do?"

"It was in those moments of intimate prayer with the Lord where he revealed entirely that he was calling me to be a Catholic priest," Nick said.

But Nick wasn't ready to make the leap. He joked, "I told the Lord, 'Look, it'd be nice to win a state championship before I go to seminary.'"

At one summer workout session in 2015, Nick asked Coach Cook how he viewed his job.

"Nick," he said, "I've always seen my coaching, wherever I was at, as a ministry."

That helped Nick put his coaching experience into perspective. "It was a call that initially scared me because I thought I had my life figured out," he said. "I realized that the Lord was going to use the gifts that I had cultivated as a coach and now I was going to be coaching souls. The stakes would be higher, but it would be the same line of work."

Meanwhile, offensive line coach Todd Gray went to Cook and said, "Coach, you need to talk to Nick. He's talking about going into the seminary. He thinks he's getting a call."

"The call ain't coming from no cell phone," Cook replied. "He ain't getting a text. That's the Big Guy calling. Little Jesus don't mess with Big Jesus."

Nick cited the adage that the Lord doesn't call the qualified, He qualifies the called. "Having the gift of coaching in my life, especially at Notre Dame, really allowed for my transition out of coaching into seminary to be a lot smoother than most guys who come from different backgrounds."

The Pios blanked eight out of fourteen opponents in 2015 to go undefeated and win the state 3A title. Nick entered the seminary in 2016 and was ordained as a priest in 2022.

"We grow up by imitation," Nick said. "I hope Coach Cook can see in me the imitation of the way that he has lived his life. I hope the way I minister to people is a direct reflection of how he has treated people. I've seen the things he's done and the way he's acted and applied them to my ministry.

The souls that the Lord saves through me and his priesthood, will also be because of Coach Cook, who took the time to form a young man."

At five-eight and 165 pounds, Will Fruge was another of Notre Dame's undersized overachievers, starting at strong-side linebacker as a junior in 2009 when the Pios won the state title and as a senior in 2010. He inherited the position from his brother, Seth, who went on to play at LSU as a walk-on and, later, became a plastic surgeon. Brothers Scott and Mitchell also played at Notre Dame, as did their father, John.

"When Will crossed over the line, he wasn't a priest," said teammate Jake Molbert. "He looked like a gladiator. He hit hard."

Co-valedictorian of his class with a perfect 4.0 grade point average, Will was on the Louisiana High School Athletic Association All-Academic team as a senior.

"Will was quiet and a lot like Nick—intense, smart, a heads-up player," Cook said. "They always went the extra mile whether it was training or preparation for the game. Both are very devout, prayerful guys. They were everything you hoped to have in a player."

After the pregame meals on game days, Will and Cook's youngest son, Stu, slipped away to the school chapel to pray the Rosary together.

"If you'd given me those three guys [Schu, Nick, and Will] and said which one was going to be the priest, right out of the chute my pick would've been Will," Cook said. "Will and Nick weren't a surprise, but I didn't see that coming with Schu."

That's because Schu was in a fraternity not known for producing choir boys, let alone priests.

Will followed his brother Seth to LSU and got a bachelor's degree in chemical engineering. Becoming a priest "came and went in waves" his last two years in college. "I was waiting for some kind of sign or communication from God, whether he wanted me to pursue marriage or priesthood," he said.

After graduating from LSU, he went on a year-long pilgrimage to Europe, visiting various Catholic churches, Adoration chapels, and a monastery near Grenoble, France. "I went on a retreat and explored the spiritual side of things. I started to really seek the Lord in prayer, reading the scriptures and the recordings of retreats."

Will returned to the United States and studied at Notre Dame Seminary in New Orleans for two years, expecting to become a traditional Diocesan priest working out of a Catholic church. This changed when he felt drawn to a stricter way of life in a religious community requiring vows of poverty, chastity, and obedience.

"Things are shared in a religious community," he explained. "You don't have personal money or belongings. Everything belongs to the community, and you share."

He wound up at the Community of Jesus Crucified (CJC), an enclosed, monastery-like compound located in the center of St. Martinville, Louisiana, with nine other men and women called brothers and sisters. Will began wearing the habit of the religious order and changed his name to John Paul. He is not yet considered a priest.

The clothing and the new name signify his transition from "more-or-less a free man" to a life dedicated entirely to God through CJC. "We're all tempted at times to go back on our gifts or forget who we are," John Paul said. "My name is a great reminder of the gift I made."

John Paul has a rigid daily schedule that begins at 5:15 in the morning with prayers and ends at 8:30 in the evening with monastic silence. He doesn't follow Notre Dame football anymore, but he acknowledges that it helped prepare him for the highly structured life he now leads.

"You live a disciplined life on and off the field—going to summer workouts, showing up at practice, being a team player," he said. "In a religious community, you have a lot of the same things lived out in a different way."

Loyalty, honesty, and sacrifice are shared themes.

"Being there for one another and taking responsibility for our actions," John Paul added. "Communicating and encouraging one another. All these little things are very simple, but they build character in a very real way."

He remembers Cook discussing virtues such as sacrifice, generosity, and gratitude. "He'd always tell us to be thankful."

Cook pulled the potential out of his players, "called them to their dignity," John Paul said. "He wasn't afraid to say, 'You can do better than that.' He did it in such a way that was matter of fact. He knew what we had, and he believed in us. It made you want to do better, to give all you had."

Brother John Paul has lofty goals. "I just want to live a life of faithfulness," he said. "I want to be a saint. One of the things I hope for is to share with others the gift of grace that God has given me."

Some of Cook's former players claim there are still grass stains on their knees from kneeling during his long-winded talks. Most had no idea of the impact they would have on their lives.

"There's a rhythm to his life, and that rhythm is rooted in commitment and consistency," Father Nick said. "Young men struggle to commit to something and see it through. They struggle to be consistent in their emotions and decisions. You always knew Coach Cook was going to have a word or some type of message for you. He's just a rock of stability."

Most people choose to be a coach. Louie Cook was chosen. Coaching is his calling, not his profession.

"He's a man who didn't have selfish ambition, was authentic to who he was and who God was calling him to be," Father Schu explained. "He was called to be a football coach in Crowley, Louisiana, for Notre Dame High School most of his life and that's what he did. Because of that he changed a lot of souls. He changed heaven."

4

🏈

Rayne Man

Picture the television town of Mayberry on *The Andy Griffith Show* and you have a snapshot of Rayne, Louisiana, when Louie Cook was growing up there in the fifties and sixties.

Businesses were named after the people who owned them—Claude's Barber Shop; Dot's Beauty Shop; Simoneaux Meat Market, to name a few. If you dialed 4444, Batson's would deliver groceries to your door.

Like Mayberry, Rayne was a place where kids could leave their bicycles unlocked outside the movie theater and their parents didn't worry about them staying out after dark.

Louie spent most summers playing sports during the day and then, at night sitting in the yard with his buddies, shooting the breeze until it was time to go to bed.

Within a five-block area of where Louie lived, there were fifteen kids around the same age. He pumped gas at his father's car dealership in the morning and went home for lunch. "Y'all have a pick-up game scheduled for this afternoon?" Mr. Cook asked.

He didn't want Louie hanging around the house, so he didn't have to return to work if he had a game. "I made sure we had a pick-up game every day," Louie said.

There was no air conditioning and only two television channels to watch such favorites as *The Andy Griffith Show*, *Gunsmoke*, and *The Fugitive*, which made its debut in 1963, when Louie was twelve. "That was big growing up," he said. "Came in Tuesday night at nine to watch *The Fugitive*. On Sunday nights we tuned in Ed Sullivan."

Everybody knew everybody in Rayne.

43

At the time, Rayne was known as the "Frog Center of the United States." That evolved to "Frog Capital of the World" and more recently, Rayne became the "City of Murals," all of them featuring frogs.

Jacques Weil, a native of Paris, France, came to Rayne in 1901 and with his brother, Edmond, started shipping frogs to restaurants and universities throughout the United States. The Jacques Weil Company exported as much as ten thousand pounds of frog legs a week.

Today, visitors to Rayne are greeted with a tip of a hat by Monsieur Jacques, the name for a large stainless-steel sculpture of a tuxedo-clad frog standing near the police station. Almost every business in town has a small, colorfully decorated concrete frog outside its front door.

Folks in Rayne are just as down-to-earth, easygoing, and friendly as they were in Mayberry. More than once, something happened that had people wondering if Barney Fife, Mayberry's high-strung and overly zealous deputy sheriff, was in their midst.

Take, for instance, the time a police car got bogged down in a rice field chasing Robert Cook, Louie's youngest brother, in a four-wheel-drive Jeep equipped with a winch. Knowing the police were stuck in the mud, Robert stopped and hollered, "Hey, y'all right?"

One officer yelled, "Robert, come pull us out. We won't give you a ticket."

He pulled them out and merrily went on his way.

Robert is a legend in his own right, becoming a highly reputable and successful car dealer in the Lafayette area.

He was in the middle of another Mayberry moment when two deputy sheriffs knocked on the front door of the Cook house at five o'clock one Sunday morning.

"What's going on?" Lewis Cook Sr. asked.

"We're looking for Robert," one officer said.

"What did that boy do now?"

"Well, Mr. Cook, he cut through the Texaco station near the Interstate, wiped out the ice machine, and kept on going. When y'all find him, come see us at the sheriff's office."

"Only in Rayne," Louie laughed.

Lewis Cook Jr. was born in Rayne on June 8, 1951, and, except for the three years he lived in a fraternity house at the University of Southwestern Louisiana (USL) in Lafayette, he has never left.

His Syrian father, Lewis Sr., and French mother, Josie Petitjean, met at a Rayne nightclub and dated approximately eighteen months before they got married.

"My mom was having a good time and didn't want to settle down," said Josette Cook Surratt, the oldest of the couple's six children.

Josie got an ultimatum from her mother: "Either y'all get married or break up. It doesn't look good in a small town."

They were married in August 1948. Josette came along eleven months later, followed by Louie, Dave, Cecile, Robert, and Cathy. They were born in waves, the first three separated by two years and the last three approximately a year apart. There was a four-year gap between the two waves.

"The two groups are different because the top three were much more disciplined by Daddy than the bottom three," Cathy Cook Hundley said. "Cecile and Robert were disciplined somewhat, but I wasn't that much because I was the baby."

Louie tagged them with nicknames. Josette is "Ette"; Dave is "Vitas," after the tennis player Vitas Gerulatis; Cecile is "Celey"; Robert is "Bugsy," after the mobster Bugsy Siegel; and Cathy is "Lil T." They all live in or around Rayne, except for Dave, who resides seventy miles away in Baton Rouge.

Dave may well be the first to travel the Baton Rouge-to-Lafayette section of Interstate 10 in 1973, when the road was completed but not officially opened. "Dave went around the barricades and zoomed all the way to Rayne," Louie said.

"Dad liked us to be close by," Josette said. "That's the Syrian culture. Dad always wanted us there for Sunday dinner, much to Mom's dismay. She would've liked a few Sundays off. But the more kids around, the happier Dad was."

Lewis Cook Sr. grew up about fifty miles northwest of Rayne in Kinder, Louisiana, where his parents settled after emigrating from Syria. His mother and grandmother both spoke Arabic. "There's a lot of Syrian people in this area," Louie said. "That's where we get our dark complexion—from the Syrian side."

He has a photo from his childhood, showing an older, Black boy pushing him on a tricycle. Except for their size, it's hard to tell the difference between them.

Louie once told someone he was Lebanese and his dad's sister corrected him, "We're not Lebanese, we're Syrian!"

"My aunts were mad at Dad because he didn't marry a Syrian girl," he said.

Lewis failed to pass his physical the first time he tried to enlist in the US Army, but he persisted and ended up fighting in the Battle of the Bulge during World War II. The bloody conflict claimed the lives of 8,607 Americans, roughly the population of Rayne.

"He never talked about it," Louie said. "It was a horrible experience."

Sometimes before big games, Louie tells his players about a man who was in a Houston hospital for a second open-heart surgery. Doctors gave him a fifty-fifty chance of surviving the operation.

The man hadn't shaved in several days and looked kind of scruffy. The surgeon walked in his room and said he might want to shower and get cleaned up before the surgery.

"Doc," the man said, "I fought in World War II and every time we got ready to go into battle, we just went how we were. We cleaned up after the fight. I have a battle to fight tomorrow. When I'm done with it, I'll clean up."

Louie concludes by saying, "I know the story to be true. I was standing in the room next to the man. He was my dad."

The story illustrates the toughness, pride, and fighting spirit that is at the core of the competitiveness Lewis passed on to Louie.

As a fourteen-year-old freshman, Louie started at guard on the Rayne High School basketball team. "My job was to bring the ball up against a full-court press," he said. "They'd steal it."

Louie was summoned to his dad's bedroom one night. "I'm not going to let you quit," Lewis said, "but you either need to work hard to get better or don't play basketball after this year."

During his sophomore season the local newspaper, the *Rayne Acadian-Tribune*, described Louie as "a mainstay at guard" and a "good playmaker," and by the end of his senior year in 1969 he was All-District.[1]

Even though he was only five feet five, and 125 pounds, Louie's best and favorite sport was football. On offense, he was a quick, elusive quarterback; on defense, he was an All-State safety, the first Rayne player to earn that honor in eleven-man football.

"Louie was the best option quarterback I've ever seen for a kid seventeen to eighteen years old," raved Hugh "Roland" Molbert, a star quarterback at Rayne from 1948 to 1951. "He was the backbone of the team."

Louie was so popular in Rayne that a local department store sold T-shirts with his jersey no. 14 on them. Jimbo Petitjean bought one.

"Louie was always *the* guy," Jimbo said. "If you picked a team, you definitely wanted to play with Louie, and you wanted him to be the captain and the leader because that's just his mentality."

No matter how well he played, though, Louie had to go home after each game and listen to his father critique his performance over late-night hamburgers.

"Dad had a recliner in his bedroom and Louie would go in there and replay the whole game," Josette recalled. "This play, that play, what was done right, what needed to be improved, and he would re-coach him all over again until, God knows, 11:30 at night."

In a game against Abbeville his junior year, Louie rushed for more than one hundred yards and threw for a touchdown, drawing praise from the *Acadian-Tribune* for his "lightning-fast thrusts and passing."[2]

At five feet five and 125 pounds, Louie Cook was a quick, shifty quarterback when he wasn't playing safety for Rayne High School. Louie was so popular in Rayne that a local department store sold T-shirts with his jersey no. 14 on it. *Photo courtesy of Lewis Cook Jr.*

His dad zeroed in on an interception Louie threw. "You didn't see that linebacker?" he asked. "You threw that ball right where he was."

Louie mildly objected: "Is that the only play you saw?"

"Dad was always on him," Robert said. "I don't know how Louie put up with it. He would sit there and take every piece of criticism constructively."

Five inches taller than Louie, Dave was a gifted athlete with sprinter's speed—9.7 seconds in the 100-yard dash. When his dad jumped him for winning a race in 10.1 seconds, Dave fired back, "I ran fast enough to win."

At one point, Lewis asked Dave, "What do you want to be?"

"I want to be sixty-five so I can retire," Dave wisecracked.

Dave followed Louie to Rayne and went on to play for LSU, starting at defensive back for three years. He sat through the same reviews. Robert recalled hearing Dave hollering: 'I don't want to hear about it!'"

"Always striving to be perfect," Dave said of his father.

"Dad wanted the A's, he wanted the wins, he wanted the best," Josette said.

When she got an A-minus in one class, her dad wanted to know why it wasn't an A-plus.

"You strive for excellence," Josette explained. "That was his mantra. If you're going to do something, give it your best. That's what keeps Louie striving. It's innate."

Nowadays, Louie goes to his office at Notre Dame after games and rehashes key plays with a handful of friends and assistant coaches. He doesn't eat a hamburger until he gets home.

"He probably plays it over as if Daddy was there," Josette suggested. "What did I do that I could have done differently? They always covered the mistakes over those late-night hamburgers. We were not raised to be proud. No-o-o. Humble, humble, humble. And that's how Louie keeps his teams—humble, humble, humble. That's a large part of the way we were raised."

The only time Lewis coached his sons was in a recreational baseball league. Louie was twelve years old, and Dave was ten. "I don't know if I was the best player, but I was one of the most experienced," Louie said.

In his first at-bat of the season, he singled and then tried to steal second base. He was out.

Lewis was the third-base coach and didn't give the signal to steal. "Who told you to go?" he asked.

Louie half-heartedly gestured toward the first-base coach before admitting, "No one told me to go."

"Go sit on that bench," Lewis ordered. "Don't get off till I tell you."

Louie didn't leave the bench until the game ended.

"You do something, you take the blame for it," Lewis said afterward. "If you'd owned up, I would've played you."

Louie played baseball during his freshman year at USL for a coach named Bobby Banna. College players used wood bats at the time.

"We were taking batting practice and I cracked a bat," Louie recalled.

"Dammit, Cook," Banna yelled, "you've got more cracked bats than hits."

Louie was feeling sorry for himself when he took his position at second base, hanging his head a little bit. Banna noticed and after practice walked up to him and said, "Don't ever let me see you do that again."

"I got to thinking what a baby I was," Louie said. "Shame on me. I was nineteen years old."

When he sees a kid doing the same thing now, he tells him the story, adding: "I wish somebody would've told me that when I was ten or eleven years old."

The two incidents had a significant and lasting impact on his coaching career.

"It's not about winning at all costs," Louie said. "I see so many coaches playing kids that don't come to practice but they feel they need them to win. In the long run, it gets you."

If you don't practice or do the things that need to be done, you're not playing. "My dad didn't care that his best player was going to sit the rest of the game," he said.

The competitiveness of Lewis was counterbalanced by his happy-go-lucky wife, Josie.

"She kept the peace around there," Dave said. "She was calm and cool. She would always say, 'Just do it good!'"

While Lewis was quiet and introspective, Josie was personable and outgoing. When they went to parties, he would tell Josie they weren't going to stay long. "She'd go hide and have fun so he couldn't find her to go home," Cathy said.

Josie wanted her children to get involved in as many different things as possible. "If you look at a yearbook, Louie was Mr. Rayne High, and the class favorite every year in addition to all the athletics," Cathy pointed out.

Josie encouraged Louie to join a fraternity at USL. "That wasn't Louie," Cathy said. "But he did it and ended up loving it and making great friends."

"I got the best of both my parents," Louie said.

"His quiet reserve makes you want to hear what he has to say," observed Cecile Cook Mouton, the middle sister.

"He's a combination because he's friendly like Mom and quiet like Daddy," Cathy added. "Louie doesn't say much, but when he does, you listen. That's how Daddy was."

Louie and his father are alike in another way—a love for the people around them.

"Dad had a heart of gold," Josette said. "It may not have been the best business practice, but it showed us a lot of empathy. And all of us are like that."

Lewis owned and operated Rayne Motors, a car dealership, repair shop, gas station, and car wash all rolled into one. Louie and Dave pumped gas, washed cars, and moved them around as needed. "Y'all stay in the front in the show room," Lewis said. For safety reasons, he didn't want them to go to the back where the mechanics were working on cars.

"He didn't have to tell Dave and me twice," Louie said. "We didn't want to be there. Robert comes along and Dad couldn't keep him out of the back. He loved being around the mechanics."

It was common for someone to knock on the back door of the Cook house and say, "Mr. Lewis, I can't pay my bill this month but here's a crate of sweet potatoes."

After Louie married Faye Domingue in 1973, Lewis called his daughter-in-law and asked, "Need a freezer? Got a freezer as a down payment on a car. Josie and I don't need it."

He'd sell a car to one of his many Black customers and tell them to pay what they could weekly.

Lewis once was asked to help get someone out of jail. "Daddy would go bail him out," Josette said, "and Mom would fuss, 'Lewis, we can't pay the bills with sweet potatoes.'"

"We learned that there was no color with him," Louie said. "We had barbecues in the backyard and his Black mechanics with their families were right there with everybody else."

Louie had already graduated from Rayne High when Louisiana schools finally integrated in 1971.

"You think back, and nobody did that," Louie said. "Mom was the same way. You're a product of your environment."

One longtime friend recalls Louie buying fruit to give some needy players after practice, so they had something to eat that night.

He has made it standard procedure at Notre Dame to feed post-game meals to visiting teams from inner-city New Orleans.

At Crowley High, he often picked up players, took them out for a hamburger or pizza, and drove them home. "He was being their taxi, their mom, their daddy," Cathy said.

"Everybody in a family assumes a role," explained Josette, now viewed as the matriarch of the family. "Louie's role in our family is calm, steadying, reliable—like a rock. He's today the same as tomorrow, the same as the next day. What you see is what you get every time."

A testament to that was when Cathy had to have her left leg amputated above the knee because of complications from a water-skiing accident. Cathy was fifteen; Louie was twenty-three.

The entire family was in her hospital room the night before the surgery. Everybody was crying except Louie.

"Louie, get 'em out," Cathy said, "get 'em out."

She asked for Louie to spend the night with her. "Not my Momma who was there every night. Not my Daddy. Not my older siblings. Louie. He was just that kind of guy. I wanted him there."

What's remarkable is that none of Louie's siblings or boyhood buddies are surprised by his legendary status as a football coach.

"I knew he was going to be special," Ted Cobena Jr. said.

Ted and Louie were in middle school together at St. Joseph in Rayne, across the street from the Catholic church by the same name. They were altar boys and served mass at six o'clock in the morning, arriving at school before everybody else.

In an empty classroom, they ran pass plays devised by Louie, using an empty milk carton as a football. "Hike the ball, Ted, run five yards and turn to the left."

"Oh, Lord, he's good," Ted thought to himself, adding, "Louie could throw that milk carton."

During class, Louie would draw baseball fields and make tiny spitballs that he flipped with a finger to see where they would go.

At recess one day, Louie and Ted captained opposing football teams and chose up sides. "Louie picked the best players," Ted recalled. "I took my friends. And his team beat mine badly. He was always very competitive."

On the St. Joseph football team, Ted played center and snapped a real football to Louie at quarterback. "Louie was always thinking about football," Ted said.

Ron Prejean was one of Louie's closest friends and a teammate on the football team. Louie was the best man at his wedding.

Louie tagged him "Big Ron" after he was sarcastically called that by Rayne football coach Merrick Young during a punt coverage drill at practice.

"Even in high school, he was a coach on the field," Prejean said. "He had the respect of our head coach, who was an old-fashioned, knock-them-in-the-head kind of guy that bullied most of us around. But not Louie. He always treated Louie with respect because Louie knew what he was talking about."

Ron was tall and lean, Louie short and skinny.

"We were the two guys on the team who listened to the rules," Prejean said. "We didn't smoke, we didn't drink, we didn't eat potato chips in between games."

Prejean describes himself as "a mediocre athlete who always got the scholastic award" and Louie as "a really good athlete" who got the "hardest worker award—the MVP-type stuff."

The pair bonded like brothers, going on double dates with their girlfriends, whom they later married, and remaining close as Prejean established a highly successful accounting firm in Lafayette and Louie became a Louisiana high school football legend.

"He was a friend to everybody in school," Prejean said. "You didn't have to be a star athlete for Louie to notice you. He was just as friendly to the guys working in the cafeteria."

Students selected Louie as class favorite all four years.

"You know why?" asked Mike Bourque, one of those who voted for him. "Because he hung around with the Mire kids."

Mire is a little country community nine miles northeast of Rayne. "Mire kids were the ones everybody looked down on," Louie said.

During the lunch hour Louie played tag football with the close-knit Mire group. He quarterbacked both teams. And he hung out with the Mire guys when they weren't playing football.

"Louie was a silent leader that led by example," Prejean said. "When guys got into spats at school and either scuffling around or bad-mouthing each other, all it took was for Louie to walk up and give them a little nod. He didn't have to say anything. They got the message: Just chill."

Louie was chilling out at a Catholic Youth Organization (CYO) dance when he first met an attractive brunette named Faye Domingue. He was a sophomore, and she was a freshman at Rayne High, dating the school's star running back. "I never thought we would date because she was going with my best friend," Louie said.

Faye ended that relationship in her sophomore year. "I tried talking her into staying with him, but she was done," Louie said. "Her mind was made up."

By that time, Louie was hanging out with Ted Cobena, who had gone from catching empty milk cartons to playing the drums for a local band called 19th Street Uprising. The band traveled around the area, playing at CYO and high school dances and singing cover music of the era—Beatles, Rolling Stones, and hit songs like "Louie Louie" by the Kingsmen and "Gloria" by the Shadows of Knight.

"Back in those days, most bands had a tambourine player," Cobena said.

So, Louie drove the station wagon with all the band's equipment; operated the red, blue, and yellow lights that flickered with the beat of the music; and banged the tambourine—a triple threat, so to speak.

One night the band was playing at a CYO dance in Rayne when a nun walked up to the stage after a song and said, "The band sounds fine, but the tambourine is too loud."

"That's how much Louie was into the tambourine," Cobena said. "He beat that thing."

Louie doesn't remember that incident, but he knows the exact date Faye traveled with the band to a dance in nearby Iota, sitting between him and Cobena in the front seat of the station wagon—Saturday, August 5, 1967. They had their first official date soon after that and kept on dating until they got married on December 21, 1973.

"It was kind of a match made in heaven," Jimbo Petitjean said.

Louie Cook married his high school sweetheart, Faye Domingue, December 21, 1973, in what a cousin, Jimbo Petitjean, calls "a match made in heaven." They have lived in the same house in Rayne since 1978, enabling Louie to drive to his coaching jobs at the University of Southwestern Louisiana in Lafayette and high schools in Rayne and Crowley without uprooting the family. *Photo courtesy of Lewis Cook Jr.*

At the end of their senior season, Louie was selected to the All-State team and his friend, the running back, got a football scholarship from USL. "I'll trade," he said, preferring Louie's All-State honors.

As much as Louie wanted to play college football, he wasn't going to trade places with anybody.

"Faye and my wife, Georgette, are very much alike in that they have strong family roots and ties," Prejean said. "You go do your thing and do all you want to do, but I'm not leaving home."

Faye and Louie have lived in the same house since 1978. "Rayne is the perfect place for us," she said.

For nearly a half-century, Louie has coached at USL in Lafayette and high schools in Rayne and Crowley without uprooting his family. "I get to I-10 and turn left or right," he joked.

"Going from Rayne to USL was a no-brainer," he added. "Once I got there, I realized that staying in college was not what I thought it would be or worth moving my family around. I could get what I wanted from coaching and not have to do that."

The bottom line for Prejean, an accountant, is that nobody works as hard as Louie.

"You hear about the Saban Way," Prejean said, referencing Nick Saban, the University of Alabama football coach. "Well, there's the Cook Way. And he will outwork anybody."

During the summer the head coach at most schools is not going to be at the gym or the weight room at 5:30 in the morning. Louie is there. He wants to be there as an example for the kids and make sure everything is all right.

Faye remembers a principal telling her when she started teaching that if she could bottle her enthusiasm and match it with her experience later, she'd be awesome. "You start off with such enthusiasm and joy and it peters out," Faye said.

"But not that one," she noted, pointing to Louie. "He's still in the hunt."

She recalled the scene in the movie *Patton*, when the general, played by George C. Scott, was looking over a battlefield and reminiscing about the preparations for war.

"That's him," Faye said. "He's General Patton, prepping for every game. That has never changed. He has never lost that enthusiasm."

Neither has Faye.

After Notre Dame won one of its four state championships, Josette sent Faye a thank you note, saying Louie couldn't have done it without her support. "All too often the wife takes a back seat," Josette said. "She has been awesome, and I wanted her to know the family understands what she does, and we appreciate it."

When you live in the same town your whole life, everywhere you go brings back memories.

The abandoned Joy theater in downtown Rayne reminds Faye of riding her bike to the movies and on the way home stopping at a giant mulberry tree behind the post office to pick berries for her aunt to make tarts. "It was a wonderful little town to grow up in," Faye said.

Louie used to go hunting where I-10 passes through Rayne. Before the highway was built, it was a straight shot down Main Street. Now, there's the dreaded "S Curve," so-called because of its shape and the threat it poses to tipsy drivers.

"People would be flying down Main Street and hit the fence in front of our house," Louie said. "When my grandma would catch us sittin' on the fence, she'd come with a belt and yell, 'Get off!' I'll betcha people crashed into our yard four or five times when I was growing up."

On evening walks Faye and Louie often go past the football field at Rayne High. As an eighth grader in 1964, Louie played in the first game at Wolves Stadium and then, as a freshman the next year when it officially opened, he was one of the first to use the locker room and step on the field in a Rayne Wolves uniform. Etched in his mind is the exact spot where his parents sat to watch him play.

Next to St. Joseph Catholic Church is the so-called "Wrong Way Cemetery." All the above-ground graves face North–South, the opposite of traditional cemetery plots. Louie and Ted attended seventh and eighth grade at the school across the street, so they were altar boys at funeral masses held during the week. "I started many a day in the graveyard," Louie said.

From the front steps of the church, you can see where Lewis Cook's car dealership, Rayne Motors, used to be. With a little imagination you can smell the savory biscuits that once came out of the oven at Paco's Café. "I'd have two Paco biscuits and a Chocolate Soldier drink after weekday mass," Louie said with a grin.

"Scores of friends," the *Acadian-Tribune* reported in 1970, "come from everywhere to share Paco's coffee and biscuits and his marvelous philosophies and witticisms."[3]

All the world's problems supposedly were solved at a "table of knowledge" that can now be found at Gautreaux's Doughnut Kitchen.

Louie and Faye go to mass every Sunday morning at seven o'clock. Afterward they swing by Gautreaux's. Faye goes inside to get a dozen hot glazed donut holes plus a large cinnamon roll set aside for Louie, who stays in the car, a safe distance away from the table that may well be causing the problems that need to be solved.

Around noon Louie and Faye have a festive lunch at home with sons Lew, Jeff, Stu, and their families. It's the kind of scene Lewis Cook Sr. cherished and one that keeps the spirit of Mayberry alive in Rayne.

5

⬤

From Bottom Lines
to Goal Lines

Louie Cook could've been the poster boy for obedient sons.
He never talked back to his father, Lewis Cook Sr., and always did what he was told even if it meant getting out of bed late at night to go find his younger brother, Dave, who had a habit of getting home just past curfew. "If Dad said, 'Be home at 11,' he meant five to 11 because at 11 he was going to look for you," Louie said.

"There were no questions, no doubting or arguing with Dad," added Josette Cook Surratt, Louie's eldest sister. "His word was law. And that's how we were raised. Ultimate respect and obedience in the sense of this is what the boss said to do."

So, when it was time for Louie to attend college, his dad had everything planned for him. He would major in accounting at the University of Southwestern Louisiana (USL) in Lafayette and on graduation, he'd go to work for his dad's best friend, Braxton "B. I." Moody III, who owned a prosperous accounting firm. "Go to work for Mr. Moody, you'll be set up for life," Lewis told his son.

It was a brilliant plan because Moody would become president and chief executive officer of Chart House, Inc., a nationwide restaurant group that included Burger King, and an icon of Louisiana's business community, serving on the boards of numerous banks and companies. The College of Business Administration at Louisiana at Lafayette, previously USL, is named after Moody.

Dutiful son that he was, Louie majored in accounting his first three semesters at USL. "I just knew it wasn't for me," he said. "I was drawing baseball and football fields in the sixth grade. I kind of felt the calling right there. I wanted to be a coach."

At age eighteen, fresh out of high school, he coached a Babe Ruth League baseball team with kids only three years younger than he was. The same summer he was the sports editor for the *Rayne Acadian-Tribune,* a biweekly newspaper. This led to another summer job as Rayne's recreation director, organizing and running every aspect of the city's baseball leagues.

He wanted to play college football, but he was too small. So, he joined the Lafayette Area Football Officials Association and over the next five years refereed high school games, doing everything from operating the clock to holding the chains to being line judge and head linesman.

"There wasn't a moment Louie wasn't doing something sports-driven," said Josette, who also was attending USL and was aware her brother wanted to change his major from accounting to health and physical education.

"I knew he was miserable," she said. "He was a round peg in a square hole. My brothers were brought up playing sports year-round. They went from football to basketball to track and then summer baseball. They didn't pursue other hobbies because sports were it. They loved sports. They were good at it."

Louie decided to tell his father he was switching majors before refereeing a freshman football game at Rayne High. Josette went with him.

"Louie was the oldest son, but he didn't defy Dad," Josette explained. "Changing his major really was defiance."

They walked into their father's bedroom together and Louie quickly said what was on his mind: "I'm not enjoying accounting and I'm not doing well. I'm going to be a coach."

His dad's response was predictable: "Louie, you're going to live month-to-month, you're never going to get ahead. It's a no win. You win a game, and this daddy is mad at you because Little Johnny didn't play enough. Or you lose a game, they're mad because you should've won."

Louie stood his ground: "I'm almost twenty years old. Tomorrow I'm going to get my schedule for the next semester. I'm not doing this anymore. I'm switching."

Josette reminded her dad that she'd changed majors.

"Get out of the room, Josette, just get out," he snapped. "This is between Louie and me."

Father and son went back and forth, Lewis finally pleading: "You're not going to have any money. You're going to be poor."

Louie calmly answered: "I'd rather be poor and happy than be rich and miserable."

By the end of the game Louie officiated, his dad had a change of heart: "What do you need me to do?" he asked.

"It wasn't that Louie was going into something that Dad had no affinity for," Josette said. "He loved sports. He just wanted Louie's future to be more financially viable. The irony is that Louie is very fiscally oriented. He knew exactly what his plan was going to be."

"I wish I'd never let you coach that Babe Ruth team," Lewis said at one point during the argument. That wouldn't have made a difference, but it got Louie started on the calling to be a coach that he'd felt since the sixth grade.

"I look at it like this," Louie said. "The Good Lord said, 'Louie, you're going to be a coach. And I'm going to make sure you're healthy and nothing distracts you from being at practice every day.'"

Louie has missed just one practice during his entire coaching career. "Birth of kids, weddings, funerals, there's nothing I had to miss that I should've been at. That's fall and spring practice—one time in nearly fifty years. That's from above."

In late July 2021, he was sitting in his Notre Dame office preparing for the August practices. Earlier that day two former players had visited him—Lane Anzalone, the Pios' starting quarterback in 2006, and Kade Comeaux, a six-foot-six, 300-pound offensive lineman who was offered a scholarship by LSU after his sophomore year at Notre Dame in 1997.

"My dad saw the financial side of coaching and it's not pretty compared to being an accountant with Mr. Moody's firm," Louie said, reflecting on their life-changing conversation. "Over the years what are the rewards? Is it the Hall of Fame? No, the rewards are seeing Lane who studied at the Mayo Clinic and is now an ear, nose, and throat surgeon and big Kade, a hardworking guy who's a successful businessman. That's what makes you feel good."

It may well have been divine intervention that brought together Louie and his coaching mentor, Larry Dauterive.

They were on the sidelines together for several games at Clark Field in Lafayette when Dauterive was head coach at Our Lady of Fatima and Louie was moving the chains.

When Dauterive spoke at a football theory class Louie was part of at USL, he invited the students to come visit him and talk football. Louie showed up the next day and kept coming. "We're all products of having a mentor," Dauterive said. "Some guy has got to push that button and open that door for you."

Dauterive busted the door wide open. "There's only one first impression, right? And you could see the gleam in his eyes and a thirst for knowledge."

Louie did his student teaching at Lafayette High, where Dauterive also was the head baseball coach. "He knew more baseball than I did," Dauterive said. "He'd sit by me on the bus going to games and we're talking football even though it's baseball season."

They formed a bond. "Every time I turned around, he was there," Dauterive said. "He was always there. I thought to myself, 'There's something special about this guy.'"

Dauterive went on to coach at Louisiana Tech and in the Canadian Football League for the British Columbia Lions, where quarterback Doug Flutie, the 1984 Heisman Trophy winner, was one of his pupils. "He taught football," Louie said. "Tech put in a new passing attack one year and he gave me the whole deal. He is the guy I leaned on as a young coach."

Dauterive was the first person Louie called in April 1974 when Rayne High head football coach Ted Brevelle offered him a job as running back coach. The year before, Brevelle was voted Southwest Louisiana Coach of the Year for leading the Wolves to the state semifinals for the first time in twenty-nine years. "Louie, a bird in the hand is better than two in the bush," Dauterive reminded him.

Louie had just gotten married and was living in Rayne with his wife, Faye, who was teaching at a local elementary school.

"I didn't want to go back home to Rayne," Louie said, "but it was hard to get a job and Brevelle had turned Rayne around. I wanted to go somewhere where I could learn."

Louie took the job, and a month later Brevelle left Rayne to join the coaching staff at McNeese State University. Louie informed Dauterive of the opening, unaware Brevelle had already recommended his assistant, Byron Ronkartz, to succeed him.

Dauterive backed off as soon as he found out. But Ronkartz wasn't feeling too kindly toward Louie.

"I bebop to the stadium at Rayne to meet him and he's mad," Louie recalled.

"I hear you were pushing Dauterive for the job," Ronkartz snarled.

Louie explained what happened.

"What do you know about linebackers?" Ronkartz asked.

"I think they run on the field when the other team has the ball," Louie cracked, trying to ease the tension.

"You're going to be the linebacker coach," Ronkartz blurted out.

"That's fine," Louie replied despite feeling he was being punished. "Do we have a playbook . . . a scheme?"

Ronkartz pulled out a crumpled sheet of purplish mimeograph paper and shoved it at him. "Here, this is our defense."

Louie knew nothing about linebackers or defense. He started researching everything he could, poring over *Scholastic Coach* magazine articles,
studying game films, and talking to people. "If I'm going to do it, I'm
going to do it the best I can," he said.

Ronkartz was twenty-four, one of the youngest head coaches in Louisiana Class 3A. He was a bone-rattling linebacker on the first Notre Dame
High team in 1967, played at McNeese State, and handled the defense his
previous two seasons at Rayne.

Louie still remembers playing against Ronkartz as a sophomore in high
school and getting hit by his lightning-like strikes that knocked him back
but not down. "I'd run and bang! He didn't wrap his arms around me,
and I bounced off. He hit me twice."

Ronkartz hired another coach to run the offense, freeing Louie for
defensive duties. "I ended up appreciating the fact that he put me with
the defense and the linebackers because he really needed someone experienced to call the plays," Louie said.

Louie coached three years under Ronkartz, the first two as defensive
coordinator and the third overseeing the offense. "By having to learn the
defense, that helped me a great deal when I became the head coach," he
said.

One summer morning on his way to USL for a class he was taking to be
certified for teaching business, Louie stopped by his dad's car dealership.
B. I. Moody was there.

"Son, how you doin'?" Moody asked.

"I'm doing good, Mr. B. I."

"What you up to?"

"I've got my first year of coaching done and I gotta go to school," Louie
explained. "Ironically, I need one more accounting course."

"Go get your course, have your fun coaching, and when you're done
with that, come work for me," Moody said. "Go, get you a few years of
coaching in—get that out of your system."

In Louie's second year in 1975, Rayne was undefeated (13–0) going into
the state championship game against Lutcher on its home field.

As the Rayne bus rolled into Lutcher, a town of about 3,200 people,
Louie saw signs reading "No Chance for Rayne" and kids grabbing their
crotches greeting the team with their middle fingers. Lutcher won, 28–14,
the players celebrating on the field afterward with champagne and cigars.

By happenstance, one of the Rayne players involved in that game
showed up at Rayne's Wolves Stadium on the same day Louie was there
to talk to the media about the upcoming 2021 season. Morris Godeaux, a
starting defensive end for the Wolves in 1975–1976, was showing a friend
around when he spotted his former coach.

They reminisced about the Lutcher game and "the ditch"—a space between some bushes and the scoreboard at Wolves Stadium where there was a ditch that usually was filled with water.

"If you were slacking off or you wanted to challenge somebody for a position, take them to the ditch," Godeaux explained. "It was all-out war in the ditch."

"It was a linebacker thing," Louie noted.

Ronkartz would stand in the middle between the two combatants and drop his cap to start the brawl.

"It was anything goes," Louie said. "Wrestling. Punching. Grabbing."

"Fightin' it out until you couldn't breathe no more," Godeaux added. "You couldn't kick."

"I would get fired for doing that now," Louie said. "But back then, hey, the poor kids endured a lot."

Godeaux mentioned a pep talk Ronkartz gave the team before playing Central of Baton Rouge in the semifinals of the state playoffs in 1975. "He was standing on top of a big box fan and had a can of Coke in his hand. He got so excited that he bit off the top of the can."

"After y'all ran out on the field," Louie said, "he came to me: 'Got any gauze? I think I'm bleeding.'"

Godeaux then said goodbye to his former coach, leaving Louie to reflect on Ronkartz and the ditch.

The Wolves thrived under Ronkartz in 1974–75, winning twenty-five of twenty-eight games, before faltering in 1976 with a 4–6 mark.

"The kids liked Ronkartz," Louie said. "He was a good guy, unique in his own way."

Louie didn't consider the ditch useful in getting players ready for a game, so he ditched it as soon as he became head coach in 1977. "In all my years of coaching I don't know that I made a kid any tougher than when I got him," he said. "I'd like to think I've prepared them to be able to endure a little bit more and develop more mental toughness to push themselves a little harder. But if a kid had a mean streak in him, he had a mean streak. I didn't add any toughness. Some of them will punch that wall because they think it makes them tough. Some don't want to get near the wall."

Ronkartz resigned at the end of the school year in late May 1977, catching everybody by surprise. Louie had already declared he was going to coach at Lafayette High, the biggest school in the area. "I was a goner," he said. "I had a contract in my hand."

Lewis Cook told his son to apply for the Rayne head coaching job.

"Nah," Louie said, "I'm not ready for it."

"You're ready," Lewis said. "You're always selling yourself short."

Louie threw his hat in the ring.

"The first week of June goes by, the second week goes by, and they still hadn't named a head coach," Louie said. "I'm holding a contract. Nobody is working out the kids. Several of the coaches are leaving. There was no leadership."

Tabbing Louie to be head football coach at Rayne should've been a no-brainer. He'd served as an assistant in baseball, track, and football; established Rayne's first girls' basketball team; and then transformed a losing boys' basketball squad into a twenty-six-game winner, producing the school's first district crown ever.

"Everything we did was based on what he had learned from others," said Robert Cook, Louie's youngest brother, who was on the basketball team. "If he didn't have the knowledge, he went and got it."

Louie had a former coach watch a practice and tell him what needed to be improved. The coach pointed out that after scoring a basket, his players were running back up the court on the outside instead of the middle. This enabled opponents to fast break down the middle and score. "Sure enough," Robert said, "they never got any fast-break points on us anymore."

At the end of the third week in June, Louie was finally offered the job by John Bertrand, the superintendent of schools for Acadia Parish.

"Coach," Bertrand said, "I'm going to appoint you head coach at Rayne High for one year."

"I'm not taking the job for one year," Louie said politely. "We're not going to win a game at Rayne High this year."

"What?" Bertrand exclaimed.

"Rayne High will be lucky to win a football game," Louie repeated. "Vince Lombardi could be the coach and they would have a hard time winning. We had a terrible spring training. We've got to hire coaches. The kids haven't been working out. Nobody in their right mind would take the job in Rayne right now."

Lombardi was synonymous with winning after he led the Green Bay Packers to back-to-back Super Bowl wins in 1967 and 1968.

"I'm going to know in three years whether I can do this job or not," Louie continued. "And if I'm not the guy, I'll come in here, shake your hand, and tell you thanks for giving me this opportunity. This is my career. I'm not just doing this for a check."

Bertrand clarified the terms of the contract: "We're just going to evaluate you after one year."

Louie replied, "If you tell me you're behind me, I'll take the job. If it depends on what happens this year, I don't want it."

Rayne won two of ten games in 1977, the only losing season in Louie's career.

He inherited a roster with only ten seniors, most of them seeing their first action. "It was one of those where I said I don't know what I'm going to do next year as a second-year head coach, but I definitely know what I'm *not* going to do. I learned a lot about what not to do."

One learning was don't kick a vendor's metal drink carrier lying on the locker room floor. Upset by two unsportsmanlike conduct penalties committed by his team, he booted one during half-time of his first game as head coach. "I don't know if my toe was broken but it sure felt like it was," he said. "I never did that again."

There was no hesitation in making other changes. He spread books out all over the living room floor of his house and designed an off-season workout program. Immediately after the Thanksgiving holidays, he had the entire team on the field working out. "We worked about as hard I thought we could work," he said.

Louie always asks his players: "What motivates you to be as good as you can be?"

Even though he has never failed, the fear of failure drives Louie. "I fear failing so I'm going to bust my butt."

He tells his players, "I hope never to put y'all in a position to where you're going to be embarrassed by what you do."

The Wolves lost their first two games in 1978, prompting Louie to tell Faye: "I'd better figure out something else to do for a living. Obviously, I can't coach."

They rebounded to win six of their next eight games, finishing with a 6–4 mark.

The Wolves were 7–4 in 1979 and 6–5 in 1980, making the state playoffs both years and stringing three winning seasons together for only the second time in school history. Overall, Louie's record at Rayne was 21–21.

Even as a young coach, Louie was ahead of his time.

Watching an LSU–Texas football game on television, he noticed ball carriers slipping through the grasp of tacklers, leaving them with a handful of fabric from their tear-away jerseys. "We're going to get some tear-away jerseys," he announced to his coaches.

No high school could afford to buy the number of tear-away jerseys needed for a team, so Louie arranged to buy blemished white T-shirts from Fruit of the Loom and assigned a coach to make the jerseys.

They were soaked in chlorine so a finger could be punched through the cloth and then a purple number was applied. For the team's purple jerseys, sheets of used purple ditto paper were retrieved from the trash and soaked in water with the white shirts until they came out purple. Gold numbers were pressed on these jerseys.

It became a tradition at Rayne for students to gather remnants of the jerseys after a game and hang them on the crossbars of the goal posts. Some students even wore the tattered jerseys around town.

"Any high school could've done it," Louie said.

Only one other school in the area did until the tear-away jerseys were banned permanently by the NFL in 1979 and colleges in 1982.

"I was always looking for that edge," Louie said. "How can I stay ahead?"

Ron Prejean has had a front-row seat watching his buddy go from playing and coaching at their alma mater to being an assistant at USL and back to coaching in high school.

"Nobody can figure him out," Prejean said. "All of these opposing coaches, they're looking for the Louie Cook angle. And there is none because the big angle is hard work. He shows up early, stays late. He coaches his coaches and then lets them go and do their thing."

In 2019, Louie went to see B. I. Moody at his home.

"Mr. B. I.," he said, "forty-six years ago you told me that when I had enough of this to come see you and you'd take care of me. Well, here I am."

Moody laughed and said, "You went down the right path. You've sure done a whole lot of good for a whole lot of people. I'm awfully proud of you. I know your dad was, too."

6

Getting a PhD in Football

Louie Cook didn't realize it at the time but the two years he was line-backer coach at Rayne High provided a blessing in disguise.

The blessing was a linebacker Cook coached—Randy Champagne, a six-foot, 230-pound human wrecking ball. "He was the meanest and toughest football player I've ever coached," Louie said. "That son of a gun was mean."

One day he noticed the purple paint on Randy's football helmet was chipping off and told him he was going to have it repainted.

"Oh, no, Coach, don't do that," Randy protested. "By the end of the year, I want to have all that paint chipped off. I'm going to hit 'em. And when I hit 'em, the paint flies."

Randy was so dominant as a senior in 1975 that he was voted all-district on both defense and offense and selected the outstanding offensive player, an honor that usually goes to a quarterback, running back, or receiver. He was also the top shot-putter in the state, heaving the twelve-pound iron ball fifty-three feet to win the title.

Cook was Randy's shot-put coach as well as his business-class teacher who convinced him to minor in accounting at the University of South-western Louisiana (USL).

The USL coach who recruited Randy happened to be defensive coor-dinator Sam Robertson, who became head coach of the Ragin' Cajuns in 1980. Robertson got to know Cook, leading to an impromptu conversation at a USL track meet and Louie being invited to join USL coaches at a sum-mer camp for boys. "I'm the only guy from the outside," Cook said. "It's all the USL coaches and me."

Just before the camp started, Robertson married Rosalind Moody, the daughter of B. I. Moody III, best friend of Cook's father and a successful businessman who had a job waiting for Louie when he wanted it. "It was kind of like marrying into the family," Louie said of the closeness between the Moody and Cook families.

At a luncheon on the last day of camp, Louie and Sam were seated at the same table.

"Louie, how you going to be this year?" Sam asked.

"I don't know, Coach, we lost a bunch of guys."

"You'll always win, Louie."

Cook knew the names of all the kids at the camp, so he handed out the certificates. There was one left over.

"That little sonofabitch ran out on us," complained the coach in charge of running the camp.

"I don't think he came to the camp," Cook said.

"Oh, yeah, he had to be here," the same coach said. "They got a certificate for him."

"Coach, I don't remember meeting this guy," Cook persisted.

When Cook's youngest son, Stu, started teaching, he told him: "The first thing you need to do is learn everybody's name. They have a name for a reason. Use it."

Cook was right about the kid. He never showed up at the camp. The certificate was printed by mistake.

Robertson saw how diplomatically Cook handled the situation. A week later he offered him a job, coaching USL's receivers: "Louie, I think you'll be a great recruiter."

Cook's coaching ability took a back seat to his people skills. USL had been criticized for not having local coaches and not working hard enough to recruit players from area high schools. "I had the right accent to coach in Lafayette and I was an alum," he said. "Kind of killed a couple of birds with one stone."

Looking back, Cook said: "I was blessed that Sam hired me. The Good Lord took care of me. I'd been a head coach for only four years. What do I know? When we ran a play and it worked, it was one of two things: we either outexecuted them or I got lucky and called the right play. I didn't know to call that play. I just knew that this is what I wanted to run and hoped it worked."

Cook coached four seasons at USL: 1981–1984.

"It was like working on your PhD for football," he said. "I learned to understand the game a whole lot better, I made a lot of contacts, and later on it gave me credibility with high school kids because I had been a college coach."

Louie Cook was a great recruiter, a masterful communicator, and a caring coach his first four years (1981–1984) at the University of Southwestern Louisiana (USL). He enticed Elton Slater, a coveted defensive back from Texas, to play at USL; helped star receivers Clarence Verdin and Greg Hobbs deal with an incident that almost got them kicked off the team; and encouraged several others, including running back Kenny Lee. "He was doing stuff for everybody," Lee says. "Ain't nobody knew." *Photo by Brad Kemp.*

Cook always dreamed of coaching in college. "I was fired up," he said. "And six months later I was ready to leave."

During those six months, the Ragin' Cajuns had what the *Lafayette Advertiser* termed a "plane wreck of a season."[1]

The Cajuns posted a 1–9–1 record in 1981. "The theme that year was the Big Red One," recalled Rennick Tuck, a freshman receiver who later switched to defensive back. "The Big Red One won only one game."

Robertson called it his most disappointing year as a coach. "The morale on the team is bad," he said with two games still to play. "My morale is bad."[2]

Things were so bad that Robertson acknowledged "some of the players have hung it up mentally" and are saving themselves for "deer hunting after the Thanksgiving holidays."[3]

Cook was working "from the crack of dawn to late at night" when he wasn't recruiting the "Golden Triangle," a goldmine of high school football talent in Southeast Texas that ranges from Beaumont and Orange in the north to Port Arthur in the south. "I'm watching a game in Beaumont Friday night and hustling home the next morning for an eight o'clock breakfast meeting with the team," he said.

His wife, Faye, was teaching school and pregnant with their first son, Lewis III.

"It was a different lifestyle," he added. "I was miserable."

At one point he said to himself, "Man, this ain't what I thought it was going to be."

In a game at Arkansas State midway through the season, he benched receiver Clarence Verdin (pronounced *Ver-DAN*), a speedy, pint-sized playmaker who would become a two-time All-Pro kickoff and punt returner for the Indianapolis Colts in the NFL.

Clarence claimed to have a bum ankle, but he never saw the trainer for treatment. "The whole week I couldn't get him to do anything at practice," Cook said. "So, I didn't play him."

USL didn't score a touchdown in a 14–3 loss. "We've got to figure a way to get our playmakers in the game," Robertson said, obviously referring to Verdin.

Cook thought to himself: "The best way I know is not to play his ass."

He told Verdin: "Where I come from, I don't play a kid that doesn't deserve to play. You didn't deserve to play."

Two weeks later the Cajuns were shellacked, 41–0, by Southern Illinois. "We played with no heart and no brain," Robertson said. "We didn't have our heart in it, and when the heart is not beating you can't get blood to the brain."[4]

The Cajuns had a blocked field goal nullified by a penalty for twelve players on the field, eventually leading to a Southern Illinois touchdown.

Defensive coordinator Dave Dunkelberger was furious, directing a profanity-laced tirade at Mike Doherty, a graduate assistant, as they were walking to the locker room at the half. "Gawd-damn, Doherty, you've got one frickin' thing to do and you screw it up."

Cook overheard the tongue-lashing and tried cheering up the dejected Doherty. "At least you've got one thing to do," he joked. "Why am I here?"

He asked a similar question of junior quarterback Dwight Prudhomme, whom he dubbed "Dante" after Dan "Dante" Pastorini, a fun-loving quarterback for the Houston Oilers in the 1970s who was always in the doghouse with his head coach. Prudhomme started the season opener and then languished on the sidelines the rest of the way.

Cook was standing near Prudhomme in the dressing room during half-time of a game against Lamar University, when he suggested a play to the team's offensive coordinator. "He just blew me off," Cook said.

On turning around, Cook noticed Prudhomme, wearing a baseball cap backward and slouched by his locker with a smirk on his face.

"Dante, why are we here?" he asked.

"Coach," Dante replied, "I was just thinking the same thing."

"Coach Cook could say funny things with an underlying seriousness about them," Prudhomme said. "The tag, Dante, was funny but it also was his way of telling me, 'You need to kind of toe the line a little bit.' He always had a little humor involved."

Cook shared an office with Lee Rodgers, the offensive line coach. "If it weren't for Louie's sense of humor, I'd probably blown my brains out a couple of times," he said. "But we were able to laugh things off and not get so uptight about everything, and a big part of it was his sense of humor in the office."

The '81 season was brutal for players and coaches.

"It was basically a free-for-all," Prudhomme said. "We were losing, people were getting frustrated, practices were just a big-time burden."

In one practice, running back Kenny Lee was hit out of bounds on a kickoff return play, tearing the ACL (anterior cruciate ligament) in his left knee.

"It was a dirty shot," Prudhomme said.

"It was maybe not so much a cheap shot as something that didn't need to happen," Cook said, noting the tackler was mad and crashed into Kenny recklessly. "If he wasn't all wound up, it probably wouldn't have happened."

"It split the team a little bit," Kenny said.

"My heart was broken that day when you got hurt," Cook told Kenny forty years later.

"That's why you're still coaching and winning," Kenny replied. "You cared about us. We knew that."

At the end of the year, Louie considered going back to Rayne High, which was looking for a head coach again. His brother Dave urged patience. "Louie," he said, "you've got to pay your dues."

It was sound advice. Things got better in 1982, as Cook landed Elton Slater of Lincoln High School in Port Arthur, Texas, one of the most prized recruits in the country.

Cook was a natural on the recruiting trail with his aw-shucks personality, Cajun accent, and humor.

"Coach Cook beat some big schools in the Golden Triangle," said Gerald Broussard, who coached with him at USL. "Every momma loved him."

The mommas cooked for Cook.

"Let me tell you, I've eaten some bad food and smiled, too," Broussard said. "I learned that from Coach Cook. If they want to feed you, you eat! You could've just had a steak. That's all right. You eat!"

The mommas laughed at his stories and made sure their boys went to see him in Lafayette.

"They didn't go visit USL," Broussard said. "They went to visit Coach Cook. When people would come and get a feeling for Lafayette, it was always good. It was just his ability to get 'em in the car. You had to get 'em in the car and get 'em to Lafayette."

At Lincoln High, Cook met head coach Joe Washington Sr., father of Little Joe Washington, an All-American running back at the University of Oklahoma from 1972 to 1975.

"Who you recruitin'?" Coach Washington asked.

"Tim McKyer and Elton Slater," Cook said.

"You might get McKyer but Slater, you can color him Texas orange or Oklahoma red," Coach Washington said.

Both were blue-chip cornerbacks and Slater was a prep All-American in both football and track and field.

"Boom, McKyer committed to us right away with the stipulation Slater wasn't coming," Cook said.

"I've been in Slater's shadow for four years," McKyer explained. "I don't want to do that anymore."

Nobody gave USL a shot at getting Slater, who was hotly pursued by perennial powerhouses such as USC and Nebraska in addition to Oklahoma and Texas.

Oklahoma conducted what amounted to a campaign, assigning assistant coach Lucius Selmon, the oldest of the famous Selmon brothers, to look after Elton, and flying Head Coach Barry Switzer into town to woo his parents, Emma and Ernest Slater. When Elton visited the OU campus in Norman, they entertained him with a Little Joe Washington highlight film.

"Coach Cook was the littlest man on the totem pole," Elton acknowledged. "Everybody else was from a major university."

That didn't faze Cook. "Elton was kind of a homebody guy. He wasn't comfortable with the big time. Miss Emma was from St. Martinville, Louisiana, and I'm a coon ass from Rayne."

Emma Slater was a cook at a cafeteria in Port Arthur. Whenever Cook was in town, he went there to eat and chat with her. "Emma, your boy's here!" a coworker announced as he entered the restaurant.

"I'd go when the crowd was down and two or three of the gals would take their break and bring me some pie," Cook said. "I'd cut up with them."

Broussard remembers Cook telling him, "Brim, them cafeteria ladies, they got the spoon. Be nice to them."

On national signing day, Emma was nice to Cook. "Now you can make your decision," she informed Elton, "but I prefer Mr. Lewis Cook."

So did Elton. "I went with my heart," he said. "And it was Coach Cook. He was very kind, honest, and straightforward. You could talk to him. On a scale of one to ten, I gave him a twelve."

McKyer ended up at the University of Texas–Arlington. "He called me after the first year and wanted to come to USL," Cook said. "I talked him out of it. I said, 'Tim, you played as a freshman. As much as I'd love to have you, it's in your best interests to stay.'"

McKyer remained at Arlington and went on to play twelve years in the NFL, earning three Super Bowl rings.

Cook found college coaching more to his liking in 1982, working alongside Lynn Amedee, the team's new offensive coordinator. Amedee made Louie running back coach, put Prudhomme back at quarterback, and got the ball to Verdin so he could make some big plays. The Cajuns responded with a 7–3–1 record.

"Cookie," Amedee said, "you and Rodgers handle the running game and I'm going to handle the passing game."

Instead of working late every night, he let the coaches go home shortly after practice. "He knew what he wanted," Cook said. "We didn't have to stay all night."

Amedee played quarterback for LSU from 1960 to 1962 and was quarterback coach at the University of Tennessee in 1979, when he and head coach Johnny Majors tried to entice Prudhomme to play for the Vols. They were sitting in the living room of Prudhomme's home in Lafayette.

"I need you in Tennessee," Amedee said.

Majors coached the University of Pittsburgh to the national title in 1976. He took off his championship ring and tossed it to Prudhomme, who caught it. "Prudhomme," he said, "look at that ring right there. You come to the University of Tennessee; you have a chance of winning one just like it. If you go to USL, you don't have a chance."

Prudhomme laughed in telling the story. "That's all he said."

He turned down Amedee at Tennessee and now he was playing for him at USL.

"Lynn saw the potential in Prudhomme," Cook said.

"I don't know what you've been doing here the past three years but that guy down the hall doesn't like you," Amedee told his new pupil, referring to Robertson. "We're going to start fresh."

Amedee had Prudhomme pick out several seniors who could be trusted and he took them out for pizza and beer. "He told us his plans and ideas and wanted us to be his disciples to turn everything around," Prudhomme said. "The funny thing is he didn't even give Sam a playbook."

Amedee said: "He's an old linebacker. Let him go coach the defense."

Prudhomme completed 52 percent of his passes for 1,320 yards and eleven touchdowns. "We turned things around to win seven games and set thirty-one offensive records with the same team that won one game the year before."

In 1983, Amedee left for greener pastures, Prudhomme had a fling with the New Jersey Generals of the United States Football League, and Robertson was waving a white towel on the sidelines.

With eight seconds left in the third quarter of the season opener against Northeast Louisiana (University of Louisiana–Monroe), Robertson conceded defeat. His team had just received two fifteen-yard penalties, committed six turnovers in the first half and trailed 31–6. "The white flag was symbolic of an exasperated coach," he explained.[5]

If the '81 season was a "plane crash," the '83 season started like a train wreck. The Cajuns lost their first five games.

The night before the debacle at Monroe, the Cajuns' two top receivers, Verdin and Greg Hobbs, missed the team curfew because they were out partying. They claimed they were in somebody else's room at the hotel.

The following Monday, Robertson called Hobbs to his office. On his way there, Hobbs saw Verdin, who answers to the nickname Skeet or Skeeter. "Skeet, Coach Sam called, and he wants to see me. Come on, you're going with me."

Hobbs had a great relationship with Robertson, who helped get him a summer job at a bank run by the Moody family.

Verdin had a checkered past. He once missed the team bus leaving for a game against Southern Mississippi in Hattiesburg, Mississippi. He caught up with the bus on Interstate 10.

He also had another go-around with Cook because he pouted after he didn't start a game. "I look around for him and he's sitting on the bench," Cook said. "He's mad. So, I said, 'Stay over there.'"

They were walking to the locker room at the half and Verdin said, "Hey, man, what's up with this?"

"What language are you talking," Cook said, "and who are you talking to? You ain't talking to me, not like that. I told you why you weren't starting but you were going to play. When I turned around and saw you, I read in your body language: 'Screw this team. I don't care about the team. I'm upset.' You're back there hanging your lip. That just tells me how selfish you are. I'd like to play you in the second half but I ain't playing you with that attitude."

Verdin came out the second half, patting his teammates on the butt and yelling, "Let's go! Let's go!"

"Get your little ass in the game!" Cook groused.

Verdin caught two passes for forty-five yards, including a thirty-one-yarder for a touchdown.

On their way to the meeting with Robertson, the two seniors rehearsed their alibi that they were at the hotel but in somebody else's room.

When they got to Robertson's office, Hobbs could see he was upset and disgruntled. "Clarence, you stand outside. Hobbs, you sit down."

Robertson didn't mince words: "Hobbs, let me tell you. I know everything that went on. If you tell me anything different from what I know already, I'm going to kick you off the team and send you back home and tell the press that you got kicked off the team."

"I was never more scared in my life," Hobbs said. "So, I told him everything."

"Okay," Robertson said, "get out of here. Call Clarence in."

As Hobbs left Robertson's office, he whispered to Clarence, "Tell the truth."

"I figured if Coach broke it down to him like he did to me, there would be no problem," Hobbs said.

The next thing Hobbs heard was Robertson shouting, "You lying sonofabitch!"

Clarence stuck to the story. "To this day, he rags me for not sticking to the story," Hobbs chuckled. "I rag him for being a fool and not doing the right thing."

"Robertson wanted to kick me off the team," Clarence said. "He told me flat out: 'I want your ass out of here.'"

They were both in the doghouse.

"We went to practice that evening and the coaches were treating us like dogs," Hobbs said.

Hobbs missed a block on a punt coverage drill and one of the coaches grabbed him by the shoulder pads and threw him to the ground. "I'm gone," Hobbs thought to himself. That night he called his mom in New Orleans to tell her he was heading home.

And then, Cook pulled Hobbs aside.

"He gave me the talk," Hobbs recalled.

"Hang in there," Cook urged. "It's not going to be that bad."

"Coach Cook changed my mind," Hobbs added.

Verdin was demoted to the scout team, a group of inexperienced and lesser-skilled players tasked with emulating opponents in practice, and then he was cut from that. "How low can you go?" he laughed.

Verdin was down but he wasn't out.

"Thank God that Coach Cook was there," he said. "I probably wouldn't have played pro ball if he didn't speak up for me. I put him in some bad situations, but from his goodness and kindness, he hung in there with me and believed in me. Like: 'Skeeter, you're a great athlete. Come on, man, just tighten it up.'"

Verdin and Hobbs finished the '83 season one-two in pass receptions, as the Cajuns won four of their last five games to end up with a 4–6 record.

The most memorable win was over Louisiana Tech on a late November night when sheets of rain from a torrential thunderstorm flooded the playing surface, knocked out the power at Cajun Field, and threatened to wipe out the game. The players waited in the locker room.

"Go in there and keep them loose," Robertson told Cook.

He kept them loose with his extensive repertoire of Little Johnny jokes and stories about two slow-witted Cajuns named Boudreaux and Thibodeaux. He tells the stories with an exaggerated Cajun accent that makes them even funnier.

One story has Thibodeaux coming out of church on Easter Sunday and walking past Boudreaux without saying anything.

"Thibodeaux, you not going to say hello?"

"Boudreaux, that you?" Thib asked. "You lost some weight."

"Yeah, you know, Lent just passes by," Boudreaux said. "I gave up on that boudin, cracklings, and rice. I feel good. What did you give up, Thib?"

"Well, me and Louise decided we give up sex," Thib said.

"Whew, man," Boudreaux said, "you kept that up for forty days and forty nights?"

"I gotta be honest," Thib said. "I went into Winn-Dixie with Louise. She had one of them Menzie skirts on with them transparent drawers. When she bent over to get some meat, I couldn't hold back no more."

"Thib," Boudreaux said, "that's a serious offense against the Church, breaking your penance like that."

"I don't know about the Church," Thib said, "but they sure ran my ass out of Winn-Dixie."

Mention Winn-Dixie to any of the players and they immediately think of Coach Cook and the laughter in the locker room that night.

"He made everybody laugh and feel comfortable," Verdin recalled. "I tried telling them when I got to the NFL, but I couldn't tell them like Coach Cook."

After a fifteen-minute rain delay, the relaxed Cajuns beat Louisiana Tech, 13–9.

"He's not just a coach," Verdin said.

In his four seasons at USL, Cook was a father to many of the Black players, a caring and empathetic man to all.

"The door was always open," Verdin said. "You felt free to talk to him. If we felt something wasn't racially right, we went to him. White or Black, he'd sit down and talk to us. We had some neat conversations."

"Get your education," Cook told Verdin. "I can't change your situation, but I'm going to teach you how to be a man. We're going to deal with this like a man."

When Rennick Tuck was ill in his dormitory room, Cook went and sat with him until he felt better.

When Elton Slater was redshirted his freshman year after tearing a hamstring muscle, Cook encouraged him through the injury and afterward. "You need to be yourself," he reminded Elton. "Play well, play hard, and play smart."

Cook had a talk with Kenny Lee after he tried to come back from the serious knee injury incurred in practice. "I've always been truthful with you," he told Kenny. "We've got a lot of young players that look faster than you. I'm going to play you when I can, but I can't play you in front of the other guys."

Cook paused and then said: "You ought to think about coaching. You're a good guy and you can help a lot of people because you've got a lot of character."

"I don't want to coach," Kenny said. "I want to play."

"Think about it for a week or two," Cook said. "You can start off as a student assistant. Your school will still be paid for. We don't want to lose you."

When Kenny got hurt, he thought about quitting. "I was out there on crutches because you had to be at practice. I'd almost given up. He encouraged me every day. One of his sermons was: 'Get your education; football isn't everything.' I had to look at life from a different perspective."

Kenny was a student coach for two years, eventually got a bachelor's degree in behavioral science, and then returned to his hometown of Greensburg, Louisiana, to be the head football coach at his alma mater, St. Helena Central High, for four years. He ended up working twenty-four years for ExxonMobil.

"He made a spot for me to get into coaching," Kenny said. "I used to tell my kids: 'If I just teach you about football, I've failed you. I've got to teach you about life and being a man.' That's what Coach Cook did."

Cook worked for four offensive coordinators in as many years at USL. He and Rodgers applied for the job in 1984 and neither got it. Rodgers resigned; Cook stayed and became the quarterback coach.

He inherited backup quarterback Donnie Wallace, a senior who helped spark the Cajuns' late-season resurgence in 1983. He was making a strong bid for the starting role in spring practice when he sustained a shoulder injury that required surgery.

Cook was walking by the training room one day, saw Wallace with his injured shoulder in a harness, and asked if he was alright. "He put his hand on my shoulder and said, 'All I can tell you, Donnie Wallace, is cream always rises. You've got to keep doing what you're doing.'"

The next game starting quarterback Donnie Schexnider went down with a season-ending knee injury. Wallace took over and passed for 1,127 yards and five touchdowns the rest of the year.

"I think back and it's rewarding to know that as long as Louie Cook was around, I'd probably never be in a bad headspace because he's thinking about those things," Wallace said. "He has compassion—genuine compassion."

A field goal with four seconds left in the final game of the season beat Tulsa and gave the Cajuns a winning record for the year (6–5). A month later, Cook announced he was leaving USL to become head coach at Crowley High School. "My mind was set that it was probably time to go," he said.

He left behind a legacy that many of his Black players are keeping alive. For Kenny Lee, Rennick Tuck, Clarence Verdin, Greg Hobbs, and Donnie Wallace, the passage of time has awakened their memories of Coach Cook, not dimmed them.

Every November around high school playoff time, Kenny Lee phones Coach Cook to encourage him because he knows his former coach would do the same thing for him if he was still coaching. "He's one man I met in my life that I can really say doesn't look at color," Lee said. "He looks at human beings. And that's what I love him for."

Lee gets emotional talking about Coach Cook. "My dad was an alcoholic," he explained. "He was around, but he wasn't around. I didn't have a dad that I could talk to."

But he could always talk to Cook. "He was more than a father to me," Lee said.

Lee, Verdin, Hobbs, and Tuck keep up with each other and found out in recent years that they have similar stories to tell about Cook. "We kept it a secret until we got older and started talking about stuff he did for us—how he helped us physically, mentally, and spiritually, and made a difference in our lives," Lee said.

"He did that for you?" they say to each other and laugh.

"He was doing stuff for everybody," Lee said. "Ain't nobody knew."

Rennick Tuck has an analogy for that. "Coach Cook does everything with ease, so nobody knows the back story or what's going on. It's like when you're watching a duck on the pond, and he's so graceful and everything. But underneath the water, his feet are paddling really hard."

Tuck was in the locker room when Cook told the Boudreaux-Thibodeaux joke about Winn-Dixie. At the end of the 2021 season, he texted him a humorous Cajun story he'd come across in a magazine and then called to ask why he wasn't getting the "Lincoln Riley treatment" for all the titles his high school teams have won.

Riley, head football coach at Southern Cal, had just signed a contract worth an estimated $110 million, including a new house and use of a private jet.

"You should have a six-million-dollar home and everything," Tuck said.

"Nah," Cook laughed, "they wouldn't do that for me."

"Well, at least they could've given you a little pirogue," Tuck teased.

"Words can't describe the man," Verdin said. "He made me laugh. He made me smile. He was always happy. Win or lose, the man has kept his integrity."

Hobbs now owns and operates a bunch of Popeyes chicken restaurants in Texas and Louisiana and traces his success to how Coach Cook treated him and his teammates. "Anybody can make mistakes, but you've got to treat people like people," Hobbs said. "And that's Coach Cook. No matter who you are or how you look, he's going to treat you the same."

Wallace is an executive for the PGA Tour. "Most coaches these days at every level are trying to manage talent," Wallace said. "Coach Cook was coaching men. There is a difference because if you're trying to manage talent, you're not developing it. He was the other end of that spectrum."

Elton Slater ranked among the nation's top defensive backs with eight interceptions in 1986 and got a look-see as a free agent from the Miami Dolphins the following year. He worked thirty years for the city of Port Arthur and then on February 15, 2022, he was killed in a car accident. He was fifty-seven.

"If I had to do it all over, yep, I would," he said six weeks before his death. "But it would've been so much better if Coach Cook was the head coach because he knew football and how to explain things in a mild tone of voice without cursing and hollering. He would've been an excellent head coach."

Of course, Cook didn't get the top job at USL. But he got his PhD in football, and he took with him to Crowley as an assistant the former linebacker, Randy Champagne, the blessing in disguise who made it possible.

7

"They're Laughing at Us"

Louie Cook was walking out of the Superdome in New Orleans with his friend, Carroll Delahoussaye, head coach at St. Martinville High School in Louisiana. Delahoussaye was carrying the state championship trophy his team had just received for winning the Class 3A title in 1984.

"Are you taking the job at Crowley?" Delahoussaye asked.

The two coaches had talked before about the football program at Crowley High and agreed that the right guy could take it from the outhouse to the penthouse.

"There's a good chance I'm going to take the job," Cook offered grudgingly.

"We're not playing you," Delahoussaye said.

"You're worried about that right now?" Cook laughed. "You're holding a trophy saying you're the best team in 3A and I'm going to take a team that hasn't won a game in two years."

With a twenty-one-game losing streak, Crowley's football team was the butt of jokes. "If you were going to give an enema to football in Louisiana, you'd given it to Crowley," said Larry Dauterive, the coach who mentored Cook early in his career.

"They're laughing at us," James Griffin, the superintendent for Acadia Parish schools, told Cook at their first meeting to discuss the job. "I can't pay you what you're making now, but I'll personally go to the Boosters Club and see what I can do."

The proposed salary was $6,000 less than what Cook was making at the University of Southwestern Louisiana (USL).

"I'd prefer not to do that," Cook said. "I don't know if we can win a game. I'm not sure what the problems are. I really don't want to be obligated to anybody. I'm going to look at it and if I can afford to come, I will."

He asked for help in hiring two assistant coaches he wanted to bring in from Rayne High—Randy Champagne and Randy Thibodeaux. "I'm not a miracle worker," he said. "I can't do it myself."

A few days later Cook was watching basketball practice in the Crowley High gym and noticed a king-sized player moving gracefully around the court.

"What does he play in football?" Cook asked.

He found out the guy wasn't on the football team.

"No wonder they haven't won any games in two years," he commented.

After practice, Cook walked up to Tracy Boyd, a six-foot-four, 240-pounder, and introduced himself as an assistant coach at USL.

"Tracy," he said, "do you know who Dale Brown is?"

"Yeah, he's the basketball coach at LSU," Tracy said.

"How about Bill Arnsparger?"

"I don't know who that is."

"He's the football coach at LSU," Cook said. "Not to knock your basketball ability, Tracy, but you're the post player, the center on the basketball team. There are no 6-4 centers in the SEC [Southeastern Conference]. If Dale Brown was here watching, he'd say, 'Boyd, good-looking athlete, but I can't recruit him—too short to play basketball at LSU.' He'd have walked out of here in ten minutes. If Bill Arnsparger came in, he'd likely be waiting to talk to you about football."

Cook said he might become the head football coach at Crowley. "I'd love for you to play football."

"Coach," Boyd said, "I played when I was little, but I haven't played in a long time."

"Well, I'm not sure I'm going to be the coach," Cook said, "but there's a chance I will be."

Cook took the job. At the first team meeting, Boyd was sitting in the front row. He started at tight end Cook's first year at Crowley in 1985 and then played at Elizabeth City College in North Carolina. The New England Patriots selected him in the sixth round of the 1992 National Football League draft. He ended up playing in the Canadian Football League.

Boyd was the harbinger of things to come at Crowley High over the next seven years.

"I never doubted he'd turn Crowley around," said Mike Doherty, who coached with Cook at USL. "Crowley had a lot of talent walking the halls. I knew Louie would get the kids on the field and they were going to play as hard as they could for him."

Shane Garrett, Crowley's best and most versatile player when Cook arrived, recalls him walking the halls, looking for big-bodied guys to try out for the team. "Guys that had never played, they came out and turned out to be good players."

One of those hallway finds was Joel Sinclair, a humongous freshman who was in the marching band at Crowley High. Sinclair played football in junior high but was giving it up to concentrate on playing the tuba in the marching and concert bands.

Cook talked with Sinclair in the hallway. "If you don't play football, you'll never know what you could become or how far you can go," he said. "If you come out and try, you'll at least know what it is and can make a better decision."

That made sense to Sinclair. He played both football and the tuba as a freshman and for the next three seasons, 1989 to 1991, he was a six-foot-four, 285-pound fixture at left tackle. "Next thing you know I'm signing a scholarship to go to Michigan State," he said.

The outgoing head coach at Crowley recommended that Louie get rid of his assistant coaches. "Ain't a one of them can help you," he grumbled.

Cook kept three of them—Kevin "King" Magee, Bob "Czar" Czarnecki, and Donald Adams. "Everybody sees things in different ways," Cook said.

"Coach Cook brought the right temperament of men with him to coach us," said Sinclair, who went on to become a high school football coach. "You had the funny coaches. You had serious coaches. You had the fun-loving. But all the coaches cared about us. He orchestrated that for us. He basically created a whole new system of family for us playing football at Crowley High School."

Magee was quiet, but funny. "He was passionate about defense, but he wasn't over the top like some of these guys," Sinclair said. "Coach Czar was the coolest cat in the room. He had a charisma about him. He loved the kids."

Known as "Coach A" and "Love," Donald Adams was particularly important to the coaching staff because he's African American and from West Crowley where the team's Black players lived. "He was that bridge from the Black community into Crowley High for us as athletes," Sinclair said. "We knew Coach A. So, we trusted Coach A. And Coach A always showed us love."

Sinclair remembers Coach A pulling him aside and saying: "'You may be a coach someday. One rule you must live by is always show the kids love.' That's what I do now in my coaching career. I try to show the kids the same kind of love that those coaches gave to us."

At first, Ron Prejean was puzzled by his high school pal's decision to take the Crowley job. "You're in college," Prejean thought to himself. "Why are you going back to high school?"

Prejean went to Crowley High to see for himself. "You could see Louie's excitement about doing something good in a place that was at the bottom."

"We cannot go any lower than we are now," Cook admitted.

And yet he was oozing with enthusiasm.

Prejean left saying, "He knows what he's doing."

The locker room was given a badly needed makeover with new paint and hunter green carpet trimmed in old gold, the school's colors. The players painted their own lockers. "If any of you clowns write on any of these lockers, it's going to be your ass," warned Garrett, Crowley's ace wide receiver and punt-kickoff returner.

Name plates were placed on the players' lockers as if they were pros.

A wall was built to conceal a screened-in area used to store equipment and do laundry. On the wall, Magee painted Crowley's newly designed white football helmet with a stripe and three-dimensional "C" in green and gold. "When people see that C a few years from now, they're going to know that Crowley was in town," Cook said.

Magee decorated another wall with a drawing of the state of Louisiana, highlighting the Superdome in New Orleans where the championship finals are held every year. On it, he inscribed the message: "Believe it!"

"Everybody thought we were crazy," Cook said. "You ain't won a game in two years and y'all are paintin' the Dome."

Cook played baseball his freshman year at USL and one of his teammates was Ron Guidry, a three-time twenty-game winner for the New York Yankees in the late 1970s and early 1980s.

When Cook took the job at Crowley, Guidry phoned and asked, "Louie, can you use some weight equipment?"

Guidry was building a new house and needed to get rid of some Nautilus equipment the Yankees had given him. The weights were trucked to Crowley High the next day. "We had nothing," Cook said.

The second day of spring practice was so bad that Cook apologized to Champagne and Thibodeaux, the coaches who had left Rayne to join him. "Guys, I'm sorry for bringing y'all into this," he said. "I've never seen anything this bad. I've got to be losing my mind. I gave up college ball for this?"

In a meeting with students, both boys and girls, he said, "Why don't I see anybody wearing Crowley High shirts around town? All I see is Notre Dame shirts. You know why that is? We haven't won any football games.

"How many of y'all heard of John Curtis?" he asked, referring to a private school in the New Orleans area coached by John Curtis Jr., one of only two prep coaches to win six hundred games in his career.

A bunch of them raised their hands.

"Why do you think y'all know about John Curtis?" he continued. "Because they win football games. Everybody here is not a football player. But I want y'all to understand that what we're going to do is going to affect you. Let's all be together. We all can help one another."

Crowley High is located near exit 80 on Interstate 10, about three miles from where most of the Black players lived in West Crowley. Adams picked them up for practice in a used fifteen-seat van. "I knew where they lived," he said. "And I was going to get 'em. I didn't want to hear no excuse for missing practice."

Changing the culture in any organization must start at the top. Cook teamed with the school's principal, Eric Stutes, to schedule physical education classes so they could be optimized for training and practice purposes. This gave the coaches four hours of instruction and practice time each weekday during the football season and one and a half hours of training daily for the rest of the year. "He gave us a chance to succeed," Cook said of Stutes. "He trusted me, and I knew he was there to help me."

Cook inherited twenty-five varsity players (eight juniors and seventeen sophomores), but one of them quit the first day. Eighteen freshmen joined the squad plus eight seniors. "They were guys that played before and quit," he said. "I let anybody that wanted to play come back."

Shane Garrett, a versatile baseball player with pro potential, was going to quit football until he found out he couldn't play either baseball or basketball if he did.

"O and 20 my first two years," Garrett said. "Practices were rough. The coach was tough. People would just walk off the field because they didn't want to deal with it. So, we started losing a lot of players. We know we're not going to win."

Garrett also knew the losses would be lopsided—50–6; 47–8; 42–0, for example. They were blanked in seven of the twenty games and outscored 362–70 in 1983 and 329–41 in 1984.

Going into the '85 season, the Crowley Gents hadn't won a game since October 31, 1982—Halloween.

They didn't fare any better in the season opener, losing 14–7 to Welsh. The headline of a story in the *Crowley Post-Signal* summed up the game: "Crowley Comes Close—Still No Cigar."[1]

The Gents snapped the losing streak the next week on Friday the 13th and then lost another close game prior to playing arch-rival Rayne High, where Cook played and started his coaching career.

He stood on the visitors' side at Wolves Stadium for the first time and looked at the spot in the stands where his mom and dad always sat. They weren't there. Lewis Cook Sr. had died of congestive heart failure three months earlier—Thursday, June 6, 1985, two days before Louie's thirty-fourth birthday.

"Your birthday's Saturday," Josie Cook announced to her son. "I'm burying him tomorrow."

"We need to have the funeral Saturday or Monday," Louie said.

"I'm not burying him on your birthday," Josie persisted.

The funeral was the next day—Friday. Lewis Cook was sixty-five.

"It was weird," Louie said of being at Wolves Stadium and his father not there to watch him. "I was on a mission because that little girl said I was going to be a loser."

That "little girl" was a cheerleader at Rayne High.

At a basketball game in Rayne shortly after he became head coach at Crowley, she walked up to him and said, "I can't believe you're the coach at Crowley."

"Everybody has got to work somewhere," he replied.

"You come over here with these losers?" she asked.

"Well, I'm trying to see if we can do something about that," he said politely.

"Coach," she sniffed, "you're going to be a loser just like them."

Now, he was angry: "Week four at Rayne—Crowley and Rayne. Be at the game. I know you're going to be graduating. Come to the game. We'll find out who the loser is."

At halftime of the Rayne game, Cook was seething because the Gents were up by only one, 7–6.

"It's frickin' Rayne!" he exhorted the players. "You're from Crowley. We're better than Rayne. We're going to win the game if y'all just get out there and play."

Rayne had won the last four games between the two schools and the sting of the girl calling him a loser was something he'd never forget.

The Gents won, 30–6. The girl wasn't there to see the game, so she read about it in a newspaper story headlined: "Crowley's Blowout Wasn't Expected."[2]

"We never lost to Rayne in the eight years I was at Crowley," Cook said proudly. "It's not fun playing Rayne. It's a no-win for me."

The Gents went on to win six games before losing in the first round of the state playoffs to finish with a 6–5 record. "Who would have ever thought a team with a twenty-two-game losing streak could wind up in the Class AAA state playoffs at season's end?" the *Post-Signal* mused. "The Gents thought so."[3]

"When you play for a losing team, you lose the sense of team," said Dammon Stutes, the Gents' starting quarterback from 1984 to 1986. "You are motivated by your individual achievements. We had great athletes, even as a losing team. And to lose with great athletes showed us we're not playing as one."

Stutes and Garrett had another year of eligibility left. Tracy Boyd missed the cut-off date by three days. If he remained in high school for his senior year, he couldn't play football.

"What should I do, Coach?" Boyd asked.

Cook recommended going to Pearl River Junior College in Poplarville, Mississippi, so he could play for at least two years. That's what he did. From there, he went to Elizabeth City College and the Patriots in the NFL.

Meanwhile, the Gents rolled to ten victories in 1986, losing twice, the first and last games of the season.

In the season-opening loss to Welsh, Garrett hardly touched the ball. "We were in a two-back offense with Shane the split end," Cook said. "They double covered him all night long and we couldn't get him the ball."

On the bus ride home to Crowley, Cook kicked himself verbally. "I'm a helluva coach. My best player touches the ball only three times. What a dumbass! I've gotta do something to get him the ball."

Shifty and swift, Garrett was a threat to score any time he got the ball. Cook changed the offense so Garrett had more options as either a wide receiver or slotback. The next week he got the ball seven times on Crowley's first series of downs. "From that point on, it was hard to stop us," Cook said. "I could throw it to him, hand it to him, pitch it to him."

The Gents clinched their district title and a spot in the state playoffs for the second straight year when Garrett scored on a ninety-three-yard punt return that, according to Bill Webb of the *Lafayette Daily Advertiser*, "bore an eerie resemblance to Billy Cannon's 1959 game-winning return against Ole Miss."[4]

Cannon's legendary punt return on a muddy field helped him lock up the 1959 Heisman Trophy and has come to represent the spirit of LSU football. Garrett's jaunt on a gimpy ankle helped define Crowley football under Coach Cook.[5]

"We were playing Westlake, first home playoff game at Crowley in fourteen years," Cook said as he began to retell the story. "Shane rolled his ankle early in the game. He was crying. He was hurt. He was slowed. And he was upset."

The ankle was taped twice so Garrett could continue playing. With the score tied 14–14 and seven minutes left in the game, Westlake punted.

"Let it go, let it go!" Cook yelled, knowing Garrett's condition.

"My thing was: they punt the ball, I don't care where it's at, I'm going to get the ball," Garrett said. "But I was hurting and didn't expect to do much."

He was on his own seven-yard line and briefly thought about signaling for a fair catch, but instead caught the ball and took off. "I saw all the blockers lining up on the left side," he said. "So, I got behind the wall."

Cook was now hollering, "Go, go, go!"

Garrett saw a crack in the wall.

"Zing!" Webb wrote in the *Daily Advertiser*. "Into the crack he went. Zing! Through a wall of Rams [Westlake Rams] seemingly cemented into the ground. Zing! Past the safety and into the end zone. Zing! Crowley won 20–14, and many wondered if they hadn't just seen the ghost of Billy Cannon."[6]

Garrett wasn't done. With about a minute to go in the contest, the Gents needed about five inches for a first down that would seal the victory if they made it. "If we don't make it, they're going to get the ball close to midfield with a chance to tie or win the game," Cook said.

"I never asked for the ball," Garrett said. "This particular time, I said, 'Coach Cook, give me the ball. Let's go get it.' I got the ball, and they were on me. I stuck my foot in the ground, accelerated, and just shot up in the air."

Garrett slapped his hands.

"It was like a human missile," Cook said. "He went pushing into that pile with his head down."

"Barely got it," Garrett smiled. "That was the ball game."

"When I talk to the kids about leadership, I bring up Shane's name because you don't have to run your mouth all the time to be a leader," Cook said. "You can lead by example. And I tell them that story. The best player on the team hardly said a word."

"I couldn't get a word in with all the talkers we had around," Garrett joked.

Garrett's numbers for the '86 season were eye-popping: thirty-eight receptions for 821 yards and ten touchdowns; fifty-seven carries for 637 yards and seven scores; nine punt returns for 127 yards and two tallies; and five kickoff returns for 240 yards, including a 76-yard TD. He went on to play at Texas A&M and professionally for the Cincinnati Bengals in the NFL and for three teams in the Arena Football League.[7]

"When Coach Cook came, hey, it was a blessing!" Garrett said. "I ended up getting a scholarship. That probably wouldn't have happened if he hadn't come to Crowley."

Stutes completed 76 of 153 passes for 1,286 yards and fourteen touchdowns in 1986, while running back Kirk Landry rushed for 1,040 yards and fifteen touchdowns.

"It just shows the difference in coaching because we had the same players," Garrett said. "We couldn't win a game those first two years."

The perseverance of Garrett, Stutes, and Landry during the famine and their resurgence under Cook served as an inspiration for those who followed the next five years. The Gents went on a roll: 9–3 in 1987; 10–2 in

1988; 12–3 in 1989 to win the state 4A title; 8–3 in 1990; and 12–3 in 1991, losing in the state finals by two points.

Joel Sinclair was in junior high and remembers what it was like BC— Before Cook. "I knew nothing about Crowley High football until he got there," Joel said. "All of a sudden Shane is on the news. You saw his punt return. He was a superstar."

Wes Jacob and David Martin were misfits in junior high who fit perfectly with Cook at Crowley High. Wes was a prep All-American receiver his senior year in 1988. Martin wore the same jersey number 5 as his hero, Garrett, and played like him in 1989, returning five punts and kickoffs for touchdowns.

"If Coach Cook knew you could do better, he'd push you to do better," Martin said. "If he figured you couldn't do better, he'd teach you how to do better."

Cook's approach trickled down to the seniors who passed it on to the younger players. "The older guys were the foundation to the change Crowley High was going to have," Sinclair said. "So, us winning the championship in '89 was inevitable. It was part of what was drilled and drilled into us since '85. Those upperclassmen taught us how to win."

It was the school of hard knocks for Sinclair, a second-string offensive tackle and scout team member as a sophomore in 1989. "I got rocked in practice twice that season," he said, recalling hits by linebackers Ronald Perrault and Marlon Mayfield. "They hit me so hard I felt I could survive anything after that. They taught me a lesson I never forgot."

In the spring of 1989, Cook stared at the game schedule he keeps on his office wall, trying to figure out what five games the Gents could win to break even.

The '88 season ended in a heartbreaking one-point loss when the Gents failed on a two-point conversion attempt. Gone from that team were fourteen starters and twenty-two seniors, including Jacob, the Class AAA MVP; All-State quarterback Edward "Tiger" Hollier, who accounted for fifteen touchdowns and 1,719 yards of total offense; and star defensive back Kevin Quebodeaux. They were products of Cook's first freshman class and considered his best chance of getting to the championship game in the Dome.

The closest thing to a high-profile player on the '89 team was Martin, the Gents' top rusher as a junior with 538 yards on fifty-seven carries and eight touchdowns. Orlando Thomas, a future All-Pro in the NFL, was still a diamond in the rough at free safety.

The new quarterback was Joey LaFosse, who reminded Cook of himself in high school because of his size, generously listed at five feet eight and 160 pounds.

Quarterback Edward "Tiger" Hollier, *left,* **and running back–receiver Wes Jacob,** *right,* **were both All-State performers and cornerstones of Crowley's 1988 team that Louie Cook considered the most likely to win it all. Unfortunately, a last-minute two-point conversion attempt failed, and the Gents lost by one, 14–13, in the quarterfinals to Wossman High, the same school they would topple the next year for the state crown.** *Photos by Brad Kemp.*

He played guard on the junior high football team, but Cook had other plans once he saw him running at track meets. "I picked Joey out to be the quarterback pretty much because of the way he competed," Cook said. "He didn't always finish first, but he battled to the end. He'd push and push."

There was a slight problem—LaFosse threw the ball sidearm. "Don't throw another pass," Cook cautioned at the end of his freshman season. "I'm going to retrain you to get over the top of the ball."

Cook worked with LaFosse on his throwing motion every day for six weeks during the winter. "He was a student of everything," Cook said.

By his senior year, Joey was a decent passer, but his size and perceived frailty kept Cook from moving backup quarterback Hal Morgan from outside linebacker to the middle spot. "I was afraid to put Hal in the middle because he'd take more hits," Cook said.

He also was concerned LaFosse wouldn't make it through the season without getting hurt, necessitating Morgan to take over at quarterback. "Finally," Cook said, "we just bit the bullet and said, 'Heck with it, we'll worry about it later.'"

The Gents had a 2–2 win-loss record at that point and tried four different players at middle linebacker. "We started week five with Hal in the middle and we never lost again," Cook said.

LaFosse didn't miss a single play in the fifteen-game season. "He was a lot stronger than you would've thought," Sinclair said. "He was very cerebral, and he was strong."

On long drives LaFosse would pop into the huddle like the Energizer Bunny, look at Sinclair and the other weary linemen, and wink. "You could play for Joey because you trusted Joey. He was the ultimate captain . . . him and Orlando Thomas. They were our captains."

"And they were," Cook agrees. "Joey on offense and Orlando on defense. But I don't name captains. We don't vote on it, and we don't talk about it. The captain of a team should emerge just like Shane emerged. He was silent but everyone knew that Shane was the guy. Orlando was the safety, Joey the quarterback. Their personality and their drive just dripped out of them. You knew it. You could see it."

The Gents won four playoff games to get to the Dome, beating Jennings 14–7; Rayville 33–14; Mansfield 3–0; and outlasted Broadmoor High of Baton Rouge in the semifinals.

The Gents muffed the opening kickoff against Broadmoor, putting them on their own five-yard line, prompting Cook to say: "Rayville ran the opening kickoff back. We fumbled the first play of the game against Mansfield. So, I guess it's fitting we start on the five-yard line."

The Gents fumbled on the next play, virtually giving Broadmoor a touchdown and the early lead. LaFosse answered by marching the Gents down the field on an eleven-play, sixty-seven-yard drive to tie the game. Crowley went up 13–12 early in the second quarter and managed to fend off Broadmoor comeback attempts the rest of the way and win 34–26.

Part of the lore of the Broadmoor shoot-out is an incident that took place before the game.

The Gents were doing their walk-through in front of the Crowley gym when one of Cook's former coaches at Rayne High showed up with a young, buffed-up guy he'd never met. "This is our first chance to go to the Dome," he said. "I'm nervous as all get out."

Cook's pregame routine usually consisted of going into his tiny office and sitting quietly in a lounge chair, doing his final prep for the game. Instead, he had to deal with the visitors who followed him into his office.

"Coach, I had a good day today," the unknown muscleman said. "I bench pressed 300 pounds."

"We need to get this guy a trophy," Cook thought to himself.

Kevin Magee, the Gents' defensive coach, was nearby. He and Cook have worked together so long that they can often read each other's minds.

"Kevin, what are you looking for?" Cook asked.

"I'm looking for a medal to pin on the sonofabitch's chest," he said.

There weren't enough medals to go around after the Broadmoor game.

LaFosse rushed for three touchdowns and completed all seven of his passes, including a thirty-seven-yard scoring toss to Mike Meaux; Jason LeJeune racked up 114 yards on twenty-one carries; David Martin snagged six tosses for 106 yards; and Orlando Thomas had two interceptions, the second a pass in the end zone near the end of the game to wrap up the victory.

"The Road to the Dome Is Complete," proclaimed a banner headline in the *Crowley Post-Signal*.[8]

"This one was sweet, but wait till we get to the big house," said Gents' defensive end Sean Morgan.[9]

Richard Pizzolatto, a Crowley High coach and teacher, summed it up neatly: "We're going to 'the room' to play for the 'ship."

Cook tried to tone down all the hullabaloo over playing in the Dome. "We're going to New Orleans to win the championship," he told the players. "The Dome just happens to be where they play the game."

The day of the game there was a sign on the exit 80 on-ramp to I-10 heading east to New Orleans: "Last One to Leave, Turn Out the Lights."

Some five thousand locals, about half of Crowley, flocked to the Dome to see if the Gents could beat Wossman, the Monroe, Louisiana, high school that had become their nemesis, knocking them out of the playoffs two straight years. "They beat us in '87, they beat us in '88 and here it's '89," Cook said.

The third time was a charm, the Gents winning 17–15 with unheralded players responsible for most of the heroics.

Running backs Jason LeJeune and Mike Meaux stepped up when the Gents' biggest playmaker, David Martin, went down with a knee injury in the second quarter. LeJeune ran for seventy-four yards on twenty-one carries and Meaux seventy-one yards on fifteen rushes, each scoring a touchdown.

Vietnamese placekicker Visith Luangphone booted a thirty-seven-yard field goal with sixteen seconds left in the second quarter to give Crowley a 10–7 halftime lead.

Punter Brady Thibodeaux averaged forty-five yards on seven punts, the blockbuster a state championship game record seventy-two-yarder

Crowley High split their first four games in 1989 and then reeled off eleven straight wins to capture the Class 3A state crown. Pictured here with Coach Louie Cook, *foreground*, are, *left to right*, cornerback Brian Quebodeaux (3); running back David Martin (5); defensive end Sean Morgan; safety Orlando Thomas; and offensive tackle Louis Monceux. Quebodeaux and Thomas sparked the Gents' playoff run with key tackles and interceptions. *Photo courtesy of Brad Kemp.*

in the fourth quarter that got the Gents out of a hole deep in their own territory.

Meaux and Brian Quebodeaux intercepted passes in the last two minutes of the game to stop Wossman drives. An interception by Orlando Thomas in the first quarter set up the Gents' first touchdown.

"Hal Morgan made two or three tackles that if he doesn't make, might've been touchdowns," Cook added.

The one play that sticks in Joel Sinclair's mind is Joey LaFosse escaping a tackler in the end zone to lunge out with the football and avoid a safety that would've given Wossman two points and tied the game. "He had the wherewithal to get out of the end zone before he came down," Sinclair said.

It didn't matter that LaFosse completed only one of nine passes for thirteen yards. His heady play in the end zone enabled Thibodeaux's booming punt that followed. "It's still the longest punt in the championship game at the Superdome," Cook said. "And it flipped the field completely around."

Carroll Delahoussaye, the St. Martinville head coach, went down on the field to congratulate Cook and saw the baby-faced LaFosse without his helmet on.

After allowing 101 points in the first five games in 1989, the Crowley Gents' defense got stingy, limiting the next 10 opponents to only 83. Leading the turnaround were assistant coaches, *foreground, left to right*: Danny Smith (defensive line), Kevin Magee (defensive coordinator), and Randy Thibodeaux (defensive secondary). Behind them are the players who made it happen. *Kneeling, left to right*: Chad Perkins, Marcus Senegal, Wallace Jones, Visith Luangphone, and Brian Quebodeaux. *Standing, left to right*: Orlando Thomas (13), Kevin Simon (61), Marlon Mayfield (25), Troy Harmon (55), Ronald Perrault (44), Sean Morgan (11), and Hal Morgan (6). *Photo by Brad Kemp.*

"That's your quarterback?" Delahoussaye asked.

"Yeah, number 10," Cook said.

"I know where I want my boy to come play quarterback," Delahoussaye said. "If you can do it with him, I'm going to let you have mine."

Afterward, an emotional Cook told his players: "You showed this state that there are no individuals at Crowley High School, but a team . . . a team that wasn't satisfied with just getting here. A team that wouldn't quit until you'd won it all."[10]

Looking back now, Cook said, "Wow, what a ride! It's a grind. It's a journey. That's what I liked so much."

He was thirty-eight years old at the time and had already achieved the three goals he set for himself coming out of USL: (1) be a head coach; (2) win the state championship; and (3) coach in college.

He expected it to be in that order because he didn't play college football. "I thought I'd have to win big in high school for any college to recognize my ability," he explained.

He floundered through the 1990 season. "It was kind of like someone took the flag out of the hole," he said. "I'm hitting these golf balls and I don't know where the hole is."

The Gents struggled as well, losing 13–7 in the second round of the playoffs to Carroll, another Monroe, Louisiana, high school.

"We didn't have the same bond as we did the year before," Sinclair said. "We were still a good team but there wasn't the same level of enthusiasm and senior leadership as there was in '89."

The crushing blow was six players stealing six pairs of Isotone gloves at a Crowley department store. Cook found out about it after the last regular-season practice and confronted the players: "I would've thought one of y'all could've figured out that if you want six pairs of gloves, let's put up enough money to buy one pair and steal the other five. But, no, y'all stupid asses all went in there.

"I could run y'all off the team," he continued. "I could make you run gassers, suicides, roll on the ground. I'm not wastin' my time. But let me tell you what's going to happen. One or two of y'all or maybe more are going to screw up in a game and we're going to get beat. You've got no character; no class; and we're going to get beat and the season will be over long before it should be."

That's what happened.

The winning twenty-yard touchdown run for Carroll was a sweep around two of the players involved in the shoplifting incident. They messed up on the play. "Where were y'all?" Cook asked. "Y'all goin' lookin' for some gloves again instead of making a play?"

Cook took it personally. "I thought maybe being part of this team would've given y'all a chance," he told the six players. "But obviously I failed y'all, too."

He questioned himself: "You always wonder if your calling is the right thing."

Immediately after the Thanksgiving holidays he gathered the players returning for the '91 season and told them it was back to the basics. "We'd drifted from where we needed to be," he said. "We refocused and ended up playing for the championship again."

On the way there, Crowley hooked up in the second round of the playoffs with St. Martinville, coached by Cook's friend, Delahoussaye, who didn't want to play against him. The Gents proved why, winning 27–7.

The season is best remembered for what is known as "The Play"—a pass in the title game against South Terrebonne.

Trailing 14–6 midway through the third quarter, Gents quarterback Brannon Woodward fired a bullet to tight end Sherard Joseph in the end zone. The ball was batted in the air, Joseph dove for it and appeared to have control of it before hitting the ground.

Officials even asked Joseph if he caught the ball. "Yes, I did," he said.[11]

They looked at each other, shrugged their shoulders, and then ruled no catch. "I guess they didn't believe me," Joseph told *Lafayette Daily Advertiser* sportswriter Brad Hawkins.[12]

"High school football doesn't use instant replay to correct an official's embarrassing call," Hawkins wrote, "but maybe they should consider the use of a polygraph machine on the sidelines."[13]

Hawkins went on to observe "the officials in the end zone, seemingly out of position to make any call, showed indecisiveness" and "looking at each other in total confusion" before ruling the pass incomplete.[14]

The Superdome's Jumbotron scoreboard and television replays confirmed Joseph caught the seven-yard pass for what would've been a touchdown, trimming South Terrebonne's lead to 14–12. That was the final score after the Gents added a fourth-quarter touchdown.

Three decades have passed and Rev. Sherard Joseph, the pastor of two Baptist churches in Crowley, is still asked about "The Play."

"Cost us the game," he said. "Cost us another championship."

"I would've had two rings," said Sinclair, a member of the '89 championship team who, playing left tackle, was right in front of Sherard and got a close-up look. "I know he caught that ball. I don't care what anybody said. He caught the ball. The referee that was closer to it, he signaled touchdown. The guy came from the other side said he didn't catch it."

Cook is philosophical about "The Play," the opposite of his wife, Faye.

"It wasn't like it was the last play of the game," he said. "It was the third quarter. We still had time to go win the game."

Faye isn't as forgiving: "Still very angry. Not for Louie, but it cost those kids a championship. Six men and not one of them was able to make the call in the end zone. Six men; twelve eyes. Nobody saw it."

She saw "The Play" over and over again on television. "I just felt so bad for the kids," she said. "They worked hard and earned it. But they weren't going to have another chance."

A poignant photograph on the front page of the *Daily Advertiser* showed a helmet-less Joseph leaning over a distraught Woodward, both hands touching his helmet, as he tried to console his quarterback after the loss.

"I didn't think too much of it because at that time I was a junior," Rev. Joseph said. "So, I had another year. Brennan was a sophomore. I went over and patted him on the back and said something like, 'Hey, we'll get another chance at this next year.' That's how I felt—we'll get another crack at this."

The next year Cook was back at USL as offensive coordinator and the Gents were eliminated in the second round of the state playoffs.

Carencro High School, located in a suburb of Lafayette, made its first trip to the Dome in 1992 and Cook was asked to speak to the team the week of the championship game.

"I've been on both ends," he began. "We went to the Dome in '89 and won it. We went in '91 and lost. We came back after that win; there were five hundred people waiting for us in the gym. Two years later we lost, got back to the gym, and had to give kids a ride home. Understand that it's nice to go to the Dome," he continued. "That will stay with you for about four or five days if you don't win. If you win, it'll last you a lifetime. One day you may be down and out. You may not even be able to find your championship ring. Somebody might steal your car. Or you might lose your house. But the one thing they'll never take away from you is that for one night you were the best that there was, and you were state champions. No matter what happens to you, if you win that game, it'll be with you the rest of your life."

Carencro won its first state championship, just like Crowley in 1989.

8

🏈

"There Goes His Redshirt"

A football tradition at the University of Houston is for its mascot to do pushups for every point the Cougars score in a game.

This was a concern that became a laughing matter to Louie Cook as the Cougars piled up forty-nine first-half points against the University of Southwestern Louisiana (USL) in their game at Houston in October 1992.

Earlier in the year, Cook returned to USL as offensive coordinator for head coach Nelson Stokley, a star quarterback at Crowley High and LSU before entering coaching. Another addition to Stokley's staff in '92 was Ron Brown, a wide receivers coach affectionately called "Brown Brim" by Cook because of his name and skin color.

Cook watched from the press box and Brown the sidelines as the Cougars scored four touchdowns in the first quarter to set a school record of twenty-eight points. As a result, their mascot, Shasta, had to do twenty-eight more pushups on top of the forty-two he'd done for the first three scores. By halftime, Shasta was up to 322 pushups with another two quarters to go.

At the half, Brown waited for Cook outside the Cajuns' locker room.

"Brim, where were you?" Brown asked.

"The cougar grabbed me," Cook said.

"The cougar grabbed you?"

"Yeah, the dang cougar grabbed me," Cook said. "He wants to give the kids a pep talk. He says if we don't start doing better, we're going to kill him. I think they got him on an IV right now."

Houston won 63–7, the mascot doing 119 more pushups in the second half to total 441 for the day. All the USL coaches needed an IV by the time the Cajuns finished the season with a 2–9 win-loss record.

"We're getting smoked and I'm talking about the cougar," Cook said, laughing. "You've got to keep your sense of humor. If you don't, you go crazy."

The Cajuns even had a walk-on quarterback named William Sirmon whom Cook good-naturedly called Maniac. One day at practice Cook said, "Maniac, if the cops show up at your house tonight and they want to arrest you for murder, plead guilty because you're killing me."

It wouldn't be the last time he used that line.

Stokley coached at USL for thirteen years, from 1986 to 1998, his teams compiling a 62–80 mark and producing future NFL stars such as quarterback Jake Delhomme, kick returner Brian Mitchell, safety Orlando Thomas, and his son, Brandon Stokley, a wide receiver.

Nelson was offensive coordinator for Clemson's national championship team in 1981 and guided the Cajuns to winning records his first four years before going 5–6 in 1990 and 2–8–1 in 1991. "His strength was he let his coaches coach," said Boo Schexnayder, a sports performance consultant. "His weakness was he let his coaches coach."

Sometimes this led to confusion, craziness, and chaos.

If the Houston debacle was an embarrassment, a 14–10 loss to Cal State–Fullerton at home two weeks later was an insult, slap in the face, and kick in the butt rolled into one.

"Cajuns' ineptness reaches Titanic scale," proclaimed a headline in the *Lafayette Daily Advertiser*.[1]

A related story reported the Cajuns "reached the bottom of the barrel in the Nelson Stokley era."[2]

Stokley agreed: "No question it's the most disappointing loss. It's about as tough as they come."[3]

The week before, Cal State players threatened to boycott the Cajuns game if school officials didn't stop the program entirely or drop to a lower division.

In six previous games, Cal State lost twenty-four of forty-five fumbles, including three returned for touchdowns. This led to nicknames such as "Cal State Disneyland" and "Cal State Fumbleton" as well as a candid assessment by Gene Murphy, the team's head coach who retired at the end of the season: "It's a primary case of self-abuse. We continue to shoot ourselves in the foot. We've had forced errors, unforced errors, bad quarterback-center exchanges. It's gotten to the point now where it's starting to affect us emotionally and mentally."[4]

The Cajuns were now reeling emotionally and mentally.

"Poor Stokley," Cook said. "You would've thought he got shot with a thirty-ought-six rifle, laying in the locker room after the game."

Stokley told his coaches: "If I was y'all, I'd find a way to protect yourself because we're probably going to be fired after last night."

Cook was calling the plays for the offense he inherited and didn't feel it was best for the team's personnel. He came up with a new plan and presented it to Stokley the following Monday. "I trust you, Louie," he said. "Do what you want to do."

Those were the only words Stokley spoke to Cook all week. The worst was yet to come if you looked at the Cajuns 0–38 record against Southeastern Conference schools and lopsided losses to Auburn in three previous meetings: 52–0, 49–7, and 50–7.

So, you can imagine the shock of 74,327 Auburn fans when the Cajuns jumped to a 24–10 halftime lead on three long touchdown drives and a field goal on the last play of the first half. The field goal provided a glimpse of Cook's competitiveness.

Stokley wasn't wearing a headset, so he had one of the other coaches tell Cook to run out the clock.

"We're going for points," Cook said as he called for a shovel pass that was completed for a thirteen-yard gain, setting up a thirty-nine-yard field goal.

"What are we doing?" a puzzled Stokely asked.

Still, Auburn won, 25–24, on a last-second field goal.

"We made a statement but making a statement by winning was what was most important," Stokley said.[5]

"Everybody is thinking moral victory," Cook said. "I'm pissed because we should've won the game. We didn't score in the second half, and I'm upset about that. I can remember thinking to myself: 'We just don't do things right all the time.'"

The Cajuns didn't do much right the last three games, losing them all to finish with a 2–9 record. "That was a bad offense," Cook said of the '92 team. "Only threw eight touchdown passes the whole year. Only scored fifteen touchdowns. Averaged thirteen points a game."

The Cajuns needed a quarterback who could lead them out of the darkness of the bayou. Cook knew just the right guy for the job—a slender teenager named Jake Delhomme who smashed every passing record at tiny Teurlings Catholic High School in Lafayette.

Jake guided Teurlings to the 1992 Class A semifinals, completing 218 of 394 passes for a whopping 3,351 yards and thirty-two touchdowns. He also ran for 265 yards and eight touchdowns. For his high school career, he passed for 6,703 yards and sixty-five touchdowns.

Cook was going to see Jake practice and invited Stokley to go with him.

"Who else is recruiting him?" Stokley asked.

"I hope nobody," Cook said. "Then we'll get him."

Jake wasn't on LSU's radar screen or any other SEC school. Besides USL, three other Louisiana colleges were pursuing him—Tulane; Northeast

Louie Cook recruited Jake Delhomme to play at the University of Southwestern Louisiana and then lobbied hard for starting him at quarterback as a freshman in 1993. Jake completed 56 percent of his passes for 1,842 yards and fourteen touchdowns to lead the Ragin' Cajuns to an 8–3 record and a share of the Big West Conference title. He went on to play for eleven years in the NFL. "Coach Cook's greatest strength," Jake said, "is making a young kid a man and believe they are better than they could possibly be and not letting him down while they achieve that along the way." *Photo by Brad Kemp.*

Louisiana University (now Louisiana-Monroe); and McNeese State University, where his older brother, Jeff, played as a wide receiver.

"He was intelligent; he was highly, highly competitive; he was athletic; he was a winner; he made people around him better," Cook said. "Every box you want to check except for size and speed, Jake had."

Jake was six-feet-two, 170 pounds at the time.

He beat teams with his passing, running, and field goal kicking, and he even blocked a last-second field goal to topple arch-rival Notre Dame. "You look for a guy to do whatever it takes to win a game," Cook said. "And that was Jake."

Cook bonded early with his future quarterback.

Jake dreaded telephone calls from some of the coaches trying to recruit him. "I hated when they would call and say negative things about other schools," he said. "I don't like negative people. I can't stand to be around them. They bother me. They irk me."

Cook is the exact opposite—upbeat, positive, and caring. "I couldn't wait for that phone call to come from Coach Cook," Jake said. "I knew we weren't going to talk about anything negative. We were going to talk about football—the game tomorrow night. We had a conversation like I was talking to a buddy. It's almost like he became more of a friend."

Cook was the main reason Jake selected USL. "It felt right to play for him," he said. "There was something about him."

That something could be the reassuring, grandfatherly tone in his voice or his innate intuitiveness or how he masterfully deals with sticky situations such as the decision to redshirt Jake, holding him out of games as a freshman so he could develop and mature physically and mentally.

Redshirting is used widely by colleges to give athletes an extra year to complete four years of eligibility. The first redshirt, and the basis for the term, was purportedly Wayne Alfson of the University of Nebraska, who elected not to play in any of the Cornhuskers' games in 1937 while still practicing in a Nebraska redshirt without any number.

The rules for redshirting have varied over the years, but for Jake in 1993 it was simple—one play and done, his eligibility for the season gone.

Jake verbally committed to play at USL on his birthday, January 10. On the same day, Jason Sanborn announced he was transferring to USL from Foothill Community College in Los Altos, California. Sanborn compiled some impressive statistics at the junior college level, completing 52 percent of his throws for 3,942 yards and twenty-six touchdowns in eighteen games.

Initially, Jake wanted to redshirt. He changed his mind sitting in the stands with his father, Jerry, watching Sanborn and the other quarterbacks play in USL's spring football game in late March. Halfway through the intrasquad scrimmage Jake looked at his dad and said, "I'm not redshirting."

"What do you mean?" his dad asked.

"I'm better than these guys," Jake replied.

He was right.

The plan entering August practices was to redshirt Jake while Sanborn started, and Reggie Hayes and Danny DiPace backed him up. Of the three, only Hayes had playing time with the Cajuns.

Jake went along with the plan, saying: "If they want to redshirt me, fine. If not, and they need me to play, that's fine, too. I'll do whatever it takes to help us win. I cannot *stand* to lose."[6]

That was music to Cook's ears: "When I recruited kids, I'd say, 'As a high school player, what's most important to you? I'm hoping to hear: 'To win.' If they say, I want to be All-State or I want to rush for a thousand yards,' that's nice, you want kids to have goals. But you'd like for them to say, 'I want us to win.'"

It didn't take Cook long to realize that Jake was at least the second-best quarterback on the Cajun roster. He said as much at the coaches' weekly meetings to evaluate personnel.

"Whoa, stop!" Stokley said. "We're redshirting Jake. We've got to get the other guys ready."

Cook believed Jake was the Cajuns' only chance to win if Sanborn couldn't do the job or got hurt. He pulled Jake aside one practice and, using his favorite term of endearment, said, "Brim, you be prepared to play. We hope we don't have to play you. But you'd better be ready."

"I just knew through training camp and two-a-days I needed to be ready," Jake recalled. "I could tell the way Coach Cook was handling me."

Cook continued to bring up Jake's name at staff meetings.

"Whoa!" Stokley stopped him again. "I don't want to hear about Jake. We're redshirting him."

Sanborn started the season opener against Utah State in Lafayette and threw three interceptions in the first quarter. "He was throwing the ball in places where we'd never seen him throw it before," Cook said.

He was in the press box scratching his head when Stokley hollered through his headset: "Get him out of there!"

Hayes was next and quickly had a pass intercepted.

"Get him out of there!" Stokley yelled.

DiPace followed and threw another interception.

"Three quarterbacks and five interceptions the first half of the first game," Cook lamented to Gerald Broussard, the tight end coach on the sidelines. "These people got to be thinking we're the dumbest coaches. Who are these guys? Who does that?"

Cook left the press box with slightly more than a minute to play in the first half. "If we get the ball back," he instructed Broussard, "just fall on the sonofagun. I'm going down to the locker room."

By the time he got there, a beleaguered Stokley was in Cook's office sitting behind his desk.

"Louie, what are we going to do?" Stokley asked.

"Coach, we gotta go with Jake."

"I told you we're redshirting Jake," he said, pounding the desk with his hand.

"For whom, Coach? We're not going to coach him. We can't win with these other guys. If we don't win this year, we're all gone. We've gotta go with Jake."

"Do what you want," he said, dropping the "F bomb" and slamming the door on his way out.

Cook liked Stokley and didn't want to be disloyal. He was frustrated that the decision to play Jake had come down to a confrontation he tried to avoid.

"Louie, what are you going to do?" one of the other coaches asked.

"Oh, it's just me?" Cook snapped. "I thought it was us. I'm going with Jake. Maybe I'll get lucky, and he'll fire me after the game. If we don't go with Jake, we've got no shot. It ain't going to matter. I'll be home and they can pay me the rest of the year and y'all can suffer through this because I'm not doing it."

Cook marched into the locker room where the quarterbacks were waiting for him. "You three had your chance," he said to the trio who had already played.

He looked at Jake and nodded, "You're in."

"I was ready to go when we came in at halftime," Jake said. "He walked in and through those droopy eyes, he just looked, and it was like, 'Put the clipboard up. You're in.'"

When Jake took the field for the first snap in the second half, Stokley moaned: "There goes his redshirt."

In the press box a grateful Cook sighed, "Thank God."

Jake was an answer to prayers. He saved the season and the coaches' jobs. The Cajuns went from a 2–9 record in 1992 to 8–3 in 1993 and a share of the Big West Conference title. The six-game turnaround was the best by a NCAA Division 1-A team in 1993 and among the top twenty in 1-A history.

"It turned out for the best, thank the Good Lord," Cook said. "It was a crazy way to get there."

Jake avoided an interception in the second half of the Cajuns' 34–13 loss to Utah State while completing eight of seventeen passes for 110 yards and a touchdown, giving Cook hope for the rest of the season.

Cook was aware of what happened to Dwight "Dante" Prudhomme, another homegrown quarterback who was rushed into action his freshman year at USL in 1979 and had thirteen interceptions, or nearly one for every nine passes he tossed.

Going into Jake's first start against Miami of Ohio, Cook made it clear his play-calling would be conservative, adding: "I'm not breaking that kid's will his first game."

Jake looked like a seasoned veteran through the middle of the third quarter, guiding the Cajuns to a 28–3 lead but then rookie mistakes, including three interceptions, enabled Miami to rally and win, 29–28. "We beat them up and down the field, just not on the scoreboard," Jake said.[7]

The Cajuns won eight of the next nine games, the lone loss a 61–14 blowout to Florida at "The Swamp," the nickname for the Gators' football stadium.

"We weren't lighting up the board, but we were just good enough to complement the defense," Cook said about the '93 season. "One game we ran the ball forty straight plays."

Orlando Thomas spearheaded a stingy defense, intercepting nine passes to lead the country's major colleges in that category. "Orlando willed the defense," Cook said. "He and Jake were the same type of guys. They got after each other. But they were winners. Both made everybody better around them."

Jake completed 56 percent of his passes (145 of 259) for 1,842 yards and fourteen touchdowns. He had twelve passes intercepted.

"I'm eighteen years old, a 170-pound freshman, they think I'm God's gift," Jake said. "So, I was treated with kid gloves."

But at practice late in the season he was having a rough day, making uncharacteristic mistakes. Cook tapped him on the shoulder and calmly asked for his room number at the conference center where he lived. "Brim," he added, "if the university police knock on that door tonight, and want to arrest you for murder, just put your hands out and let them cuff you because you're killin' me."

It was the same message he delivered the year before to the quarterback called Maniac.

"That was Louie Cook's way of dog-cussing me," Jake said. "He has that magic, that charm, that way. You can feel it. It kind of oozes from him. I never felt so bad for letting somebody down. And that's the thing about Coach Cook. You didn't want to let him down."

The Cajuns faced another redshirt dilemma in 1994. This time it was whether they hold out Nelson's son, Brandon, a five-foot-ten, 155-pound wide receiver who only played football his freshman and senior years in high school.

Obviously, Nelson wanted to coach his son, the sooner the better because of the ups and downs of his coaching career. With Jake at quarterback for three more years, it was a good time to be a receiver.

"What do we do?" Stokley asked Cook.

Brandon was sure-handed, fast, and slippery. Defensive backs didn't like going against him in one-on-one drills because he was a headache to cover.

"We need to redshirt Brandon," Cook said.

He suggested suiting up Brandon for emergency use only the first four games and if he wasn't needed, keep him out the rest of the year to retain all his eligibility.

"I was happy with that," Brandon said about redshirting. "It gave me an extra year to mature, learn the game, get bigger and faster, so it ended up being the best thing for me."

Brandon sat out the '94 season while the Cajuns won five of their last seven games to finish with a 6–5 mark.

In 1995, Jake and Brandon became a record-setting duo, Jake completing 54.1 percent of his passes (190 of 351) for 2,761 yards and twenty

From 1992 to 1995, Coach Cook, *center*, was offensive coordinator at the University of Southwestern Louisiana under head coach Nelson Stokley, *far right*. Two of the biggest decisions they made pertained to redshirting the record-setting duo of quarterback Jake Delhomme and wide receiver Brandon Stokley, Nelson's son. Cook was for redshirting Brandon but not Jake. "I always thought redshirting was the best thing for me," Brandon says. "It gave me an extra year to mature, learn the game, get bigger and faster." Brandon ended up playing fifteen years in the NFL, earning two Super Bowl rings. Standing in the background are running back Isaac Benefield (32) and lineman Sam Heinen (51). *Photo by Brad Kemp.*

touchdowns and Brandon catching seventy-five tosses for 1,121 yards and nine touchdowns. "Those two were on another planet," Cook said.

Jake remembers a fourth-down play with two minutes left against Tulane in the Superdome. He was looking to throw a short pass for a first down but when he saw Brandon get open deep, he heaved the ball to him for a game-winning thirty-seven-yard touchdown.

Jake put on a headset to talk with Cook in the press box. "Brim," he said, "there are certain times in games where people have to make plays. That was a time a play needed to be made. That's not where you were supposed to go with the ball, but you made the play. That's what big-time players do. When it's time to make a play, they make plays. And you did it."

Afterward Cook quietly congratulated Jake in the locker room. "That's a Louie Cook deal—shake your hand, look you in the eye and nod like, 'I'm proud,'" Jake said. "That meant the most. That's what he does to players. They believe that. They see that. They feel that. They know that's real."

It was déjà vu the next week against Louisiana Tech, Jake and Brandon connecting on a twenty-one-yard touchdown pass with under two minutes to play. The win was the Cajuns' fifth straight and assured them of a winning season.

That seemed impossible after a gut-wrenching 25–24 loss to Northern Illinois in the fourth game of the year that left the Cajuns with a 1–3 mark and the coaching staff in turmoil.

At halftime of the Northern Illinois game, one coach complained, "I can't wait till this season is over . . . get rid of these turds."

At a practice the following week, there was bitching, bickering, and backbiting among the coaches. "Everybody is on edge," Cook said. "They're all moping around. It's like the damn season is over."

He couldn't sleep that night and wrote down some notes. "I might be back early today," he told his wife, Faye, as he left for work.

"You don't have practice?" she asked.

"We have practice but what I'm going to say in this meeting today probably is going to get me fired," he replied. "I love Stokes but he ain't going to say nothin'."

Cook was the offensive coordinator, not the head coach, but he decided something had to be said.

"If nothing I say makes any sense," he began, "it's because there's a lack of blood flowing to my brain because it's leaking out of the stab wounds in my back. The way I see it right now it's every man for himself."

He cited the lack of discipline on the team and circumventing school policy to keep certain players on the field. "If our own children were going out with some of these guys on the weekend, we'd be scared to death," he said.

"If it wasn't for the jersey number on some of the kids' backs," he continued, "we couldn't even get their attention because we gotta go, 'Hey, 82, move over here.' We don't even know what 82's name is. But we're going to ask 82 to bust his ass for us."

Cook ended his remarks by saying: "It's a shame. When you walk down the hall, you gotta walk with your back to the wall because you don't know where that next blade is coming from. That ain't how it's supposed to be, guys."

He closed his notebook and walked out of the room.

Afterward, Cook told Stokley, "We're acting like the season's over. We can win the next five games."

And the Cajuns did just that to wind up with a 6–5 record, the same as the year before and their third straight winning season.

Jake wasn't at the meeting, but he knows the story. "Basically, he MF'd every one of those coaches on that staff and called them out," he explained. "But he did it in Louie Cook's way. He's all-encompassing. He sees it all. He gets it all. And he just has a way."

Marcus Prier and Troy Gisclair can attest to that.

Prier was the Cajuns' top running back in '95, rushing for a team-leading 979 yards and fourteen touchdowns. He gained only two yards on nine carries and fumbled in the first half against Northern Illinois. Cook gave him a pep talk at halftime: "Get your head up, quit moping around, feeling sorry for yourself. I'm giving you the ball. I don't care if you fumble it every time. Take the dang ball and go. You're too good to be playing the way you're playing."

Prier's thirty-six-yard run in the third quarter set up a go-ahead touchdown. He finished the game with fifty yards rushing on thirteen carries. "I felt like my college career had come to an end," he wrote in a letter to Cook in 2004. "You gave me some encouraging words at halftime, and I bounced back."

Prier "applied the same principle" to a failed marriage that he referred to as the "worst fumble of my life." He got past the "fumble" by going to graduate school. "I wanted to thank you and let you know that I am proud to have played for you," Prier concluded.

Gisclair caught only one pass in five years as a walk-on receiver at USL. "One target, one catch, one hundred percent," he said. "It's called perfect."

A mix-up on the sidelines prevented Gisclair from playing in the spring intrasquad game. Cook felt badly about it because Troy's parents had traveled 125 miles from their home in Larose, Louisiana, to see him play.

"You had me to run a play in and they had a time out," Gisclair reminded Cook.

"I'm sorry, Troy, that's all on me," Cook said. "Hopefully one day I can make it up to you."

In the second game of the '95 season against the University of Alabama–Birmingham, the Cajuns led 49–7 entering the fourth quarter. Cook called for a short pass to Gisclair. Backup quarterback Brian Soignier flipped the ball to him for a six-yard gain.

"It all worked out like it was supposed to," Gisclair said. "Everything happens for a reason, right? I got that one opportunity. It just so happened the team photographer catches on film the only catch I made in five years."

Gisclair tells the story with a sense of awe: "Coach Cook was so genuine and always a man of his word. Whatever he told you usually was going to happen. Even though we weren't all equal, he was fair and treated us all the same."

"The Good Lord, he takes care of fools sometimes," Cook said. "He gave me a chance for redemption."

Gisclair is white, Prier Black.

"Everybody went to his office," Jake said. "The white guys. The Black guys. The offensive guys. The defensive guys. It was like a funnel to his office because they knew there was an ear there and a life lesson always to be learned."

One of many lessons Jake learned from Cook is the importance of believing in someone. "I believed in him, and I tried carrying that over whenever I would call plays in the huddle," Jake said. "There are ten other sets of eyes that are staring at you and if they don't believe in you and what you say, it's not going to work."

He learned something else: "Coach Cook's greatest strength is making a young kid a man and believe they are better than they could possibly be and not letting him down while they achieve that along the way. To me, that was always the definition of Louie Cook. There's never a panic in a situation. I got emotional playing, like all players. My heart was on my sleeve. But playing football or in life, never get too high or too low. Try to stay more high than low. You've got to keep a level playing field. I got that from him."

Cook left USL to return to Crowley High at the end of the '95 season.

"When you have somebody like Coach Cook leave, there's a big void," Brandon said. "But when you are a great coach, you leave a foundation. My dad saw that. We had something good going and he wanted to keep some consistency there. And that's what we were able to do. But the foundation of what we had going on was laid down by Louie Cook."

Jake was a senior and Brandon a sophomore beginning the '96 season. They broke their own records, Jake completing 53.3 percent of his passes (201 of 377) for 2,901 yards and twenty touchdowns and Brandon catching eighty-one passes for 1,160 yards and seven touchdowns.

In four years at USL, Jake completed 52.6 percent (655 of 1,246) of his tosses for 9,216 yards and sixty-four touchdowns, a preview of his stats for eleven years in the NFL—a pass completion rate of 59.4 percent, 20,975 yards and 126 touchdowns. He quarterbacked the Carolina Panthers to three playoff appearances and the 2004 Super Bowl.

Four games into the '97 season Brandon tore the anterior cruciate ligament (ACL) in his left knee, sidelining him the rest of the year. Because he redshirted as a freshman, he was able to come back in 1998 and finish his four-year career with 3,702 receiving yards to become only the second player in Division 1-A history to average 100 yards per game.

The Baltimore Ravens selected him in the fourth round with the 105th overall pick of the 1999 NFL draft. He went on to play fifteen years in the NFL, earning Super Bowl rings with the Ravens in 2001 and Indianapolis Colts in 2007.

Cook was invited to a party celebrating Brandon's good fortune in the draft.

"Louie, I appreciate everything you did for Brandon while you were there," Nelson said. "I'm glad you had the foresight to redshirt him, or we wouldn't be having this party."

"Coach," Cook said, "the good Lord has got control of all of us."

9

🏈

Psychologist of the Year

It was 1996 but to Louie Cook it seemed more like 1956, when segrega-tion laws in Louisiana required Blacks and whites to attend different schools, sit apart on buses and in restaurants, and use separate public restrooms and drinking fountains. Those laws also prevented them from playing against each other in sports.

As the Crowley High players lined up to stretch at the first spring practice, the four years Cook was away at the University of Southwestern Louisiana (USL) might as well have been forty. The Blacks were on one side and the whites on the other, just like in the 1950s.

Donald Adams, an African American known as Coach A, was an assis-tant coach during Cook's first stint at Crowley as well as his second go-around with the Gents.

"Chief, what's with this segregation?" Cook asked, using their nick-name for each other.

"Man-n-n, 'The Reap' got it so screwed up, Chief, they don't want to be around nobody."

"The Reap" was short for "Grim Reaper," the moniker given to the head coach who preceded Cook. That evolved into "Brim Reaper."

Upon taking over at Crowley in 1993, The Reap declared he was "not Lewis Cook or Kevin Magee, thus that's how I plan on running things."[1]

The difference between The Reap and Cook "was night and day," according to Greyson Augustus, a six-foot-five, 270-pound offensive tackle who sat out his junior year in 1995 because he and The Reap didn't see eye to eye. "There was a lot of yelling, a lot of screaming, a lot of pun-ishment for doing things wrong. I'm not going to make it seem like Coach

Cook was this big soft Mr. Rogers–type coach. He would yell if he needed to. But it was more of a teaching environment."

The Gents posted an 11–2 win-loss record in 1992 under Magee, a loyal Cook assistant. The Reap compiled a respectable 22–15 mark and made the playoffs each of his three years at Crowley but left behind a racially divided team.

"He not only individualized a team sport, but he also racialized it," said Walter Sampson, a linebacker Cook converted to fullback. "Everything was about him, and he considered us Blacks as the lower class on his team. He didn't treat us the same as he treated the white guys on the team. So that's what created division."

"Where we were from, you really were taught not to trust white people," Augustus said. "I was blessed not to think that way, but I was always taught to be cautious."

Meanwhile, some of the white players believed The Reap catered to the Blacks by playing them in games despite skipping practice.

Pappy Morgan, a white strong safety, was pulled off the team by his father after he was benched for missing a couple of practices because of an illness.

Cook saw a difficult situation. "The Black players didn't trust the white players. The white players didn't trust the Black players. Neither one trusted the coaches."

The next day at practice Cook gathered the team around white and black lines he had drawn on the field.

"I don't know what all this is about but when y'all on that field, I better not see any kind of segregation," he said. "We're a team. I don't care what color you are. In fact, when we're in the huddle we're holding hands and when you stand in the back, y'all are going to hold hands. I better not see all the whites on this side and all the Blacks on the other."

The team reflected both the town of Crowley and the school, which was nearly 50 percent Black. White folks lived on one side of town, Blacks on the other. There also was a clear division at school.

"When Coach Cook got there, all that shut down," Augustus said. "He brought the two different sides of town together—getting us to see each other as a brotherhood. He looked at us through an equal lens. If you were the best player, dude, you were the best player. Our defense was one of the best in the state of Louisiana that year. And we had two white linebackers [Scott Carboni and Brady Broussard], a Hispanic linebacker [Almando LeJeune], and a Black linebacker [A. J. Richard]."

Cook called his Black players "the brothers."

"You've got to be compassionate to the situation the brothers came up in," Cook said. "I never gave them more than anyone else, but I tried to understand what they were dealing with because their world is different than my world. What I had growing up, very few of them ever had. People say, 'You've got to treat everybody the same.' No, you don't. You should be fair to everybody but you're going to handle everybody differently."

Cook's return to high school football wasn't as shocking as his decision eleven years earlier to coach a Crowley team that had lost twenty-one straight games. It was no secret he wanted to coach his sons, Lewis III, who entered Crowley High in 1996, and Jeff, two years behind him in seventh grade. The door opened for him to do this when Crowley High principal Eric Stutes called to ask for help in finding a new coach.

Cook's star pupil at USL, quarterback Jake Delhomme, had one year of eligibility remaining, and his favorite target, Brandon Stokley, was a redshirt sophomore.

"What do you see coming in on defense?" Cook asked Jake.

"There was nothing coming in," Jake said in retrospect. "He could see the cupboard was bare."

They were subtle hints intended to soften the blow for what was to come.

"When he told me he was going back to Crowley," Jake said, "it was like, 'Hey, I'm leaving you in good hands. Trust me, you're going to be fine.' I have a very dominant personality. He knew I was going to take over. I wasn't going to let anything slide."

The Cajuns had a 5–6 record Jake's senior year but won only three games the next two seasons.

"Louie was made for high school football," said Harold Gonzales Jr., publisher of the *Crowley Post-Signal*. "He was made for nurturing and coaching teenage boys and girls at the high school level. He was successful in college, but I don't think he was as happy in college as he is coaching high school kids."

A headline in the *Post-Signal* declared, "He's back!"[2]

One of the first things Cook did was meet with all the male athletes in the school gym to introduce himself and share his beliefs and vision for the football team and the players personally.

"I was sitting there thinking, 'I'm not playing football,'" Augustus said. "I had played football my entire life. I was done with football."

As the gigantic young man was leaving the gym, Cook called out, "Hey, Brim, give me one second."

Augustus slowed up so Cook could tell him he had good coaches such as Coach A and Magee on his staff and invited him to practice and see for himself what was going on. "One of the things he said—and it's something that sticks with me till this day—is that he could see me doing some really good things for the team," Augustus remembered.

Up to that point, coaches always commented on how Augustus could be a great football player because of his size. Nobody ever mentioned the good things he could do for the team. "I gave him a shot," Augustus said.

So did James Martin, a quiet, easy-going six-foot-four, 240-pound defensive lineman who was a whipping boy for The Reap.

"I ain't playing, Coach," he said. "The man wore me out."

"James," Cook said, "it's going to be different now. Give it a couple of weeks."

Martin stayed on the team and, along with Augustus and Morgan, earned all-district honors at the end of the season.

"We were frustrated," Augustus said. "All that talent was sitting there, and Coach Cook got us all together."

It took a while. "There was no trust," Cook said. "They were kind of like an abused child. Afraid to come out of the corner. What's going to happen now?"

Nick Dugas was a dual threat at quarterback; Bill Phillips, a workhorse at tailback; Walter Sampson, a stud at fullback; Joe Domingeaux, a force at tight end; and cousins Marcus and Wayne Wilridge, both dangerous receivers and kick return specialists.

"I'd have to select an all-star team from my first seven years at Crowley to match those guys at the positions they played," Cook said. "There weren't enough balls to go around for all of them."

It was the same group of guys that Augustus grew up and played football with through middle school and Crowley High "never quite getting it done but had a ton of talent."

Most observers believe the '95 team, The Reap's last at Crowley, was the most talented of all. In addition to the players Cook inherited, the Gents had Jerry Doiron, a two-time All-State receiver who racked up 2,538 yards and twenty-eight touchdowns on 143 catches in three years. He later changed his last name to Johnson and played at the University of Michigan.

"If Coach Cook had that '95 team, we would've won it all," said Melvecchio Guidry, a running back and safety. "We had the talent."

That team wound up with a disappointing 6–5 record, losing in the first round of the state playoffs.

"It's not the same at Crowley as when Louie was here," The Reap told a colleague. "In fact, Little Jesus himself could come back and wouldn't win."

A *Lafayette Daily Advertiser* headline billed Louie's return as "Cook's second coming."[3]

"It had changed a lot the four years I was gone," Cook said.

When things finally calmed down, he asked Joe Domingeaux what the players were told when they learned he was coming back to Crowley.

"I thought I was back at USL (University of Southwestern Louisiana)," Louie Cook recalled on first seeing the size of the offensive linemen on Crowley High's 1996 roster. Shown here are, *front row, left to right*: Joe Domingeaux, tight end (87); Jeremy Broussard, center (66); and James Martin, backup tight end (91). *Back row, left to right*: Greyson Augustus, tackle (72); Collin Thibodeaux, guard (74); Jonathan Bellot, guard (79); and Michael Pitre, tackle (78). "We looked good getting off the bus," says Augustus, a six-foot-five, 270-pounder. Domingeaux was listed at six-five, 245; Martin, six-four, 240; Bellot, six-one, 240; Pitre, six feet, 235; Thibodeaux, six feet, 230; and Broussard, six feet, 210. *Photo courtesy of Greyson Augustus.*

"They said, 'Coach Cook is a good dude but he don't play around,'" Domingeaux replied. In other words, if you don't do it right, you don't play.

Obviously, the message had yet to register for twenty-nine of the fifty-nine players who showed up late for the first practice in August. Cook found some of the stragglers in the gym sitting in the stands and others in the locker room. "It was a horrible practice," he recalled.

Afterward, the players gathered around him.

"When you walk back in the gym, look up on the wall at that banner from the '89 state championship team," he began. "Look at it good and understand this: there's more talent on this field—way more talent—than that team had. Y'all won't have no banner up there."

He paused to let them think about that. "How are we going to win? You can't even get to practice on time. I'm not going to have y'all disrespect the guys that wore the same helmet with that C on it. My name's on there, too. I ain't got nothing to prove."

He had the players who were late for practice line up at the end of the field to do a dreaded drill called suicides. "When the whistle blows, take off running," he instructed. "Every time you hear the whistle, lay on your belly, get up and keep running. When you get to the other end, turn around, and when the whistle blows, come back."

"Coach, I'll jog four laps," Marcus Wilridge volunteered. "I ain't diving on my belly."

"Marcus, go in with those guys," Cook said calmly, motioning to the players who didn't have to do the suicides because they were on time. "We'll figure out what's going to happen when I get in there."

Cook walked to the end zone where the twenty-nine players were ready to run. Marcus was the team's biggest playmaker. "I'm praying," Cook said about that day. "I've got a problem. I don't know what I'm going to do."

He turned around and blew the whistle. Marcus took off running and on hearing the whistle again, flopped on the ground with everybody else. Nobody was near him when he got to the other end of the field. "We ran four of 'em," Cook said. "Everybody was at the next practice on time."

Marcus's uncle, Tracy Wilridge, played on the '89 state championship team. "I knew of Coach Cook, but I didn't know him," Marcus said. "It was a growing process for me and him as well."

On top of his duties on offense, Marcus started playing cornerback on defense. "It's going to be on your shoulders to make plays," Cook said.

Marcus accepted the challenge.

The six-foot, 180-pounder did everything except sell hot dogs at halftime. On defense he covered opponents' best receiver and on offense he was a touchdown machine, scoring fifteen times while catching forty passes for 791 yards and rushing for 229 yards on thirty-eight carries.

The first time Cook saw Marcus's younger brother, Walter Sampson, a chiseled six-foot-three, 220-pounder, he thought he was looking at the next Lawrence Taylor, the Pro Football Hall of Fame linebacker who played for the New York Giants from 1981 to 1993.

He was fast, smart, and, for Cook, the most difficult player to coach. "The way he came around made it worthwhile."

"He had to pray a lot for me," Walter recalled. "When I first met him, I was probably a hard-headed little brat. It was hard for me to let people in. Why? Some life experiences I had. I learned that he was there for us as players. Not just on the field but off the field as well."

Walter didn't trust white people. "I didn't dislike them," he added, "but I kind of had my doubts about 'em."

"Walter could do anything he wanted to do when he wanted to do it," said Coach A, citing the time he had forty points and twenty rebounds in a Crowley High basketball game. "But he'd get in the mood sometimes when he'd get mad, and he'd just go through the motions."

Walter didn't show up for football practice the day before a state play-off game in 1995, so The Reap sent Coach A to get him. He found Walter sitting on the front porch of his house and whisked him to practice.

The saga of Walter Sampson is both instructional and inspirational.

In 1996, the Gents had a 1–2 record going into a game at Jennings High.

Walter missed one practice, went through the motions at another, and wasn't around for the game day walk-through just before lunch on Friday because he and a teammate were eating chicken at Popeyes.

Later at the team's pregame meal in the school cafeteria, Cook sat across from Walter. "That's probably not as good as that lunch you had today. Y'all left campus on my time. I told you from day one that I'm not a guy that looks the other way. You don't do right, there are consequences."

Walter was alternating between the linebacker and fullback positions. He didn't start against Jennings, but he was going to play until Cook noticed him sulking on the sidelines.

Jennings was about to score a touchdown when defensive coordinator Fred Menard asked, "Coach, you want me to put Walter out there?"

Cook was on a headset with Menard: "I don't care if they score fifty points tonight. Walter is not playing."

At halftime Walter stood outside the locker room and during the fourth quarter he left the team box on the sidelines to talk to his mother, Martha.

"Coach, you need to get that kid back in the team box," the referee warned.

Cook went to break up the conversation.

"Coach, how come Walter isn't playing?" Martha asked.

"Martha, I ain't got time to get into that with you. We're trying to win the game. But let me tell you: this young man right here is one of the smartest players I ever coached. You ask him why he's not playing. He knows."

The Gents won the game, 14–7.

Back in Crowley, Cook called Walter into his office. "You have fun tonight?" he asked. "I sure didn't. We break a two-game losing streak and I've got to deal with you."

He continued: "As smart as you are, Walter, the one thing you haven't figured out yet is why you're still on this team. You think I need you to win games? Didn't we win the game tonight? And you didn't play. Understand one thing. We're going to win games with you and we're going to lose games with you."

Cook never raised his voice.

"I've been trying to keep you around because if you stay with us, you're going to be a better person," he explained. "For sure, better than the one I met when I got here. You were the last one in and the first one out of the weight room. Never smiled. I've seen you smiling, talking to white people. I want you on the team. But I'm not doing this again."

Walter left Cook's office and then came back a few minutes later. "Coach, can I get a ride home?"

"You hungry?" Cook asked.

They went to Burger King. Walter ordered a Double Whopper with cheese.

"That hamburger changed me, my mindset, my position, our team, and the season," Walter said. "It changed a lot."

It was a turning point for Walter.

"It didn't change me just for football, it changed my life completely," he said. "It helped me to understand, make better decisions, and just stay on the right path. I was heading in the right direction, but just his teachings and little talks resonated and stuck with me."

Cook told Walter he had the power to be whatever he wanted to be if he put his mind to it. "I never really had anybody challenge me like that," Walter said. "He challenged me a lot."

Walter moved from outside linebacker to fullback and the Gents won the next ten games and wound up playing for the state championship at the Superdome in New Orleans.

In his first start at fullback, Walter rumbled like a runaway train, knocking over and dragging tacklers for seventy-eight yards and two touchdowns on nine carries. He went up to Cook after the game: "Coach, you have more fun tonight?"

"Yeah, a lot more fun," Cook said.

"Walter was a sparkplug," said Greyson Augustus. "He was fiery. He was competitive. He could have a temper sometimes, but it was because he was so passionate. Coach Cook got him to focus."

The morning after the Gents toppled unbeaten and third-ranked Eunice to win the district title, Cook got a call from the same coach who told him about The Reap's remark that "Little Jesus" couldn't return to Crowley and win.

"I guess Little Jesus CAN win at Crowley," the coach laughed.

The road to the Dome in 1996 went through Salmen High in Slidell, Louisiana, two-time defending 4A state champions, winners of twenty-nine consecutive games at home, and the Gents' opponent in the semifinals of the state playoffs.

The day before the game, Coach A was sitting in Cook's office when he got a telephone call informing him that his sixteen-year-old daughter, Andrea, had died from a rare disease called mitochondrial encephalitis that causes the nervous system and muscles to break down and fail. "I got hysterical," Coach A said.

Cook drove Coach A to the nursing home where his wife, Jacqueline, was sitting on the bed next to Andrea, who died in her sleep.

"My wife was crying," Coach A said. "Coach Cook was crying, too. He took both of us in his arms. I knew right then I had a special, special friend."

Coach A listened to the game on the radio. "It killed me not to get on that bus," he said. "But them brothers got fired up and ready to kill Salmen."

Before the Salmen game, Cook got a phone call from Larry Dauterive, his friend and mentor. "I gave Louie a heads-up," he said. "It's a different animal playing there."

In 1994, Dauterive's Opelousas High team traveled to Salmen for a semifinal game and got pummeled, 41–9.

"It's intimidating," Dauterive told Cook, describing the smoke, lights, and loud music that greeted the Salmen players as they stormed onto the field toward his team. "Man, Louie, you need to tell your kids about that."

He did, except he didn't provide any details. "I hear when they come on the field, it's a spectacle," he told the players. "I want to watch. So, we're going out five minutes early and check it out."

The entire Crowley team locked arms across the fifty-yard line. There was a cannon-like boom and then strobe lights flashed through the fog as the music got louder and louder, pumping the players higher and higher. "They'd better turn it off, Coach!" several of them hollered. "They'd better turn it off."

Blaring throughout the stadium was the rhythmic drum beat and haunting voice of Phil Collins singing "In the Air Tonight." It was the same song played at Crowley home games.

"I don't know whose job it was to play the music, but they failed," Augustus said. "That was our song. I locked eyes with Marcus Wilridge. One single tear dropped from his eye, and we lost our minds."

"There's something about that song that gives me chills," Joe Domingeaux said. "I could listen to it today and my mind always goes back to Crowley High football."

Walter said the whole team was fired up. "From the kickoff to the ending whistle, we laid it on 'em."

The Gents' upset heavily favored Salmen, 32–22.

Walter was the secret weapon, catching three passes for fifty-eight yards and a touchdown in addition to rushing nine times for forty-two yards and a score. "When he went to fullback, that solidified the offense for us," Cook said.

A tip from Domingeaux, the Gents' unselfish tight end, set up three big pass plays by quarterback Nick Dugas, including a twenty-seven-yarder to Walter.

"Hey, Coach, they're double covering me," Domingeaux told Cook. He suggested running a corner route that left Walter wide open.

On the way back to Crowley, the Gents' bus was at the top of the Interstate 10 bridge crossing the Mississippi River in Baton Rouge. Most of the players were sleeping when the usually quiet Domingeaux yelled, "Coach, stop the bus! Stop the bus!"

"What's the matter, Joe?"

"I think I saw The Reap about ready to jump off the bridge because we're going to the Dome."

The Reap liked to tell the players he was going to get them to the Dome.

"I ain't never got nobody nowhere," Cook said. "I tell them, 'Hey, thanks for the ride, guys, because I don't make a play. I ain't thrown a pass or made a tackle in a long, long time.'"

The Gents were headed to the Dome with Little Jesus where they would meet the almighty John Curtis Christian School Patriots, led by J. T. Curtis Jr., currently the winningest active coach in America with 615 career victories and counting. The win against Salmen was the one-hundredth of Cook's career.

The 1996 championship game is the only time the two legendary coaches faced each other. "Four times we were one game from playing each other in the playoffs," Cook said. "We lost twice, and J. T. lost twice."

The Patriots were 13–0 and seeking their thirteenth state title. The Gents were 12–2 and on an eleven-game winning streak.

Coach A stood on the sidelines, the signature green towel that he waved at Crowley High games slung over his right shoulder. He buried his daughter, Andrea, on Monday. It was now five o'clock Saturday—kickoff time. "I was looking up in the Dome and said, 'My little girl's up there and I'm down here with Coach Cook.'"

They were both in heaven as far as Coach A was concerned. "That was one day I remember losing but so full of joy," he said. "The kids gave it their all. We were so full of joy."

The Gents scored first and trailed only 14–7 until the last seven minutes when the Patriots tacked on two more touchdowns to win, 28–7. "They beat us up in the fourth quarter," Cook said. "We moved the ball but couldn't finish."

Cook was selected Coach of the Year by the Louisiana Sports Writers Association. A friend called to congratulate him. "They made a mistake," he said. "I should've got Psychologist of the Year."

Joe Domingeaux went on to start four years at tight end for LSU. Marcus Wilridge starred at wide receiver for USL, catching 130 passes

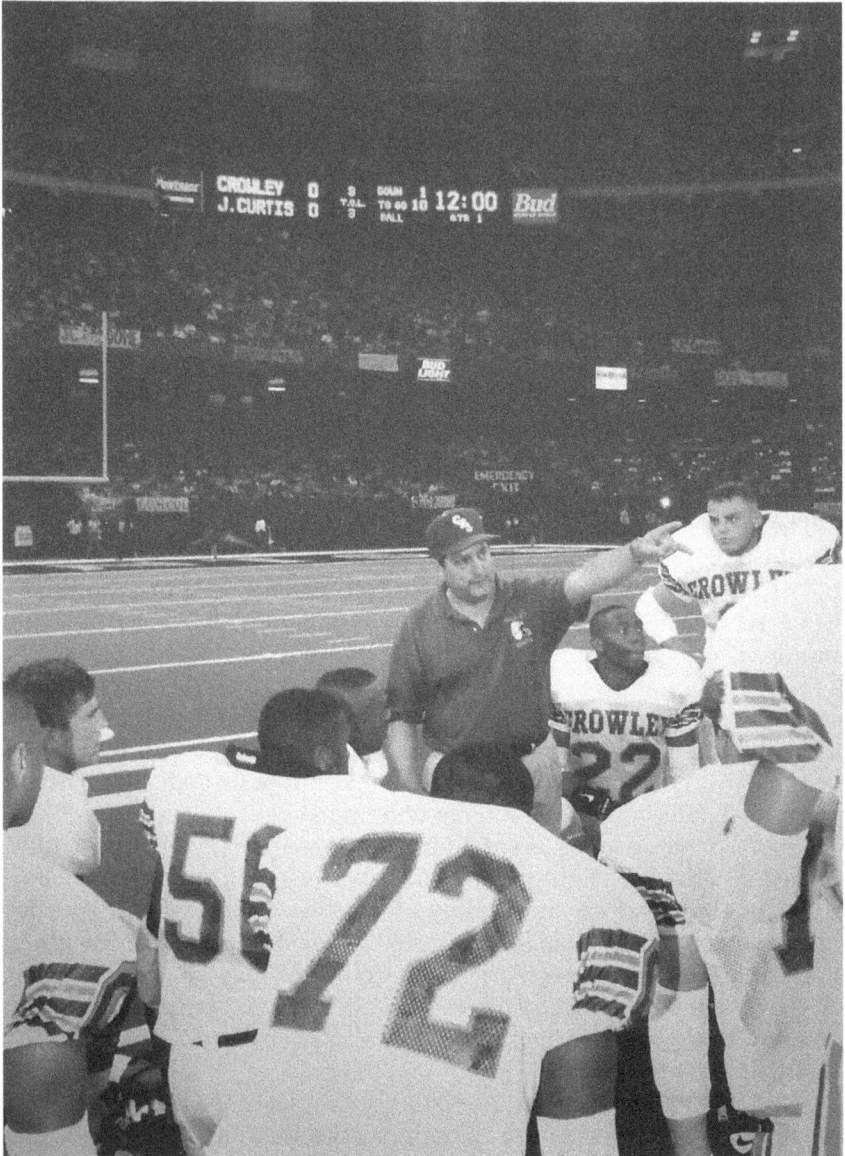

Louie Cook had one hundred career wins going into Crowley High's 1996 state championship game against John Curtis Christian School, coached by John T. Curtis Jr., the winningest active coach in America with 615 victories through the 2022 season. John Curtis won the only meeting between the two legendary coaches, scoring two fourth-quarter touchdowns to prevail, 28–7. Crowley players facing the camera are Bill Phillips (22) and Scott Carboni. *Photo courtesy of Lewis Cook Jr.*

for 1,742 yards and seven touchdowns his four years there. Nick Dugas switched from quarterback to wide receiver, hauling in seventy-five tosses for 764 yards and five touchdowns during his three seasons at USL. Greyson Augustus and James Martin also played at USL.

Walter Sampson signed as a free agent with the New England Patriots in 2003 after bulking up to 285 pounds and playing defensive tackle at USL. He totaled 135 career tackles, including thirty-two for losses and quarterback sacks. Walter never played for the Patriots, but he graduated with a degree in psychology.

"It was a blessing to have a man like Coach Cook come into my life," Walter said. "He was more than a coach. He was a dad for all of us. I call him my grandfather now."

Cook may well have been Teacher of the Year in 1996.

"We went from segregation to playing for the championship in the Dome," he said. "The players started trusting again."

Greyson Augustus said it best: "Coach Cook came in and he gave us all one thing to believe in. He gave us accountability. He gave us standards, which is still something that sticks with me till this day, whether it was comparing us with guys that were on his championship teams from the past or in the classroom. Whatever it was, he gave us standards that we had to live up to. And he respected us, and he loved us on a daily basis. We went out there and had a special season. It was awesome."

10

🏈

Here Come the Sons!

The scene is familiar in college and pro football.

The head coach stands frowning or grimacing on the sideline as if he's got hemorrhoids. Every now and then he rips off his headset to unleash a flurry of obscenities at a referee or at one of his players or coaches. Even the joy of winning is dampened by the obligatory bath of cold Gatorade.

"You think they are living the dream?" Louie Cook asked, quickly answering his own question. "Most of them are miserable."

Louie spent eight years as an assistant coach at the University of Southwestern Louisiana (USL) and it wasn't fun except for the three years he teamed with quarterback Jake Delhomme, who led the Ragin' Cajuns to three straight winning seasons (1993–1995) and a pair of Big West Conference titles, setting records for passing yardage and touchdowns along the way.

During his first four-year stint at USL (1981–1984), Cook got a request from the team's offensive coordinator, who had coached previously at two major colleges: "Louie, do you think you could teach my boy how to throw? I've never taken a kid from scratch."

Louie found it odd and telling. "This guy is a quarterback coach in college and his son was in eighth grade. He'd recruit guys and tweak their throwing a little bit, but he'd never trained a young kid from the start."

It was a lesson Louie remembered as his eldest boys, Lewis III and Jeff, approached high school. Lew was fourteen and Jeff twelve in 1996 when the Crowley High job opened.

"Guys, here are the choices," he said. "I can stay at USL. Jake has got another year. I'm having fun. Lew, you can go to Notre Dame. Hopefully in a year or two, they'll be looking for a coach and I can meet you guys. Or you can go to Crowley High and play for the Gents. Six years from now, you'll both be out. Y'all think about it."

The boys grew up wearing the green-and-gold colors of Crowley High even though they attended St. Joseph in Rayne, one of the Catholic middle schools in Acadia Parish that feeds Notre Dame. "I always felt if I went back to high school, it would be Notre Dame," Louie said.

Lew and Jett told their dad they'd rather go with him to Crowley and see what happened. He took the job at Crowley and a year later Notre Dame came calling. Now, he had the decision of a lifetime to make, one that not only affected his own boys but the sons of families throughout the area, especially the African Americans in West Crowley who viewed him as a savior of sorts.

People in the Black community urged Orlando Thomas, a former Crowley High star who became an All-Pro safety for the Minnesota Vikings, to use his father-son relationship with Louie to influence him to stay. "He'll listen to you, Orlando," they said. "You can't let him leave."

Orlando didn't feel that way.

"I'm going to tell him to take the job at Notre Dame," he replied. "Y'all expect one white man to come over here and raise all your children. What have y'all done to help the man? They're in debt and he's battling by himself, raising y'all kids and all you say is, 'Coach Cook, come on back, we're going to be all right.' I'm telling him to go."

Louie had turned down two previous offers from Notre Dame and, at first, he told Eric Stutes, the Crowley High principal, that he was staying.

One reason was that Notre Dame was going from Class 2A to 3A, a move the departing head coach, Donnie Gaspard, strongly opposed. "I was a little apprehensive myself because I didn't know we could compete with some of the teams in 3A," Louie said. "At the time it was a big jump."

Another factor was that the principal at Notre Dame wasn't nearly as enthusiastic about hiring Louie as were two of the school's alumni and prominent area businessmen—Wayne Hensgens and Bryan "Buck" Leonards.

"I've got to work for the principal, and I haven't heard from him," Louie told them.

The principal wanted to promote a young assistant on Gaspard's coaching staff.

"You're going to do what?" a surprised Hensgens asked. "What about Louie?"

There were no plans to hire Louie.

"We'll see about that," Hensgens said.

The principal would later call the hiring of Louie the best move he ever made at Notre Dame. But it almost didn't happen.

Hensgens was on a deer stand in Plaquemine, Louisiana, when he got a phone call from Louie, saying he couldn't take the job. "Louie, it's 5:30 on a Friday afternoon," Hensgens said. "We're not going to hire anybody over the weekend. Give it a little more time and think about it."

School was closed the following Monday because of Martin Luther King Day, so Louie had an extra day to decide. "God, give me a sign," he prayed.

"That weekend he got a sign," Hensgens said.

A couple of incidents were more of a push than a sign, but they helped convince Louie his boys would be better off at Notre Dame.

One of them took place at a Crowley High basketball game Cook attended with Murray Morgan, a friend whose son Pappy was a star defensive back on the '96 team. They had to break up a near fight in the stands between the mothers of two opposing players, Louie grabbing one mom and Murray the other. "If you don't get your ass out of here to Notre Dame, I'm going to whip you myself," Murray half-joked.

The next day, Louie decided to go across town to Notre Dame.

"Louie could've gone anywhere in America except Notre Dame, and it would've been all right," said Richard Pizzolatto, a Crowley High teacher and coach.

"Notre Dame and Crowley High are like two countries," added Joel Sinclair, a star on Crowley's 1989 state championship team.

"Chief, I'm going to meet with the troops in the conference room," Louie said to Donald Adams (Coach A) when he was ready to break the news to the team.

"You want me to go in there with you?" Coach A asked.

"No, I want to handle this by myself."

Coach A was standing by the door when Walter Sampson, the fullback who had blossomed under Louie's leadership, came out crying and wailing, "Coach Cook is leaving!"

"Walter, Coach Cook has got to do what's best for his family," Coach A said. "Black Jesus is still here."

"Yeah, that's good," Walter said as he walked away, "but Coach A ain't Coach Cook."

Public opinion on Louie's decision was split along school color lines—green and gold for Crowley and red and white for Notre Dame.

"If you were wearing a red shirt, you were pretty happy about it," remembered Harold Gonzales Jr., publisher of the *Crowley Post-Signal*. "If you're wearing a green shirt, you were let down. And I could see both sides of it."

Louie also got some grief from Notre Dame fans unhappy to see Gaspard go because he had just led the Pioneers to a 12–2 record and the state semifinals.

The schools had never played each other in football up to that point. They wound up in the same league in 2001, Notre Dame winning nine of the eleven games they played through 2012.

"We've been to the Dome three times," Coach A encouraged Louie. "You've won a state championship for these people. You need to get across town, Coach."

Coach A eventually followed, swapping the green towel he waved at Crowley High games for a red one. Lew Cook joined his father after finishing his freshman year at Crowley.

Greyson Augustus, a six-foot-five, 270-pound offensive tackle for Crowley, reassured Lew's mother: "Miss Faye, I know you're worried about Lew staying behind because some people aren't happy, but I promise you nobody is going to hurt him."

Faye Cook said it was a good decision for her sons. "Notre Dame was a good fit for them. No regrets. But Louie really agonized over it."

A question Louie often asked himself and others when he was at USL the second time was: "Do I leave to go coach my boys, or do I stay?"

One coach said: "Well, Louie, it'll be really easy to coach them if they're either no good at all or just great. The ones that are in-between get you in trouble."

Cook's three sons covered both ends of the spectrum.

The oldest, Lew, can crunch numbers like he's eating a bowl of Wheaties, but he was never going to be pictured on the front of a Wheaties box. Jeff, two years younger than Lew, was a naturally gifted athlete who excelled in football and baseball and was recruited by LSU to play both. Stu, ten years Lew's junior, was the most valuable offensive player in the Pios' district as a senior in 2010.

"You've got two sons who are talented athletically and one that's not," Jeff said. "Lew tried hard, but it wasn't there. That wasn't easy for Dad."

When coaches now ask Louie about coaching his sons, he tells them: "If your son deserves to play, don't fall into that tendency to sacrifice him so you won't be accused of playing him only because he's your son. People are going to say it anyway—even if your son is good."

Going into the 1999 season some of the team's seniors were concerned that Louie would start Jeff, a sophomore, at quarterback instead of a senior who had worked his way through the system. "Your dad's not going to hamper us with a sophomore signal-caller, right?" one player said to Lew, who was also a senior then.

The senior quarterback started and threw six interceptions in the first three games, the Pios losing two of them. The same player who was critical of playing Jeff walked up to Lew and asked, "How long is your dad going to let this shit continue?"

Jeff ended up quarterbacking the Pios to nine straight victories before losing 28–21 to Amite High, the eventual 3A state champion, in the quarterfinals of the playoffs.

"I have two boys on the team," Louie said at the time. "One doesn't ever get in the game. And the other one is the starting quarterback. So, do I love him more than the other one?"

Shortly after losing in the playoffs, Louie got a telephone call from Mitch Downing, head coach at Benton High, who was preparing to play unbeaten and top-ranked Amite next. Downing had just received film of the Notre Dame–Amite game to review but he didn't know Louie.

"Wondering if I can pick your brain about Amite," Downing began.

"I'll send you all the reports we have," Louie said.

"Do you think you can send me your quarterback?"

"Ah-h-h, I don't know if his mom would like that."

"What do you mean?"

"I'm sleeping with that boy's mom."

"What?"

"Mitch, that's my son."

"Oh, I don't have a roster."

"He went dumbfounded on me for a couple of seconds," Louie said, laughing as he recalled the story, which illustrates how impressive Jeff was his sophomore season.

Louie's philosophy on coaching his three sons was straightforward: "Go across the white line, I'm the Coach. Get back on the other side of the line, I'm Dad."

There were no postgame debriefings like Cook had to endure with his father.

"We talked about the games, strategies, and all that stuff," Jeff said, "but he left the hard-core coaching on the field and was still Dad at home. The frustration of a loss didn't come home with us."

Jeff was a junior in 2000 when he quarterbacked the Pios to the state 3A crown and Stu was a junior tailback on the 2009 team that won it all. Both had perfect 15–0 marks.

"What's funny," Faye said, recalling their first trip to the Dome in 1989, "Louie said, 'Make sure those boys [Lew and Jeff] get on the floor. They may never get back again.'"

Stu was born December 5, 1992, two years after his namesake, Stuart Jones, died climbing Mount McKinley in Alaska, the highest peak in North America. Louie coached Jones in college as part of a private athletic program, and he was close to his family.

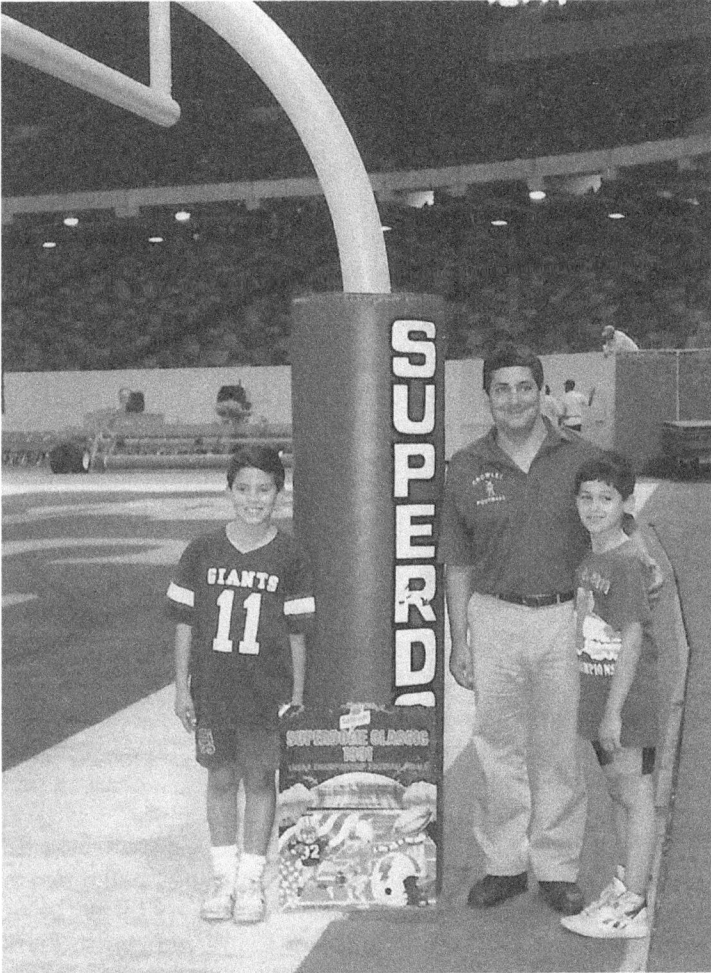

When Louie Cook's Crowley Gents made it to the Superdome in 1989, he told his wife, Faye, "Make sure those boys (Lew and Jeff) get on the floor. They may never get back again." Lew, *left,* was seven at the time and Jeff five. Lew and Jeff made it back to the Dome twice with Crowley (1991 and 1996) and nine times at Notre Dame. *Photo courtesy of Lewis Cook Jr.*

Of the three boys, Stu looks the most like his father, especially during their high school days.

"I ask myself sometimes if I didn't maybe sacrifice Stu a little bit to make somebody else feel good," Louie admitted.

"He acted more like a dad than a coach," Louie's younger brother, Robert Cook, said.

Stu usually played tailback, but he was at quarterback to open his sophomore season in 2008 because starter Ryan Leonards was out with a staph infection. Stu tossed two touchdown passes in the first quarter before a sprained ankle forced him out of the game. The Pios hung on to win, 14–12.

Leonards returned to quarterback the Pios until he broke his collarbone scoring a touchdown in the state quarterfinals. The Pios won the game, but it was obvious the backup quarterback who finished the game was not likely to get the job done against a tough Redemptorist High team in the semifinals.

Redemptorist had a star-studded lineup featuring running back Jeremy Hill and La'el Collins, an offensive tackle. They went on to star at LSU and play in the National Football League, Hill for the Cincinnati Bengals and Collins for the Bengals and Dallas Cowboys.

"You going to play Stu at quarterback?" Robert asked.

"I don't think so," Louie said.

"Louie, you can't babysit him the rest of his life," Robert said. "You've got to turn him loose."

"Dad, if you want any chance to win the game, you better put Stuart in," Jeff pleaded.

Jeff was groomed to play quarterback, Stu was not. One reason was their size—Jeff was six feet one, 190 pounds and Stu five-eight, 160.

"Stu is fiery—the most emotional of the three boys," Louie said. "That's why I didn't want to train him as a quarterback. He was up and down. Jeff was always in control. When Jeff was pitching in a baseball game, you wouldn't know if he was ten runs up or ten runs down."

At age thirteen, Jeff learned the Notre Dame offense on a car ride from Rayne, Louisiana, to Orlando, Florida, to play in a baseball tournament. "I sat in the front seat next to my dad and we went over the entire offense," Jeff said. "I didn't learn all the nuances of it, but I knew the formations, the blocking schemes, and what we're trying to accomplish. He was getting me ready."

There was no preparing him for the challenge he faced in 1998 as the only freshman to start for his father at Notre Dame.

The Pios needed an extra defensive back to have any chance against Evangel Christian Academy's wonder-boy quarterback, Brock Berlin, one of the most prolific passers in high school history with 13,902 yards and 145 touchdowns in his career.

"I couldn't believe he was putting my baby boy in there," Faye Cook said. "I was terrified."

She experienced the split personality of a wife and mother simultaneously rooting for her husband and son. The coach's wife yelled: "Don't you miss that tackle, Jeff!" And the momma said, "Get away from that

Jeff Cook (no. 8) was thirteen when he started preparing to play quarterback for his father, Louie Cook, at Notre Dame, learning the team's formations and blocking schemes. Jeff was all-everything as a junior, quarterbacking the Pioneers to a 15–0 record and the Class 3A state championship in 2000. He went on to play briefly for another legendary coach, Nick Saban, at LSU. On Coach Cook's left is his eldest son, Lew, an assistant at the school since 2000. *Photo by Brad Kemp.*

animal, Jeff," because many of the opposing players are big and nineteen years old and Jeff is fourteen.

"I don't know if he'll hit anybody but hopefully, he can get back there and help cover them," Louie said to Fred Menard, the team's defensive coordinator.

On a play at the goal line, there was a massive collision between a Pio defender and a running back for Evangel that could be heard on the sidelines some forty yards away. "Damn!" Louie exclaimed. "Who was that?"

It was Jeff.

"Got a fourteen-year-old out there making the biggest hits," observed Tommy Casanova, a Notre Dame graduate who starred at defensive back for LSU and the Bengals in the NFL.

Jeff switched to quarterback in his sophomore season and then as a junior in 2000, his first full year at the position, he passed for 1,978 yards and twenty-two touchdowns. He was on his way to another banner year in 2001 when he broke a leg in the sixth game.

It was "one of those momma moments" for Faye. She went to the hospital with Jeff while Louie stayed behind to finish the game. "He called every five minutes," she said.

The first report was that Jeff had a fracture and would be out three to four weeks. Near the end of the game, he learned the leg was broken and Jeff was done for the year.

When a broken wrist prevented Jeff from playing football in the eighth grade, he was encouraged to look on the bright side—kids who seldom play would get a chance to do so.

Jeff remembered that and asked his mother, "Why do you think it happened again?"

"I didn't have Louie's words of wisdom," Faye said. "We get home and Louie goes, 'Maybe he might've broken his neck on the next play.' That stopped the poor me."

Memories of Jeff's injury were fresh on Faye's mind as Louie contemplated starting Stu, a fifteen-year-old sophomore, at quarterback against Redemptorist in the state playoff semifinals.

"He was planning to get his learner's permit to drive," Faye said. "Guess what? He turned sixteen the week of the game."

"You've got to go play quarterback in the Dome," Louie said to Stu, hoping the Pios could make it past Redemptorist.

More momma moments lay ahead.

"I know it was hard on Louie coaching his sons, worrying about them getting injured," Robert said.

That didn't keep him from pestering his brother to put Stu at a position where he's expected to throw the ball and yet in his lone game at quarterback threw just six passes. Fortunately, he completed three for fifty-one yards and two touchdowns.

Louie simplified things for Stu: If a receiver is open, throw it; if he's not, run. "There was no other progression," Stu said. "Your second progression: Don't lose yards. At that time, running quarterbacks were starting to come in but it wasn't full-fledged like it is now. He let me just go."

On the first play from scrimmage, Stu perfectly executed a thirty-one-yard flea flicker pass to running back Nick Zaunbrecher for a touchdown. The only other pass he completed in the game was a twenty-three-yarder that set up a second touchdown. A flying tackle at the goal line by linebacker D. J. Welter on the last play of the game preserved the Pios' 17–10 victory. "Don't know how we beat them," Stu marveled.

In the championship game, the Pios were no match for Lutcher High and its sophomore wide receiver, Jarvis Landry, who caught eight passes for 119 yards and a one-handed touchdown grab that was a preview of the acrobatic catches he'd make later at LSU and in the NFL. Notre Dame was held to a Class 3A title-game low of seventy-five yards total offense and five first downs in the 17–0 loss.

Stu Cook, *kneeling,* and the Pios came up short in the 2008 championship game at the Superdome but won it all the next year, celebrating the twentieth anniversary of his father's first state title at Crowley High in 1989. Playing his natural position of tailback in the 2009 finals, Stu rushed for forty-four yards on eleven carries. *Standing, left to right,* are Faye and Louie Cook, Lew, Jeff, and his wife, Rachel. *Photo by Dwayne Petry.*

"In high school you've got to fit your system to the talent of the players that you have," Louie said. "In college, you recruit to your system."

When Jeff broke his leg in 2001, the Pios had to switch from a balanced pass-and-run offense to one that had his replacement, Patrick Hensgens, carrying the ball once in eight games. "The offense just totally flipped," Louie said. "Patrick could throw but he wasn't a threat to run. We went all the way to the semifinals with a backup quarterback."

Before the game against Lutcher in 2008, Louie acknowledged to a reporter that after Jeff left, he "didn't want another Cook at quarterback" and "it would do my heart a lot better if he was playing in the game but not starting at quarterback."[1]

Louie's reluctance to put his boys at quarterback at an early age had as much to do with putting them in the best position to succeed and not breaking their will. That's exactly what he did at USL with quarterbacks Dwight "Dante" Prudhomme and Jake Delhomme.

What's most interesting about the Cook boys is that the one who has had the most impact on their father's career is Lew, who seldom played but has become a gifted coach.

Lew has coached alongside his father since the fall of 2000. "My first year on Friday nights you could have got a chimpanzee with the ability to write that would have been as useful as I was," he said.

Lew is a jack-of-all-trades, helping his father with play-calling during games, working with the running backs, coaching the freshmen and junior varsity teams, and doing whatever needs to be done behind the scenes. "Thank God for Lew," Louie said. "I probably wouldn't be coaching if I didn't have him. He sure takes a lot off my plate."

And Lew has added some things through his mathematical wizardry and knowledge of American history that he uses as lenses to frame his ideas. "In war, the man with the high ground wins," Lew said. "In football, he who controls the edge wins the game."

Lew is constantly seeking that edge, although unlike his father, who has few secrets, he's guarded and protective of his theories. "Basically, I analyze defensive alignments and come up with offensive formations that work best against that defense," Lew explained.

"Lew is a good complement to me because he sees things a different way," Louie said.

Louie cites the time he questioned a play Lew called from the press box. "Lew, it's third-and-eight."

"Dad, I'm telling you the way that end's playing we're going to pop it."

"All right, I guess we'll run it."

The play worked for a thirty-yard gain.

"Good call, Lew."

In preparing for the 2018 state championship game against Catholic High of New Iberia, Lew figured out its defensive alignment in advance, propelling the Pioneers to a lopsided 42–21 win.

"I can do enough with these different matchups that I come up with that I'm relevant in his sphere of what he can do," Lew said. "I can actually contribute to some extent to his greatness."

Louie said he now leans more on Lew "in my play calling than I ever have. Every series: 'Lew, what you think?' So, I'm listening. I've got a lot of confidence in him now."

In drills, Lew has running backs practicing body positions and movements that lengthen their stride and make them faster and harder to tackle. "We're bi-pedal humans and imperfect machines," Lew said, sounding more like a scientist. "The cheetah was designed to run better than a human being. It's understanding where we're at in this three-dimensional reality and the limitations of movement of the human body."

Louie doesn't pretend to understand everything Lew says. "He'll wear you out with those numbers, but he knows what he's talking about."

The word that best describes Lew is *unique* "in a positive way," Stu emphasized.

"He looks at life differently," said Fritz Welter, a family friend. "Kind of like Einstein might've looked at things."

He drifts stealthily in and out of rooms, often begging the question, "Where's Lew?"

"He has this pure focus," Stu said. "Dad calls it a one-track mind."

Lew was going upstairs at home when his father asked, "Hey, Lew, what's up?"

"Me, Dad, about five steps."

Jeff's first car was a 1997 Mazda 626, one you might expect a young quarterback to drive. Lew was at the wheel of a 1996 Plymouth Breeze, a mom-and-pop type car. The cars reflected their personalities.

Lew was on the punt coverage team his senior year. "Every once in a while, he'd go in with the game on the line to rest the starter ahead of him," Louie said.

One night Louie was watching videotape of the Pios' next opponent. He heard footsteps coming down the stairs. It was Lew wanting to talk about the upcoming game.

"Dad, there's a lot of guys on the team that run down the field faster than I do," Lew said. "A lot of guys tackle better than I do. I just want you to know that if the game is ever on the line and you need to put someone else in on the punt team, I understand. I don't want to hurt the team."

It was a defining moment for both father and son.

"Lew, you've got a chance to make it and be somebody because you recognize your limitations," Louie said. "You know your strengths and you know your weaknesses. A lot of people never realize what that is. They become someone who they're not. But let me tell you one other thing: I've never put a kid on the field for charity or someone that didn't deserve to be out there.

"If I didn't have confidence in you to do a good job, I wouldn't have you on that punt team. You're not on there because your last name is Cook. You're on there because I can trust you and I know you're going to give me everything you got."

As Lew returned to bed, his father had tears in his eyes: "Here's my own son telling me, 'I know I'm not that good.'"

Other dads went to Louie and lamented how hard their boys were working and still not playing much.

"I know how you feel," he told them. "Every night I look at two boys sitting on the couch in my living room. One of them works harder than the other, but the one that works the hardest, I can't get him on the field. And his brother, who's two years younger, is the starting quarterback. How do you think I feel but how do you think he feels?"

"They all found their little place," said Faye Cook, citing Notre Dame's 2000 state championship game at the Superdome in New Orleans.

"That game is very special for me," she said. "It was Louie's first championship at Notre Dame, Jeff played, Lew coached, Stu was a ball boy, and I got to be a photographer on the sidelines. We were all a part of that game."

Stu is now a high school football coach just like his dad. Jeff is sales director of the Lafayette-based Sterling Automotive Group, managed by Robert Cook.

In 2002, Jeff played at LSU for Nick Saban, possibly the greatest college football coach of all time.

"Dad and Saban are polar opposites," he said, pointing out that he didn't enjoy playing football at LSU. "The work ethic is the same. The drive to win is the same. The difference is how they treat people. The development of kids is where my dad excels. He makes everybody better. He pulls the underdogs up."

He also lets the top dogs go where their talents lead them.

As good as Jeff was at quarterback, he was an exceptional pitcher and hitter in baseball. In fact, he only played baseball after transferring from LSU to the University of Louisiana in Lafayette his sophomore year.

One day Louie said to defensive coordinator Jimmy McCleary, "Let's be thankful we don't make them choose because we might be one championship less. Jeff might've chosen baseball over football."

Unlike many coaches who want kids to focus on one sport, Louie encourages them to play as many as possible.

"Development is part of it," said Boo Schexnayder, a sports performance consultant. "But it's more about unselfishness. People of our generation grew up playing multiple sports and you learn the value of it. Now, the cultures are all highly specialized and Louie just doesn't adhere to that philosophy. He believes that kids are better in season than when they are out of season. And he wants to see them participate in everything."

Almost every member of Notre Dame's baseball team that won the state championship in 2021 also played football.

Louie concedes that coaching your own boys can be tough, perhaps a no-win situation for some. But he doesn't see it that way.

"This is why it's a win," he said, recalling a conversation with Johnny Casanova, a former Notre Dame player who was a tight end for USL when he was coaching there in the 1980s. They were sitting in Louie's old office at Notre Dame and from his desk, he could see kids entering and leaving the locker room. Stu had just played his last game for the Pios.

"Man, we're going to miss Stu," Johnny said.

"Johnny, I can probably find somebody to make those runs and catches," Louie said. "What I'm going to miss is every day I'm sitting right here, and I hear, 'Hey, Dad.' And I get that little wave and a smile from Stu as he's going into the locker room. That's what I'm going to miss.'"

11

🏈

Early Morning Lights

It's 5:30 in the morning. The parking lot is full of pickup trucks. If not for the lights shining on the football field nearby, you'd think you were at an all-night honky-tonk. But then the field fills up with teenage boys—many shirtless and shoeless—running, hurdling, and jumping like they had scrambled eggs smothered with Tabasco sauce for breakfast.

Welcome to one of Notre Dame High School's summer workouts designed by a guy nicknamed Boo—Irving Schexnayder, an expert in speed, strength, and power conditioning with a résumé to prove it.

The workouts are legendary on their own. Coaches come from as far away as Michigan to see them personally.

On any of the twenty-four workout days in June and July, 90 to 125 boys show up at either 5:30 or 6:00. They are required to attend at least sixteen of the two-hour sessions over the summer. Afterward, about half of them go to their jobs in the rice fields. A third group of middle school–age boys arrives at 8:00 for their voluntary seventy-five-minute workout.

"What's happening at 5:30 in the morning when your ass is still sleeping?" asked Larry Dauterive, longtime Louisiana high school football coach. "Those boys at Notre Dame are out running."

Hudson LeBlanc, a starting linebacker for the Pios in 2021, calls the summer workouts miserable. "But that's how we win games," he said. "You wake up at 4:30, come to school half asleep, and then walk into the gym at 5:30. First thing is the weight room. After that you go outside to run a couple of sixty-yard sprints; work out with a med ball; do general strength exercises [push-ups, sit-ups, and leg lifts]; run hurdles; and do more med ball. By then, you can barely move."

"What's happening at 5:30 in the morning when your ass is still sleeping?" asked Larry Dauterive, a longtime Louisiana high school football coach. "Those boys at Notre Dame are out running." Every weekday during June and July, anywhere from 90 to 120 kids report at 5:30 and 6 a.m. for two-hours of weightlifting, running sprints and hurdles, and doing various general-strength exercises such as push-ups and sit-ups. *Photo by Jason Faul.*

Initially, the workouts started at 6:00, but some players wanted to begin at 5:30 so they could get to their summer jobs on time. Coming in earlier has become a badge of honor, so more and more players are now doing it.

"It's the guys before us that set the standard," LeBlanc said. "If you tried to do these workouts other places, people would quit. But we know it has been done and we see what you get out of it. It's not fun, but you do it because you want the reward."

Gerald Broussard played and coached at the University of Southwestern Louisiana (USL) when Notre Dame head coach Louie Cook was an assistant there.

"The best strength coach of all time is God," Broussard said. "The kids go from being thirteen, fourteen years old to seventeen, eighteen and Coach Cook knows how to help God along with an off-season program that challenges and develops them physically. He maximizes what their physical abilities are. Everybody is going to be playing at 100 percent because he's got you physically capable to do it."

Cook preaches that "there's no substitute for hard work" and other clichés such as "leave no stone unturned" and "good things happen to good people."

They may be time-worn adages to older generations, but to the kids of the rice and crawfish farmers in Acadia Parish where Notre Dame is located, they are nuggets of wisdom that shape them on and off the football field.

"I learned more on the football field with Louie Cook than I ever learned in any classroom," said Mitch Shoffiett, a hard-nosed linebacker at Notre Dame from 1997 to 1999 who now owns and operates a growing oilfield construction company in the Lafayette area. "Coach Cook is the reason I started this business. I would've never in a million years had the balls to go do it, but Coach always told us: 'Guys, if you believe in it, go get it—don't wait for it to come to you.'"

Cook knew Mitch didn't like school and wasn't going to college, so he got him to work harder than the next guy to overcome any shortcomings.

"If you know you're not good at something, the harder you work at it, the better you're going to be," Mitch said. "That's what I took away from Coach Cook—you might be smarter than me, you might have more education than me, but you ain't going to outwork me."

That's the motto Cook lives by and the cornerstone of the culture he has created at Notre Dame.

"My dad's a rice farmer, I'm a rice farmer," said Wesley Simon, a three-year starter at safety for Notre Dame who played on the 2000 state championship team. "You work your butt off. That's the common denominator. It doesn't for sure mean you're going to be successful just because you work hard. But it gives you a whole lot better shot to win and not just in a game, but in life."

Ryan Leonards quarterbacked Notre Dame to the state title in 2009. "You're doing stuff that's physically draining, mentally tough, and you end up bonding with each other," Leonards said of the summer workouts. "Instead of just teammates, you become like a family."

When it's the fourth quarter of a tied game against a more talented team, the Notre Dame players know their opponent didn't put in the time or effort they did at 5:30 in the morning. "It's one of those things that put us all on the same page," Leonards explained. "We worked too hard to let it all slip away. We're going to fight and claw, do everything we can to come together as a team and win."

And Notre Dame usually comes out on top.

The four years Simon was at Notre Dame (1998–2001), the Pios had a 45–9 win-loss record while the teams Leonards played on (2006–2009) were 51–4, a testament to the training program that Schexnayder developed with Cook and his coaching staff after a humbling loss in the second round of the 1998 state playoffs to Washington-Marion, a predominantly Black school in Lake Charles, Louisiana.

The Pios were ahead 7–0 in the second quarter when the Marion band arrived at Crowley's Gardiner Memorial Stadium. They got off the bus rocking and rolling and the Marion players started dancing. By the time the music stopped, they had a 27–7 upset win.

"They beat the dog out of us," said Todd Gray, an assistant coach at Notre Dame for twenty-four years. "They skull-drugged us. Ended up being ugly."

Harold Gonzales was on the sidelines covering the game for the *Crowley Post-Signal*. Dave Cook, Louie's brother and a swift defensive back at LSU in the early 1970s, watched as the Pios were repeatedly burned by Marion's superior speed. "Those are the slowest white boys I've ever seen in my life," Dave said. "They can't win until they get some speed."

Louie came to the same conclusion. The next week he told his assistant coaches: "Guys, if we don't get a step quicker and build more explosive power, we're going to fall every year around this time in the playoffs. Obviously, we've got to do something a little bit differently to help these kids."

The Pios lost in the third round of the playoffs Cook's first year in 1997. The latest defeat was to a Marion team with five losses.

At USL in the 1980s, Cook was introduced to plyometrics, or jump training, by Al Vermeil, strength coach for the San Francisco 49ers at one time and brother of Dick Vermeil, a head coach in the NFL for fifteen seasons. Jump training was widely used by Russian athletes then but was relatively new in the United States.

Cook took his plyometric knowledge to Crowley High in 1985, teaming with Brad Roll, a graduate assistant strength coach at USL, to develop a training program that was well ahead of its time.

"He was doing things at Crowley that SEC [Southeastern Conference] strength programs are doing now, and they act like they were the first ones that ever thought about them," said Roll, who went on to become the strength coach for six NFL teams. "We were doing Olympic lifts, hang clean, and power clean when nobody was doing it because no one knew how to teach it. Me and Louie learned together."

Conditioning drills had players jumping on and off wooden boxes, running in sand and varying distances each day, all timed and documented.

"The first decision Louie made at Crowley was his team had to get stronger, faster, and tougher," Roll said. "And they must understand what true work means—individual work, position work, teamwork. He taught that to those kids in the off-season program. Then it just snowballed."

Crowley went from twenty-two straight losses to a state championship in five years.

"There were a lot of very good athletes at Crowley High," Cook said. "They always had speed and were a force at the state track meet even before I was there. In my time at Crowley, we broke every record all the way from the 100-meter dash to the 800-meter relay just jump training and some of the other things we did."

Enter Boo. He and Louie first crossed paths at USL in the early 1990s when Boo coached track and Louie football.

"Louie benefits from the fact that his kids are rice farmers' kids, and they grew up working," Boo said. "They're kind of blue-collar kids. They work hard and understand the value of working because Louie just kicks that up a notch."

Boo had a system for training collegiate and Olympic-level track athletes for speed and power, plus he had a football background. "Football is still a game of quickness and power," Cook said, noting the running comes in bursts.

"Boo, I want you to come in and work with our kids," he said.

"If I work with your kids, Louie, I'm only good for a day or two, but if I work with your staff, you take it, and it becomes yours."

Shortly before Christmas 1998 Cook and his coaches huddled with Boo in a Notre Dame classroom for five hours the first day and for three hours the next.

"It was like taking a course in the physiology of exercise," Louie said. "We talked about stimulating the nervous system, the endocrine system that promotes growth. He broke speed down for us. You have speed acceleration, absolute speed, and speed endurance."

Boo stressed the importance of a rest week at the end of the next four months—January through April.

"That's four weeks—a month of training we're going to miss," Louie balked.

"It's huge that you do that," Boo said.

He demonstrated the exercises on the field, using Louie's son, Jeff, a freshman at the time, as the guinea pig.

"I did all these things none of us had ever done before," Jeff said. "I was a good athlete, but I wasn't doing any of that stuff well."

During a running exercise, Boo commented, "Jeff has a good strike angle."

"Boo, what's a strike angle?" Cook asked.

"It's the position of your foot and how it strikes the ground when your leg comes up," Boo explained.

Boo went through the entire program step-by-step, showing the coaches what to do and how to do it.

"We did things we'd never done, working muscles we'd never worked before," Louie said.

A hurdle mobility exercise, for example, works the hips to improve flexibility, rhythm, and balance.

"He went 100 percent in and did everything like I told him to do," Boo said. "And they did it with detail—that's why it has worked so well."

Most coaches cherry-pick a training program, taking what they like and leaving what they either don't understand or are unwilling to take the time to do properly.

"It takes energy to change," Boo said. "It takes effort to change. It takes self-criticism to change. And some people don't have that self-criticism as part of their personality. Louie was totally open minded about it. He just knew he had to get better with the athletes he thought he was going to have."

It was a complete revamp of the training program, and it challenged coaches and players alike.

"It's tedious and takes a long time to coach," said Gray, one of the assistants. "It's hard. It's brutal."

Andrew Schumacher was a wide receiver at Notre Dame from 2005 to 2007. "There wasn't one summer workout the first three days that I didn't throw up," he said. "It was a boot camp. They pushed us to the limits."

"They were designed to make you stronger physically, and to help you figure out, hey, I can push myself a little bit further," Ryan Leonards added. "My body will do what my mind tells it to do."

David Berken went from a five-foot-ten, 196-pound freshman to a six-foot-three, 235-pound senior at Notre Dame before going to Rice University, where he bulked up to 300 pounds and started four years at right guard. "I vomited every day for an entire summer," he recalled. "They were treacherous workouts, especially if you're a big man that's trying to move faster."

Berken improved his time in the forty-yard dash from six seconds to five. His first year at Rice in 2004, he remembers thinking, "'These guys can't touch the workouts that I was doing my senior year in high school.' We were doing things that a lot of other people weren't doing."

Kade Comeaux, a six-foot-six, 305-pound offensive tackle, was a phenom as a junior in 1998 after running the forty-yard dash in five seconds at an LSU summer football camp. He was offered a full scholarship by LSU and committed to play with two years still to go in high school. "I was super-flexible and had the fundamental skills," he said, "but the morning workouts got us stronger, faster. And [it] cemented that brotherhood and bond between us to perform as one."

The early morning workouts click because Cook and defensive coordinator Jimmy McCleary are always there when the players arrive at 5:30.

Cook gets up at 4:45 in the morning three days a week in June and July, grabs a cinnamon muffin, and drives to Notre Dame ten miles away. The players follow his example, some of them traveling thirty to forty miles each way.

"If you'd told me I'd be showing up at six o'clock workouts in the summertime, I'd laughed at you," Mitch Shoffiett said. "He's not making you do something that he's not going to do. And that's the difference between him and 90 percent of the other coaches."

Boo agreed. "It is the perfect storm when you get a special coach in a special place, and you've got these types of kids. Louie established a culture, and people come in to be part of that culture. The peer pressure in the program is extremely strong and extremely positive and only comes from culture. There's an old saying in coaching that when you get a head coaching job, you have ten chances to win games in a year, but only one chance to establish a culture. Louie is a master at establishing a culture."

"Look at what he's done," said Roll, ignoring Kade Comeaux, David Berken, and a few mountain-sized players to come out of Notre Dame. "He gets five-foot-seven to five-foot-ten white kids that weigh 165 to 190 pounds and kicks the shit out of everyone. That's the culture he brings."

The poster boy for Notre Dame football is closer to Shoffiett's size—five feet eight and 190 pounds.

"The kids Louie has at Notre Dame are 180 degrees different than the kids he had at Crowley, but he can reach all of those different kinds of kids," Boo said. "He's got a heart of gold because he takes every kid at face value. He has no prejudices about them. He can see the good in every single person."

Roll worked for nine coaches in the NFL, including Jimmy Johnson and Dave Wannstedt of the Miami Dolphins and Sam Wyche of the Tampa Bay Buccaneers. "No one can hold a candle to Louie Cook as far as being able to motivate and get players to believe and trust," he said. "Very few coaches can motivate a player or a team for one game, let alone nearly fifty years like Louie has."

The loss to Washington Marion, and the training program it produced, was the tipping point for Cook at Notre Dame.

Gerald Dill, the school's first football coach, attended a practice at the end of April. He was at the Marion game five months earlier.

"Louie, it's night and day," Dill said.

"What's that, Coach?"

"How these kids are moving and controlling their bodies. They're so much quicker and explosive."

The Pios lost two of their first three games in 1999 and then won nine straight before losing (28–21) in the quarterfinals of the playoffs to Amite High, the eventual state champion. "They gave us everything we ever imagined," Amite coach Donald Currier said. "We were fortunate to come out on top."[1]

Amite steamrolled all its opponents except Notre Dame, winning every regular-season game by at least twenty-two points and the finals, 42–7.

The next year (2000), Notre Dame was just as dominating, outscoring opponents, 392–95, and winning the state championship with a perfect 15–0 record.

The Pios lost four regular-season games Cook's first two years ('97 and '98) and twenty-one in the last twenty-four years. "That's training," he said. "We're not that good of coaches."

Cook is as humble as he is unselfish.

Hundreds of coaches have traveled to Crowley to see Notre Dame's off-season workouts and pick Cook's brain. Nick Ware observed the parade both as a player and coach.

"Coach Cook would give them everything," Ware said. "There was nothing that he held to his vest. If you wanted our playbook, he gave you the whole playbook. You wanted our off-season program, you got it all. He'd give you every single thing we did."

Cook was heeding the advice of both his mentor, Larry Dauterive, and the dean of Louisiana high school coaches in the 1960s, Faize Mahfouz, who always said, "Pass it on to somebody else."

Ware is now a Catholic priest: "In the coaching profession, you stand on the shoulders of giants. What you receive has been created, transformed, and modified by someone else. We're not the inventors. We're just the receptors. And we pass it on. Coach Cook is keenly aware of that."

Cook has one caveat. "If you want something then take the time to go get it. Don't call up and say, 'Can you send it to me?' You've got to come watch."

Jeff Wainwright was at every summer workout in 2003, the year he got his first head coaching job at Kinder High School, approximately fifty miles northwest of Crowley. His face was so familiar to the kids that Cook handed him an instruction sheet at one practice and said, "Here, Jeff, you take Group 2."

Wainwright took a truck full of assistants with him to Crowley so they could capture everything they saw. "I'd go to his workout and watch it and then, the next day, I'd teach it at Kinder. Basically, we were a day behind his workout."

Some mornings he sent his coaches back to Kinder and he stayed behind to talk with Cook about various aspects of the game and people issues that come up in coaching.

"My whole goal was just to be successful and not get fired," Wainwright said. "He has a way of talking to you in a commonsense manner and you're like: 'Yeah, that makes sense.' He doesn't ask kids to do things they can't do. And he has adapted as the game changes."

Wainwright views Notre Dame's 5:30 morning workouts as "sort of like a cult that made itself. It was nothing like: 'I'm Coach Cook. You're going to be here at 5:30!' It's like everything else he does: the kids asked for it, he supplied it."

The consistency of the workouts is what impresses Wainwright most. "Whether it's offense, defense, or the weight room, everybody is on task," he said. "And that's consistency in training. The kids know what to expect from Coach Cook. It's not going to be too high; it's not going to be too low. They know what to expect from Jimmy Mac [defensive coordinator Jimmy McCleary]. As a coach, you can feel the planning and organization in the consistency of training."

Before becoming an assistant coach at the University of Houston, Corby Meekins coached at Spring Westfield High School in Houston. He and several of his coaches spent two days watching the Pios train and then went home and added a couple of the hurdle drills to their own workouts.

"It's a well-oiled machine," Meekins said. "You don't have to tell them what the first exercise is. Immediately they're lined up. Everybody is set. Boom! They're going. That's what happens when you've got a championship program in place. Everybody knows what the expectations are and understands how you do things."

Wainwright still uses the weightlifting system and principles of offense and defense he learned from Cook.

"One of the most important lessons he taught me is the three seasons in the life of a football player and head coach," Wainwright said.

There's the football season, ultimately the most important because you must be successful. There's the off-season, and then there's the summer program, which is a season itself.

"Don't get those seasons mixed up," Cook told Wainwright. "They are separate seasons. And don't hold one season against a kid."

If a kid has a bad summer, it could be his parents' fault, not his. Put the kid back in school every day in a regimented program; he might be a great football player. There might be a kid that excels in weights but can't quite put it together on the football field. Encourage him to be a leader in the weight room.

"I've always thought about that," Wainwright said, "because your strongest and smartest kids are not necessarily your best players. Neither is the kid that shows up the most at the summer workouts."

Through the 2022 season, Wainwright's teams at Kinder, Sulphur, and currently Grand Lake have compiled a 133–83 record. He guided Grand Lake to the Class 1A state finals for the first time in 2020 and was selected Coach of the Year by the Louisiana Sports Writers Association—an honor Cook has won three times.

"I've had a lot of success in my coaching career," Wainwright said, "and a lot of it has to do with Coach Cook's time that he spent with me and the wisdom of an older coach passing it down."

That's why Boo Schexnayder calls Cook special. "The great coaches are comfortable in their own skin," he said. "They're confident enough in their abilities that they're going to help you and still win games."

Cook wants other coaches to copy his off-season training program because it will help more kids.

"Nobody is going to do it like we do it," he told an assistant coach concerned he was sharing too much information.

Cook knows the program can be replicated in theory but the way he thinks, acts, and relates to people cannot. After all, there's only one Louie Cook Jr.

12

🏈

No Place Like Dome

The Superdome needs no introduction. It's immediately connected with the city of New Orleans, the Saints of the NFL, and major sports events such as the annual Sugar Bowl and the Super Bowl, which has been played there seven times.

In Louisiana, it's the dream of every high school football coach and player to get to the state championship game, which has been played at the Superdome every December since 1981 except when Hurricane Katrina forced the finals upstate in 2005 and the COVID pandemic broke up the party in 2020.

Louie Cook was an assistant coach at the University of Southwestern Louisiana (USL) when he attended the four title games the first year they were played at the Superdome. "I can remember thinking to myself, 'If I go back to high school, I want to play for the championship here.'"

He was the defensive coordinator at Rayne High School in 1975, when Rayne played Lutcher High for the Class 3A crown. The game was played in Lutcher, a town of approximately 3,500 people about fifty miles from New Orleans.

"The only people that knew what happened at that game were the ones that were sitting in the stands that night or maybe read about it in the Baton Rouge or New Orleans papers the next day," Cook said. "You could only watch one game—4A was somewhere else, 2A was at another school. In the Dome, you can go for the weekend and watch every game."

That's why Cook was there in 1981 and Nick Saban in 2004, when he was head coach at LSU.

One of the teams Saban watched was Cook's Notre Dame Pios going toe-to-toe against top-ranked and heavily favored Amite High in the Class 3A title game. Amite scored a touchdown midway in the fourth quarter to win, 21–14. "ALMOST," blared a headline on the front page of the *Crowley Post-Signal*.[1]

The following Monday, Saban called to congratulate Cook. "Louie, I just had to call and tell you how much I enjoyed watching your kids play. Don't take this the wrong way but that team was probably three to four touchdowns better than y'all, and they were lucky to get by you."

Cook has taken twelve teams to the Dome, three from Crowley High and nine from Notre Dame. The Pios also made it to the 2005 championship game in Shreveport. They came out on top four times: 2000, 2009, 2015, and 2018. And they lost six, including four straight: 2003, 2004, 2005, 2008, 2012, and 2017.

"It really irks me when I hear somebody say, 'Oh, that coach can't win the big game,'" Cook said. "You know how many big games you've got to win to get to that final game?"

The Pios had to win four playoff games to reach the finals until 2015, when that number dropped to three and eventually two after changes to the state's playoff system.

Cook cites the Buffalo Bills and their head coach Marv Levy, who lost four consecutive Super Bowls from 1991 to 1994. "What other team has gone four years in a row?" Cook asked. "Doesn't that tell you something about Marv Levy? The guy must've been pretty good. We got there three years in a row and didn't win any of them. One of the three years we might've been as good as the team we played. The other two years they were more talented teams than we were. We were lucky to be there."

Kevin Foote was a sportswriter for the *Lafayette Daily Advertiser* at the time and he agreed: "A lot of times when they got to the finals, it was really evident that, yeah, they're a great program and he's a great coach but they just didn't have the raw talent of a lot of teams they were playing. You just can't get to the finals as many times as he did if you weren't a great coach."

The telephone call from Saban reinforced Notre Dame's reputation for producing more future doctors and priests than Division 1 football players.

"If they lost in the semifinals, that was a down year," Foote said. "I don't know how many Division 1 college signees he [Cook] had but I won't use all my fingers for the entire decade."

One of them was David Berken, an offensive tackle on the Notre Dame club that lost at the Dome in 2003 to Lutcher, a perennial powerhouse. He went on to start four years at Rice University, a Division 1 school, and to become an orthopedic surgeon.

Dr. Berken recalls Notre Dame players saying to each other, "Can you imagine how much Coach Cook would've beat our team by with the team we just played? They were so much more talented, if he was coaching them, they could've destroyed us. Look at what he's done with a few Division 1 players against teams loaded with them."

From 2000 through 2009, the Pios reached the finals six times and the semifinals nine out of the ten seasons, with the 2000 and 2009 titles serving as bookends for their dream decade. Overall, they had a 125–15 record. "We played 101 out of a possible 105 games in a seven-year period [2000–2006]," Cook said proudly.

The Pios were nearly as dominant from 2010 through 2019, again nabbing two titles (2015 and 2018) and making it to the finals four times and the semifinals seven. They finished the decade with a 111–15 mark.

"They might've been faster and more talented, but never were they better conditioned," Berken said of the Pios' opponents. "It doesn't matter what kind of game plan you're calling, if you're gassed in the fourth quarter, then you don't have a chance."

Cook is called "The Master" by Foote and other Louisiana sportswriters because of his ability to communicate with the media. That mastery extends to his players.

"We always overachieve," he reminded the Pios prior to a big game in 2021. "When we stop being overachievers, then, we're just like everybody else."

He likes to say, "It's not the size of your butt, it's the size of your heart. Fortunately, we've got big hearts."

Notre Dame's success has inevitably led to accusations of recruiting.

"We need to fire our recruiting coordinator because they're recruiting guys like me," joked Father Nick Ware, a five-foot-seven, 155-pounder who started at cornerback on the 2008 team, which lost to Lutcher in the Dome.

"If Coach Cook was at a school that actually recruited athletes, it would be dangerous," added Carson Watson, a six-foot-one, 230-pound fullback who transferred to Notre Dame from another area high school. "He would be a force to be reckoned with. Just look at the D1 [Division 1] players that have come out of Notre Dame. There ain't many."

"He could get so many kids over here if he wanted to recruit," said Cook's brother, Dave, who served two brief stints as a defensive back coach at Parkview Baptist in Baton Rouge. "But he won't do that. He plays what he's got."

"The biggest thing is the dedication of the players," said Kevin Magee, an assistant coach at Crowley who came out of retirement to help Cook at Notre Dame. "They're here because they want to be. They want to be good, and they want to work. You don't have to worry about who's going to be at practice. They're all going to be at practice all the time."

Johnny Casanova was a tight end at USL when Cook was there in the 1980s and he's had four sons play for him at Notre Dame. "Louie has done more with kids under six feet than anybody in the country," Johnny claimed.

Cook specializes in making top dogs out of underdogs. In fact, he's the ultimate underdog.

"Coach Cook is the undersized guy that was the quarterback," said Gerald Broussard, who coached with him at USL. "He's the guy that's not going to pass the eyeball test."

Cook didn't play football in college, and yet he became a highly respected college coach. When he returned to high school coaching, he went to Crowley, the outhouse of Louisiana high school football with a twenty-one-game losing streak. He led Crowley to a state title, went back to college, and, in Broussard's words, "found out it still sucks." This put him back in high school and eventually at Notre Dame with his sons.

Meanwhile, Notre Dame jumped from Class 2A to 3A and stiffer competition. "Moving up from 2A, we were a natural underdog for a long time," Cook says. "We were doing the huntin'. Now, we're the hunted. It's not much fun being the hunted all the time."

The Pios didn't make it to New Orleans in 2021, losing 17–13 in the semifinals to St. Charles Catholic, the eventual 3A champion. The following Monday, Cook met with the players in the school's chapel.

"There are going to be teams that may win a state championship and don't earn the respect that other teams earn," he said. "It's because how they went about building their program."

He recalled a comment about another Louisiana high school team with several blue-chippers coveted by elite football colleges. "Coach," the man said, "you could get some players like that."

"It's not us," Cook replied.

He mentioned a photograph of the 2000 team that won a state title. "I have a great feeling when I look at that picture, knowing that everybody in it came to Notre Dame because this is where they wanted to be. They weren't asked to come. They just came. We took who wanted to be here and worked their tails off—just like you guys did. It means a whole lot more when you do it right."

There are two things Cook always tells his players: do things right and work hard.

"The winning—and the things we want to get—will come," he said. "They may not all come at this time, but you'll find out as you get older that some of these things might help you down the line. And that's really what it's all about."

Notre Dame won two state titles in the 1970s, but they weren't Dome games. The Dome was the thing by 2000. "Everybody wanted to get to the Dome," Cook said.

To get there in 2000, the Pios had to survive a semifinal showdown with top-seeded and undefeated Breaux Bridge. "We don't belong on the same field," Cook said. "Off of that team, four guys went to LSU."

Early in the week, he told the Pios: "The one advantage that we have playing Breaux Bridge is they're going to read the same newspaper articles we do and see the same TV stations we watch. Don't read anything into what I say. All I'm going to do is pump their heads up so when we get there, they won't have any respect for us. I'm going to say how good they are, how I just hope we can hold on and be respectable."

He paused and then added: "We're good. We wouldn't be here if we weren't good."

The game was played at Breaux Bridge in front of more than six thousand people jammed into a 1,500-seat stadium. "The stands on the home side were entirely full 1½ hours prior to game time and there were fans five rows deep completely around the field," the *Daily Advertiser* reported.[2]

"I was at that Breaux Bridge game," a man told Cook later.

"You saw a helluva game," he said.

"Saw? I didn't see a play. I was so far back on the track, I couldn't see the field. I stood there, put the radio on, and tried to peek when I could."

The man missed seeing the Pios punch their ticket to the Dome with a 21–6 victory. Cook's son, Jeff, completed all five passes he threw, three for touchdowns and the other two for first downs. Safety Wesley Simon had a key pass interception and blocked an extra point attempt.

That set up the championship game against the Redemptorist Wolves of Baton Rouge, billed by the *Daily Advertiser* as the "war for perfection" because both teams had 14–0 records.[3]

The length and width of the football field in the Dome is the same as anywhere else, Cook reminded the Pios. "Your focus should be on winning the championship, not where the game is played."

He didn't say anything about the Dome's artificial turf that possibly was responsible for the tying touchdown in the Pios' 14–6 triumph.

Leading 6–0 with slightly more than nine minutes to play in the game, the Wolves botched an attempted punt, the low snap from center hitting the carpet and bouncing away from punter Kyle Hebert and over a couple of creases in the end zone before Pios linebacker Nicky Briggs pounced on it.

"We've had divine intervention all year," Cook said.[4]

Daily Advertiser sportswriter Dan McDonald suggested, "It might have been just a couple of wrinkles in the Louisiana Superdome turf."[5]

Whatever, it was a classic example of Cook preaching, "Do the right things and let the chips fall where they may."

"He truly believed that," Simon said. "It was great to win, of course, because that keeps everyone's goals in sight. But we never focused on winning. We focused on everything it took to win."

The Pios won the war for perfection, finishing with a 15–0 record, including seven shutouts. The next day Simon was still soaking in the meaning of it all.

"It was almost a feeling of disappointment," he said. "Of course, we were happy we won. But you still have that feeling of, 'Man, I just want to play another game. I want to go 16 and 0.' The ride was more enjoyable than holding and taking a picture with a trophy. Those things don't really matter. It was about the experience."

As Simon and many of his teammates came to realize, the best part of the experience was not playing in the Dome, but the journey that got them there.

"Football or just competing in general can be a snapshot of your life," Simon said. "You work hard. You don't always win. You've got to learn how to win, and you've got to learn how to lose. And just keep working."

Simon didn't make it back to the Dome his senior year in 2001 as the Pios lost to the Parkview Baptist Eagles in the semifinals. Over a twelve-year period (2001–2013), the two schools battled eight times in the play-offs, Parkview ending up with a 5–3 edge.

Twice Louie and Dave Cook faced each other, the Pios prevailing both times—21–14 in the 2003 semifinals and 28–0 in the 2005 quarterfinals.

One day the brothers were reminiscing about the 2003 game on Parkview's home field. Both teams were undefeated at the time (13–0).

"That was the best team Parkview ever had," Dave said, citing the seven D1 players on the club, three headed for LSU. "They went in there and beat us in a heck of a football game."

"That was as good a game as I ever watched," Louie said.

"We knew it was going to be a war," Dave said. "It was a high-level intensive game that came down to the first person that blinked or didn't make a play."

"We were up 14 to nothing," Louie said. "And then they came back and tied us."

The Pios' Rick Zaunbrecher scored the winning touchdown on a thirteen-yard run midway through the fourth quarter.

"It was a hard, hard game," Dave said.

Afterward, Karen Berken was watching a video of the game with her husband, Clarence. "Look at that!" he exclaimed, stopping to rewind the tape so they could see Cook kneeling by himself on the field to say a prayer.

"How many people do that?" Karen asked. "He hit a knee and thanked who got him there. That defines his success."

A week later the Pios lost 15–7 to Lutcher in the Dome.

"The Parkview game took everything out of them," Dave said. "If Louie had played 'em a couple of weeks later, he'd beat 'em."

After the Lutcher loss, the Pios gathered around their coach in the locker room.

"Everybody was distraught," David Berken recalled, "and he says: 'Guys, I'm proud of the way you played. I know we came up short but if this is the worst defeat you ever face in your life, you're going to live one amazing life.'"

Cook has a way of putting football into context with the rest of life. "Being a good person is going to last you a helluva lot longer than being a good football player," said Hunter Stover, a kicker-linebacker on teams that reached the Dome in 2008 and 2009.

Hunter's grandfather, Stewart "Smokey" Stover, was a linebacker for the Dallas Texans/Kansas City Chiefs of the old American Football League and played for the Chiefs in the first Super Bowl in 1967. Hunter's parents knew he had the potential for a career in football, so they enrolled him at Notre Dame midway through high school. "There was always this joke that Notre Dame recruits," he said. "I fit the bill—a kicker."

Hunter was no ordinary kicker. He had an extraordinarily strong leg and lived in Abbeville, a forty-minute drive from Notre Dame in Crowley. "It was all pure," he insisted. "There was no recruiting going on. People want to drive from all over to play for Coach Cook."

In a 2008 quarterfinal mudfest against Richwood High in Monroe, Louisiana, Hunter lined up to kick a fifty-eight-yard field goal. But it wasn't your average three-pointer. It was a punt–field goal, a term coined by Cook.

"It was really kind of a genius deal that Coach Cook came up with," Hunter said. "Nobody realized that if you kicked a field goal and it gets to the end zone, it's just a touchback."

Any kick, whether it be a punt, missed field goal, or kickoff that breaks the plane of the goal line, can't be returned. This was the premise Cook based the punt–field goal on.

"We set up like a field goal and try to make it," Hunter said. "The real intent was getting the ball in the end zone. Make it through the uprights, even better."

Cook put defensive end Jake Molbert at center and linebacker D. J. Welter on the edge to block like a tackle because the kicking tee was only seven yards from center. "Obviously, the ball is not going to go as high as a punt off the foot, so you need bigger bodies to protect a little bit better," Hunter noted.

Hunter was almost a sure bet to kick the ball into the end zone from midfield but if he didn't, the six-foot, 195-pounder was an outstanding open-field tackler and could be counted on to stop the kick returner. "I didn't have to worry about covering them because Hunter could do it," Cook said.

Cook trotted out his secret weapon three times in the first quarter. Hunter missed from fifty-four yards on the first try and then, two minutes later, he teed up for a fifty-seven-yarder. "Man, this is crazy," he thought to himself as the kicking tee was placed on the forty-seven-yard line.

The Richwood players seemed to be thinking the same thing. "Nobody rushed," Hunter said. "They were all playing for the fake."

Boom! The ball soared past the goal line and the goalposts, just missing to the right. "Kind of got their attention," Hunter said.

He tried from the forty-eight-yard line near the end of the quarter. This time the ball went over and through the middle of the uprights for a fifty-eight-yard field goal. "We were trying to get the ball in the end zone and eliminate a return, and Hunter puts three points on the board for us," Cook said.

"I'm glad Coach Cook knew the rules," Hunter said.

If other coaches knew about the punt–field goal rule, they never took advantage of it. "A lot of coaches want to coach Friday nights, but they don't put all the work in that goes into Friday nights," Dave Cook said.

Hunter recalled seeing Cook on the Notre Dame practice field before games on Friday. "He'd walk a hundred yards, turn around, and walk back. I'll bet he was going through the entire game in his head."

The Pios nipped Richwood, 16–12, but star quarterback Ryan Leonards broke his collarbone scoring a touchdown just before the half. "How we ever won that game I still haven't figured out," Cook said.

This forced Cook to move his son Stu from tailback to quarterback for the semifinal game against the Redemptorist Wolves.

Just before boarding the bus for Gardiner Memorial Stadium, Stu sat in his father's office going over the game plan. Posters from previous Dome visits covered the walls. Stu counted them. "We've got seven posters," he said. "All right, Dad, let's go get eight in '08."

Stu tossed a touchdown pass to begin the game and Hunter kicked a forty-eight-yard field goal in the third quarter to put the Pios on top, 17–0. The lead was down to 17–10 with two minutes left in the game when Hunter crushed a fifty-eight-yard punt to pin the Wolves on their own two-yard line. They managed to flip the field and were about to score the tying touchdown when Pios linebacker D. J. Welter came out of nowhere on the last play of the game to stop running back Jonathan Green one yard shy of the goal line.

"They ran a sweep play to the right, and I was on the opposite side," Welter said. "All their linemen pulled and went outside, and their running back cut back, and it was almost a perfect situation for me. I was coming from the back side for any cut back and gave him my best shot. The next thing I know the whole sideline was on top of me in the end zone."

In his story for the *Daily Advertiser*, Kevin Foote likened Welter's tackle to a field goal kicker "hitting a 50-yarder on the last play of the game into the wind for the victory."[6]

Cook told Foote: "I had to take a knee and say a little prayer because the Good Lord had just smiled on us."[7]

The next week Cook wasn't smiling after losing his fourth straight championship game, 17–0, to Lutcher in the Dome. But he hadn't lost his sense of humor.

"Have you ever been in front of a firing squad before?" he asked three of the Pios' defensive standouts—Jake Molbert, Bryant Gilbert, and Seth Fruge—as they were about to field questions in a post-game press conference.[8]

"Be humble and speak with class," Cook advised the players. "It's always about us, it's not about you."

In the locker room, Cook addressed the team: "Guys, look at that scoreboard. For you seniors, that'll be the last time there will be a football score on it. The scoreboard will remain on, but you'll be playing the game of life. When you become a husband and father, whatever profession you choose, the way you treat people dictates your score. Hopefully, you'll have more points doing things the right way than if you don't."

It was a great speech but Ryan Leonards, D. J. Welter, Hunter Stover, Jake Molbert, and the other juniors on the team didn't want to hear it again.

They would return to the Dome in 2009, but they had to get past Catholic High of New Iberia (Catholic-NI) in a semifinal game that's now referred to as the "Snow Bowl."

As a young boy, Cook would go to sleep at night, listening on his transistor radio to WLS, a Chicago-based station. "I woke up one night—in the middle of the night—and my radio was still going. The announcer said: 'And it's snowing. . . .' I jumped out of bed I was so fired up, and then, I realized it was on WLS. It was snowing but it was Chicago. It wasn't Rayne, Louisiana."

Cold and rainy conditions were forecast for the early December game. Catholic-NI head coach Craig Brodie lobbied to move the game, claiming the forty-mile trip to Rayne might be unsafe. He even took his case to the state police and the commissioner of the Louisiana High School Athletic Association.

It looks like Buffalo or Green Bay, but it's actually Rayne, Louisiana. To get to the Superdome in 2009, Notre Dame had to get past Catholic High of New Iberia in a semifinal game known as the Snow Bowl because of the snowy, icy conditions. "It was one of those crazy games that you never forget," Pios linebacker D. J. Welter said of his team's 43–0 victory led by quarterback Ryan Leonards (9). *Photo by Dwayne Petry.*

Cook pointed out another New Iberia high school, Westgate, had a game the same night in Lafayette. "At seven o'clock we're putting the ball on the tee," he said. "If y'all aren't there, we'll go to New Orleans next week. I'm not moving the game."

On a snow-and-ice-blanketed field, the Pios piled up 304 yards rushing, 127 by tailback Logan Venable, to roll past Catholic-NI like a snowplow, 43–0. "I don't like the decision that was made to play, but I didn't make it," Brodie grumbled.[9]

The next week the Pios beat the Parkview Baptist Eagles 14–7 to cap a perfect 15–0 record and end their title game losing streak. "Superdome no longer Pios' House of Horrors," proclaimed a headline in the *Daily Advertiser*.

Leonards completed seven of thirteen passes for 187 yards, including an eighty-three-yard touchdown toss to Zach D'Aquin, and rushed for twenty-five yards and a score. Welter made eight solo tackles to lead the defense, which blanked the Eagles after they scored on the first play of the game.

In a rare occurrence, three Pios from that team went on to play D1 college football—Welter at LSU and Stover and Molbert at University of Louisiana at Lafayette.

"Never leave a stone unturned," Cook constantly told the Pios.

"Basically, do everything you can to give yourself the best chance at success," Leonards said.

"Good days on top of good days," Stover recalled Cook saying repeatedly. "He coached us to always be humble, work hard, and leave no stone unturned."

"He always had a plan," Leonards said. "You never felt like he didn't know what was going to happen next."

There's a reason for that.

Given a choice of preparing a team for a game that you're not allowed to attend or skipping practice and coaching the game, a lot of coaches would say, "I'll be there Friday night."

Not Cook. "I'll be there during the week and y'all take them on Friday," he said.

Cook is almost always prepared for what happens next.

Consider the storybook saga of Adam Berken, a quarterback-turned-wide receiver on the Pios' 2015 championship team. "It's much more a story about Coach Cook than it's about me," Adam said. "A lot of people can throw a pass. But not a lot of people can pick the right people to be in that place. Coach Cook is the wizard in the story."

Adam grew up watching his older cousin, David, play for the Pios and dreamed of playing quarterback for Cook, who by the time he got to Notre Dame "was more of a myth than man."

Believe it or not, the rigorous workouts during Louisiana's hot, humid summers helped quarterback Ryan Leonards (9) cope with the frigid conditions of the "Snow Bowl." Shown here with Coach Cook, Leonards led the Pios to a perfect 15–0 record and the state Class 3A crown in 2009. "You're doing stuff that's physically draining, mentally tough, and you end up bonding with each other," Leonards says of the summer sessions. "Instead of just teammates, you become like a family." *Photo by Brad Kemp.*

Adam didn't get much playing time at quarterback his first two years, so he reluctantly switched to wide receiver where he alternated with another player his senior year. "Wide receiver at Notre Dame is not the best position on the field because we ran the ball about 90 percent of the time," Adam said.

He went to see Cook and express his frustration with the situation.

"Adam, keep working hard," Cook said. "One day you're going to make a play that's going to make a difference in a big game. I need you to be ready for that moment."

Adam decided it was more important to play than it was to be a quarterback watching from the sidelines.

The Pios started practicing a trick play with Adam taking a handoff on a reverse and heaving the ball downfield to Boedy Borill, the team's top receiver. "We kept practicing and practicing it," Adam said. "I'd played quarterback and I could throw the ball decently. Obviously not well enough to be the starting quarterback but somewhere in between."

In the state championship game against the Riverside Academy Rebels, the Pios trailed 3–0 with less than a minute to go in the first half. "We were really struggling to move the ball," Cook said.

He had just told his son, Lew, sitting in the press box: "Start making some notes of some first-down pass plays. We've got to start opening it up."

On fourth-and-one the Pios lined up to try and get the Rebels to jump offside. Cook walked up to Adam and asked, "You ready? If they jump, it'll be first down, and we'll run the play."

The strategy worked. Adam ran onto the field and touched the back of his helmet, signaling to his father, Kevin, in the stands what was about to happen. "Oh, my God," he shouted. "It's the play! It's the play!"

You could count the passes Adam caught all season with two hands. No fingers were needed to count the passes he threw. "I definitely was not an aerial threat," he quipped.

Adam took the handoff from quarterback Joe Faulk, ran, and then stopped and lofted the ball to a wide-open Borill for a fifty-five-yard gain to Riverside's three-yard line. The Pios scored on the next play, then recovered a fumble on the ensuing kickoff and added a second touchdown six seconds later to make it 13–3, the final score of the game.

"If you'd told me that the stands were sold out, I would've believed you," Adam said, recalling the moment. "If you'd told me nobody was in there, I would've believed you. As soon as it happened, everything kind of just got shut out. It was a 100 percent dreamlike state I was in. It feels like a dream looking back on it."

He remembers Cook saying, "I told you! I told you!" and, with tears in his eyes, hugging him on the field.

"I hadn't done much praiseworthy up until then," Adam said. "To have that moment when they needed me to do it and for them to have the trust in me to do it, that was awesome."

The Pios were back in the Dome in 2017 and 2018, losing to Catholic-NI, 33–16, the first time and romping to a 42–21 victory in the rematch.

The archrivals had played each other so often they were predictable. So, when Brent Indest, head coach at Catholic-NI, changed his defensive scheme, Cook was forced to scrap his offensive game plan.

"Forget what we worked on the last ten days," he said to quarterback Ben Broussard, instructing him to follow the plan used in a previous game.

"That's what football is," Cook said. "It's always about adapting and adjusting."

The Pios ran wild, with pint-sized running back Noah Bourgeois scoring three touchdowns and racking up 228 all-purpose yards rushing, receiving, and returning kicks. The Pios finished with a 13–0 record and

Adam Berken wanted to play quarterback, so he wasn't happy about being moved to wide receiver. "One day you're going to make a play that's going to make a difference in a big game," Coach Cook told him. "I need you to be ready for that moment." On a trick play near the end of the first half of the 2015 state championship game at the Superdome, Berken connected with Boedy Borill on a fifty-five-yard pass that set up the Pios' first touchdown in a 13–3 win over Riverside Academy. *Photo by Dwayne Petry.*

Noah finished the season with 1,700 yards rushing and twenty-seven touchdowns.

"Noah was one of the best backs we ever had," Cook said of the five-foot-six, 160-pounder. "When that sonofagun was about to get hit, he dropped his pads and delivered a lick. He was the difference in '18. Noah made everybody better."

In Cook's farewell speech to the 2021 team, he didn't mention any of the school's past stars but instead shared a story about David Guidry, a hardworking senior wide receiver who saw limited action during the 2000 season.

They were walking to the practice field for the last time before going to the Dome.

"I wish I could've got you on the field more," Cook said.

"Coach, if I had to start all over again today knowing what I know, I wouldn't change a thing," Guidry replied. "I've learned that if I get in a tight situation, I'm strong enough to be able to get my way out of it."

It was a testament to Cook and the remarkable football program he's built at Notre Dame. Winning isn't everything; winning the right way is.

13

🏈

Family Ties

Family ties go so deep in the Notre Dame football program that you almost need Ancestry.com to tell who's who.

Nine of the family names on the Notre Dame varsity roster going into the 2022 season can be traced to the school's first football team in 1967, which went undefeated (9–0) and nearly unscored on (298–6) in the regular season—Casanova, Faul, Fruge, Hebert, Hensgens, Leonards, Moody, Prevost, and Simon.

There were Leonards brothers on both teams—Al and Gregory in 1967 and Gregory's grandsons, Aiden and Hunter, in 2022. Al now collects tickets at the gate for home games.

On the 2022 team brothers Jeremy and William Prevost are kin to Charles Prevost, an end in '67; Huntson Hebert is the grandson of Jeffrey Hebert, a fullback in '67; and Jacob and Jeffrey Trahan are linked to Wayne Vondenstein, another end in '67, through Wayne's sister and their grandmother, Janet Vondenstein Trahan. Nick Vondenstein is on the freshman roster and his sister, Caroline, is a student trainer.

To confuse matters even more, the 2022 team had two players named Josh Hebert—Josh T. Hebert and Josh G. Hebert. They are not related to each other or Jeffrey Hebert.

The original Pios squad also produced the first of a parade of players named Habetz, Hundley, and Zaunbrecher.

"The same last names keep recycling through the program," *Lafayette Daily Advertiser* sportswriter Brady Aymond wrote in 2009. "Great-grandfathers built the program. Their great-grandsons have taken it to the next level."[1]

A case in point is the late William Joseph Bollich Sr., an acrobatic athlete who once did backflips around the bases after hitting a home run. He had eleven great-great grandsons on the 2022 squad, enough to form their own team.

Every now and then the classic Cajun names of Boudreaux and Thibodeaux pop up on the roster, leaving head coach Louie Cook smiling and shaking his head: "Between the Thibodeauxs and all the German names, oof!"

"Oof" is a fitting expression for a place where one player, Joachim "Schmaack" Bourgeois, is the uncle of another player, Wesley Duplechin, and yet Joachim is two days younger than Wesley.

Welcome to Notre Dame High School of Acadia Parish, where family and football are synonymous with each other.

"The kids grow up watching Notre Dame football and all they want to do is be a Notre Dame football player like their brothers, dads, and uncles," said Todd Gray, an assistant to Cook for twenty-four years. "You combine that with what Coach Cook brings and they drink the Kool-Aid."

Bryan "Buck" Leonards played at Notre Dame from 1975 to 1977 and his son, Bryan, was on Cook's first Notre Dame team in 1997. "We don't have family trees here; we have Bermuda grass," he said. "The original Germans that came married each other and then their offspring that weren't too related married each other."

Buck is one of the school's most passionate supporters. "It's inherited passion," he said.

When his grandfather butchered a cow for the family, he prepared one just for the nuns who ran the local Catholic schools.

"The Germans supported Notre Dame from day one," he said. "They were staunch Catholics and just identified with this place."

Buck estimates he was related to half of his class of one hundred, two-thirds of them Germans from the rice and crawfish farming communities of Roberts Cove and Mowata, about twenty minutes by car from the school in Crowley.

The most famous member of the '67 team is Tommy Casanova, who went on to become a three-time All-American at LSU, gracing a 1971 *Sports Illustrated* magazine cover that heralded him as the "best player in the nation." He was an All-Pro safety four of the six seasons (1972–1977) he played for the Cincinnati Bengals in the NFL.

At Notre Dame in 1967, Tommy averaged 7.5 yards rushing and thirty yards on kickoff and punt returns in addition to being "an exceptional safety" on defense.[2]

"You felt like a bug on a windshield when Tommy hit you," said Joe Guillory, a freshman defensive end for Iota High in '67. "You were never fast or strong enough to play against him. He was a monster, man."

The name Casanova is still going strong at Notre Dame with Sam (86) and Jackson (31) carrying on the family tradition that started with their grandfather Jackie, *far right*, and his brothers, Tommy and Johnny, and continued with Jackie's son, J. T., *far left*, father of Sam and Jackson. Jackie went on to play at LSU and J. T. at USL. Jackson, a sophomore linebacker, paced the Pios' defense in 2022 with seventy-nine tackles, twenty-five unassisted, and four sacks. Sam, a freshman, plays tight end. Altogether, ten Casanovas have played for Coach Cook during his twenty-six years at Notre Dame. *Photo by Jason Faul.*

Guillory was forced into action because the starter benched himself. "He was tired of getting made to look like a dummy. Playing Notre Dame even back then was like suicide. The front line stepped on you every play."

Tommy credits the German population in the area for raising "tough-assed kids."

"They will knock you on your butt," he said. "They set the stage. The rest of us just went and stuck with them. They are really a big reason why Notre Dame is the way it is."

Tommy's brothers, Jackie and Johnny, followed him at Notre Dame, Jackie going on to play at LSU and Johnny at the University of Southwestern Louisiana (USL). Louie coached Johnny at USL in 1981–1982.

One day Louie was counting the number of Casanovas he has coached at Notre Dame. "Let's see, I've coached Jackie's five boys [Jack, Will, John Thomas or J. T., Gabe, and Mike] and Johnny's three sons [Matthew, Nicholas, and Jason]," he said.

J. T. has two boys, Jackson and Sam, at the school through 2024. That's ten, one shy of an all-Casanova team.

"It's a brotherhood that spans years," Johnny said. "We all got to play in college. You assume that college is a step up, and it's really not. The family of football is here. High school is better than college as far as the pureness of football. But Notre Dame is a step above anything I've experienced."

The Casanovas are on the sidelines for most Notre Dame home games, Johnny working on the chain crew and Jackie and Tommy intently watching the action on the field. "I'd love to be out there," Tommy said during one game.

At LSU he was a running back on offense, a cornerback on defense, and a dangerous kick return specialist, returning two punts for touchdowns in a single game to tie an NCAA record.

Sports Illustrated put him on the cover of its annual college football issue, describing him as "quiet, modest, tall, dark and handsome—Casanovian in all respects."[3]

Unfortunately, he was victimized by the infamous *SI* cover jinx, pulling his right hamstring in the first game, and missing half of the '71 season. "I fooled them," Tommy said of the experts that made him the cover boy.

He's as high on his nephew, Jackson, a promising sophomore linebacker in 2022, as some folks were on him. "He's got it here and he's got it here," Tommy said, pointing to his head and heart. "He's going to be a good one."

Two of Tommy's teammates in 1967 were Dennis Hensgens and Kelly Hundley. All three families were represented on the 2003 team that went to the state finals in the Dome, J. T. Casanova starting at middle linebacker, David Hensgens at defensive back, and Steve Hundley at defensive end.

Nick Hundley Jr. recalled stories his father, Nick Sr., told him about playing at Notre Dame with Jackie Casanova in the 1970s and the season Jackie's son, Jack, was a teammate when he played there from 1994 to 1996.

The bell went off for young Hundley. "It was like ding, ding, ding!" he said on researching and finding out the three families were on the same team five times through the 2003 season. "That's incredibly uncommon."

The *Lafayette Daily Advertiser* thought so, too, and published a story titled, "Pios family tradition."[4]

For Nick Jr., family tradition is "paramount" to Notre Dame's success on the football field. "That's what tied us all together. There's a lineage that we are carrying on. We're connected beyond the game of football."

Lew Cook, Louie's eldest son and one of his assistant coaches, keeps the tradition going strong by making sure players have jersey numbers worn by their relatives. "It takes a lot of planning," Lew said. "Sometimes it doesn't work out."

Johann Hensgens had to wait until his senior year in 2022 to get the no. 14 jersey his father, Hans, wore.

C. J. Thibodeaux, a bull-dozing tailback on the 2018 and 2019 teams, wanted to wear no. 14 just like his father, Chris. It was already taken, so Lew did the next best thing and gave him no. 41.

One player told Lew he'd be "so happy" if he could get no. 43.

"Would you be 'so happy' if you can't breathe?" Lew asked. "The jersey is made for somebody that's 195 pounds and you're 225. You're not going to be able to breathe in that jersey. We'll put you in 34."

Another number has a special place in the Pios program because of Waddy Faul, a lineman from the town of Mire killed in a car accident in 1998. As a tribute to Waddy, his no. 59 is worn every year by a Mire lineman.

Jackson Casanova inherited 31, the number his father, J. T., wore as a sophomore.

Marty Bourgeois and his wife, Nancy, have ten children, including four boys: Luke, Michael, Noah, and Joachim. Older brother, Jeff, and his wife, Eloise, have three boys: Gavin, Hayden, and Waylon.

"We planned on having more but my wife got so sick with the last one, Waylon, she had to go to the hospital," Jeff said. "One ol' boy told me, 'I'd get sick, too, if I had to carry a Bourgeois."

Marty's three oldest boys wore no. 16, and when Joachim is a sophomore in 2023, he'll wear it as well.

This means Marty's grandson, Wesley Duplechin, the oldest son of his daughter, Hailey, will have to wear 18, the number for Jeff's three boys. But he'll have to wait until it's available in 2024.

The Bourgeois name doesn't go as far back as others at Notre Dame, but in recent years no family has had a greater impact on the program. All except Gavin were on state championship teams—Luke in 2009; Hayden and Michael in 2015; and Noah and Waylon in 2018.

Luke was the first of the Bourgeois clan to play at Notre Dame. "His goal wasn't to play pro or college football," Marty said. "It was to wear that Notre Dame red helmet." In fact, when Luke got engaged to his wife, Lauren, who's from Baton Rouge, he made a point of saying their kids were going to Notre Dame.

The boys roughed up each other playing football in the same horseshoe-shaped front yard in Church Point where their fathers played before them. "They used to call it Bourgeois Academy," Jeff said. "Every Saturday and Sunday people would pass by. We always had a big game going on."

Marty and Jeff were on the football and rodeo teams at Church Point High, Marty playing on the only Church Point football team to beat Notre Dame. "If they'd played us, we would've whipped 'em," Luke quipped.

Marty also was a three-time state champion in bareback-bronc riding and once in saddle-bronc. Jeff finished fourth nationally in bareback-bronc riding one year.

The boys rode whatever they could growing up—sheep, ponies, horses bareback, calves, steers, even bulls. "Waylon was the only one hard-headed enough not to give it up," Luke said.

Waylon now competes professionally. "There's really no thinking on the back of a bucking horse," Waylon said. "It happens so fast, you've just got to react."

"Rodeo made them tough," Marty said. "They learned how to hit the ground."

"I was always competing against guys older than me," Waylon said. "Michael and Hayden competed against Gavin and Luke, and I had to hang with them. Noah had to compete against us."

"When Noah was eight years old and everybody else was fourteen to fifteen, he was still out there," Luke said. "By the time he got to Notre Dame, it was easy for him. People were finally his own age."

Noah was nicknamed Crab because he could go side to side as fast as he could go forward. As a senior in 2018, he rushed for 1,700 yards and twenty-seven touchdowns to lead the Pios to the state title, beating Catholic High of New Iberia (Catholic-NI) 42–21 in the finals.

"Pound-for-pound the best player I ever coached against," said Brent Indest, Catholic-NI's head coach at the time. "He ran with balance and speed and his shoulder pads seemed to be two feet off the ground."

Indest also lavished praise on Hayden and Michael, who starred at free safety and cornerback on the 2015 team that trounced Catholic-NI 41–0 en route to the state title. "They came out with a chip on their shoulders, and they commenced to whipping our ass," he said.

"Noah was one of the best football players that I coached," Cook said. "Hayden could've done anything. They were good, hard-working, solid kids. Fun to coach because they played hard. They all were tough."

All of them played with a competitive fire that still burns when they are around each other.

Noah played on offense, so he's constantly reminded by the others that Cook puts the best players on defense.

Noah Bourgeois totaled 1,700 yards rushing and twenty-seven touchdowns to lead the Pios to a 13–0 record and Division III state championship in 2018. "Noah was one of the best backs we ever had," Coach Louie Cook said of the five-foot-six, 160-pounder. "When that sonofagun was about to get hit, he dropped his pads and delivered a lick." In the title game against Catholic High of New Iberia, Noah mugged a would-be tackler with a stiff arm as teammate Alex Roy (54) looked on. *Photo by Jason Faul.*

"I wish I could've run against these guys," Noah said.

"I wish I could have hit you," Gavin replied.

"As a freshman, the thing I remember most is catching a ball on Hayden at practice," Noah continued.

"We've got to make him feel good sometimes," Hayden said.

Losing has never been an option for the Bourgeois boys.

"That's why Notre Dame was the right school for us," Michael said.

"Other coaches will make you good," Noah explained. "Coach Cook will make you great. He's one step ahead of everybody else."

"He's one of a kind," Waylon added.

"He didn't ask from anyone anything he wasn't willing to do," Luke explained. "That meant a lot to me because it was a lot easier to get up and go do all the things he asked because you knew he was also doing so. That's what separates Coach Cook and makes him the best."

Luke was the first to travel the twenty miles from Church Point to Crowley for the summer workouts. He started in the seventh grade at the 8 a.m. sessions and then as a freshman joined the older varsity players at 5:30 and 6. "It was hard, it was tough, but it was never too much," he said.

"Not many people are putting in the work at 5:30 in the morning," Gavin said. "It's not all about talent. It's discipline and hard work."

"Coach Cook makes sure every little thing is right—what you have to do to win the football game," Hayden said. "That's what he focuses on in practice."

"If we do the little things right, we're going to win," Michael said, repeating one of Cook's favorite mantras. "When I became a good player was when I started doing the tiniest of things right."

In the championship game against Riverside Academy in 2015, Michael was covering a Black wide receiver several inches taller than he was at five feet eight. The receiver looked him over and said disparagingly, "Man, white boy, that's all you got to bring?"

"This is it," Michael calmly replied. "Go ahead and run that slant you're about to run."

"We knew exactly what they were going to do," Hayden laughed.

"Every Monday night when they came home from school, they had a booklet with every formation the other team ran on film," Jeff said. "They were so prepared defensively, it was almost cheating."

"You had to put in the work," Gavin said, "but everything was there for you to take and be successful."

Jackie Casanova recalls Cook telling him soon after arriving at Notre Dame that he was "going to get these kids to believe they can win and then we'll win some games we probably shouldn't."

"He gets them to believe," Todd Gray said. "I've never seen a place where more kids just want to be on the team and part of the program. They could care less if they get on the field or not."

There have been exceptions.

One of them was Patrick Hundley, son of Cook's youngest sister, Cathy Cook Hundley. "He didn't like football," Cathy said. "I made him play because of Louie."

She recalled how their mother, Josie Cook, pressured Louie to join a fraternity at USL. "You need the social part," Josie insisted.

The football team at Notre Dame is like a fraternity and Patrick needed to be part of it, Cathy reasoned. "Look," she told Louie, "You don't have to play him if he's not good."

Patrick has Tourette syndrome, a nervous system disorder that causes movements and sounds that are uncontrollable. "Louie worked past that," Cathy said. "He would always point out the positive."

By his senior season in 2013, Patrick was a six-foot-three, 260-pound All-District offensive lineman and played in the state's high school all-star game at the end of the year. "It was remarkable," Cathy said. "Without football, I don't know what Patrick would've done."

"You come to Notre Dame, you're almost forced to play football," Louie admitted. "Before Patrick got out of here, he loved it."

The same was true for Carson Watson, a six-foot-one, 230-pound fullback at Notre Dame in 2005 and 2006.

Carson grew up in Jennings, about twenty miles from Crowley, and started high school there before transferring to Notre Dame in the middle of his freshman season. He had to sit out a year before he could play.

The week he became eligible, Carson walked into Cook's office and announced he was giving up football. "I didn't have a great love for sports," he said, "but I knew I needed to play because I was a decent athlete."

Cook was shocked and disappointed. "He was going to be a really good player. But you could tell he had thought this thing through. His heart wasn't in it."

Cook didn't try to talk him out of it, nor did he treat Carson any differently afterward.

"He'd wave, smile, and ask me how life was going," Carson said. "He put that before football. I wanted to go back and play for him even more cause of how he treated me after I quit. So, I went back. I wanted to play for him and the school. And I wanted to play for myself."

Carson started as a junior and was the Pios' second-leading rusher midway through his senior year until he was hospitalized with ulcerative colitis. He returned to the team and suited up for a second-round playoff game against Cecilia.

"I'd probably lost fifty pounds," Carson said. "I could barely move, but I wanted to play."

He pleaded with Cook to go in the game for at least one play.

"Brim," Cook said, "you know you're not full health."

Knowing it could be Carson's last chance to play at Notre Dame, Cook put him in the game.

As the ball was snapped, Carson took off from his fullback position, tripped, and fell to the ground, knocking down a would-be tackler and clearing a path for teammate Joe David Petitjean to sprint twenty-two yards for a touchdown. "Boom! Scored a touchdown off of me messing up and falling on my face and making a perfect block out of it," Carson said with a chuckle. "It was like something out of a movie."

Carson's younger brother, Marshall, also had a storybook finish to his Notre Dame career.

A rock-solid, five-foot-nine, 210-pound fullback, Marshall was the king of the weight room, lifting over four hundred pounds. He was poised to start as a sophomore, a rare feat at Notre Dame, when he tore the anterior cruciate ligament (ACL) in his left knee, requiring season-ending surgery. At practice the following spring he tore the same ACL. The cadaver graft used to repair Marshall's knee didn't take, so he had no ACL.

Marshall was devastated. He had already missed one year and faced sitting out another. "We're going to figure something out and let you play," Cook told him. "I know some guys that play without an ACL. They wear a brace that acts like an ACL."

Cook took Marshall and his father, Paul, to see Jack Marucci, a friend and longtime trainer at LSU.

Marshall was fitted with a brace and did some drills. "If it was my son, I'd let him try it," Marucci said to Paul Watson. "He looks good. He's strong."

Without an ACL, a certain amount of muscular stability is needed so the knee doesn't slide in and out of place.

"He was a human muscle," Cook said.

Marshall played all fourteen games his junior year in 2008 and then had another surgery, this one successfully restoring the ACL in his knee. He also played every game the next year, when the Pios went undefeated (15–0) and won the state championship.

Marshall was a jarring blocker and runner. "He'd blow you up," Cook said.

"I loved it when he blocked for Stu," added Faye Cook. "Nobody was going to get him."

That's what happened early in the fourth quarter of the 2009 title game when a block by Marshall helped Stu Cook break loose on a twenty-four-yard run that was key to the Pios digging themselves out of a hole and hanging on for a 14–7 victory. Marshall also rushed for seventy-three yards, fifty-six in the second half.

"It was like Marshall just said, 'Get on my back and I'll carry us there,' and he did," Cook said later.[5]

"It's a prime example of just keep on trucking—do the right thing, do what you're supposed to do, and it'll turn out good," Marshall said, recalling Cook's words of encouragement throughout his high school journey. "Coach Cook lives his life by that. Look at him. Just a storybook career and life."

Marshall considered playing as a walk-on at McNeese State University. "The experience of Notre Dame was so good—going out like we did, winning the championship our senior year, playing in the Superdome—I decided I wanted my last football experience to be with this team and this coaching staff. It was such a positive environment."

It's the family environment that Cook cultivates at Notre Dame.

He wants a dad to watch his son practice. "That's your child," he said. "I would do it. I left college ball to coach my kids."

He encourages families and friends of players to mingle with them on the field after home games. "I want them to feel what we feel. When they feel part of the family, they hurt when we hurt. When we're happy, they're happy. We all want the same things. We're all part of it. Y'all come meet us."

You can get a glimpse of future Notre Dame stars before and during halftime of home games when youngsters are playing football on a nearby field. There likely will be a Bourgeois and Hensgens among them.

In fact, the two families are now blood relatives, Heidi Bourgeois marrying David Hensgens, who was known as Dave-O when he played at Notre Dame. They have two boys, including nine-year-old Dave-O2. Hailey Bourgeois Duplechin has a son, Gabe, around the same age, plus two more boys itching to put on the red Notre Dame helmet.

"The future looks really bright," Marty Bourgeois said.

Added Jeff Bourgeois: "They're tigers, oof!"

14

The Disciples

They are called assistant coaches, but they really are disciples, true believers, and teachers of the football gospel according to Louie Cook.

Jimmy "Mac" McCleary, the defensive coordinator, has movie-star hair in stark contrast to Wes Jacob, the receivers coach, who has no hair and is African American.

"Y'all call me Black, my friends call me white," Wes said one day while rubbing white sunscreen on his face.

"I call you Mexican!" Mac wisecracked.

"The island of misfit toys," veteran trainer Jim Dorotics calls the Notre Dame coaching staff. "Looks like a grab bag. You don't know what you're going to get with this group. The guy that brings it all together is Coach Cook. No one else could do it."

In addition to McCleary and Jacob, the cast of characters for the 2021–22 seasons included Cook's eldest son, Lew; Kevin Magee; Chris Stevens; Jake Molbert; Gus Cormier; Dustin Albaugh; Ben Boulet; and Chad Broussard.

McCleary has shadowed Cook since his second year at Notre Dame in 1998. Lew started coaching with his father in 2000 and Jacob, Magee, Cormier, and Stevens have been at Cook's side nearly a decade or more.

"That's the fruit of a coach who values people over a product," said Father Nick Ware, a player and assistant coach for Cook at Notre Dame before entering the priesthood. "They stay around because he's more interested in them as people than a game won or a championship. Coach Cook always talked about stacking good days on top of good days. He is a man who has lived his life doing that, not letting circumstances define his attitude, his approach, his intensity. All of that remained the same."

Kevin Foote, a sports talk show host as well as a sportswriter nowadays, has written enough about Cook to fill a good-sized book.

"He has such loyalty," Foote said. "There are guys on his staff that either played for him, coached with him years ago, went elsewhere and did their things, and came back and coached with him again. That means he treats people well and the right way."

Todd Gray retired in 2021 after twenty-four years at Notre Dame, but his ghost is still around.

Gray coached the offensive line and kept everybody loose with zany, irreverent comments such as the one he made on a soil-judging contest at the school. "How hard can that be?" he asked one of the judges. "What ya' got? Sand, dirt, and shit!"

"He kept it light," Cook said.

"It was hard to take Gray seriously," said Kade Comeaux, a hulking offensive tackle for the Pios from 1997 to 1999 who went on to play at LSU. "He yelled but you knew the next minute he'd be joking about something."

"He's a different dude," Mac added. "It hasn't been the same without him."

Gray chewed out ball boys for not doing what they were supposed to do, taped the ankles of players, and volunteered to fix anything that needed fixing, although in many cases he got someone else to do the job. One of the other coaches nicknamed him "The Subcontractor."

"He handled everything nobody wanted to do," Mac said. "That's why he subbed everything out. But he had it all organized."

Gray once arranged for the school's janitor, Pat Richard, to attend a playoff game in Baton Rouge.

"I'd love to go to the game, but I don't have a ride," Richard told Gray, who called him "Dawg."

"Ah, Dawg, don't worry about it," Gray said. "I'm going to hook you up with a ride."

Richard walked off and Gray went to Cook's office nearby. "Coach, you think you can hook Richard up with a ride?"

The semifinals of the state playoffs are usually held the Friday after Thanksgiving.

Gray's wife, Allison, was planning a trip to Oklahoma one Thanksgiving to see her parents. "Brim, we gotta win this week," Gray said to Cook. "If we lose, I gotta go to Oklahoma with Allison."

Notre Dame lost the game, causing Allison to lament: "Gawd dang, Coach, y'all couldn't pull it out. Now I gotta take Gray with me to Oklahoma."

Coaches Todd Gray and Jimmy McCleary, *far left and center*, are more like sons to Notre Dame head coach Louie Cook, *far right*. Gray coached at the school for twenty-four years (1997–2020) and McCleary marked his twenty-fifth year with Cook in 2022. "I'm a hot-headed Irish Catholic," said McCleary. "I can't be Coach Cook. But I value what he's shown me and emulate it as best I can." *Photo by Christell Faul.*

"Gray is like family," Cook said.

On the bus to and from games, Cook sat in the front row directly behind Gray, the driver. Cook's son, Lew, sat on one side by the window and Jimmy Mac on the other side across the aisle. "Like three sons," Louie said.

"That's what makes it special," Mac pointed out. "He looks at Todd and I like his sons. He treats us like we're his sons. He takes care of us like his sons."

As a sophomore at Rayne High, Cook backed up Todd's father, Larry, at quarterback. When Louie became the head coach, he hired Todd as an assistant. Young Todd was the ring bearer at Cook's wedding. "If I knew then what I know about him now, I would've made sure the ring was in my pocket," he joked.

Todd played quarterback in high school, so he had doubts about becoming the offensive line coach at Notre Dame.

"It'll be all right," Cook reassured him. "This is how we're going to block. Here's the play book. Things are going to be fine."

"They were," Todd said. "He had a plan since day one when we walked on that practice field. This is what we need to do, this is the attitude we need to have, this is what the kids need to see and hear. He had a plan."

Unlike the losing program Cook inherited his first stint at Crowley High, Notre Dame was a perennial winner, advancing to the state semi-finals the previous year.

"He transformed everything," Todd said, including the programs for baseball, basketball, and girls' softball. "He surrounds himself with the right people and gets the kids to buy into what he tries to do."

Jimmy Mac is the last of the coaches left from Cook's first two years at Notre Dame.

"It's a labor of love for him and for me," Mac said. "It's not what we just do. This is part of the fabric of who we are. I'm a football coach. That's what I am. I'm nothing else. I don't dance. I don't do anything else. I coach football and I love football. The kids inspire us as much as we inspire them. We owe it to them to give everything we got because they're giving us everything they got."

Mac has turned down several head coaching opportunities. "I desire success more than I desire money," he explained. "It's more important to be a part of something special than it is to elevate your own ego."

Mac's wife, Christine, a public-school teacher in nearby Lafayette, is the breadwinner in the family. "She makes more money than me," Mac said. "We laugh about it all the time."

The family environment at Notre Dame is priceless.

Mac and Christine have four boys; Todd and Allison Gray, four girls and a boy; and Chris and Jane Stevens, a girl and two boys. All of them graduated from Notre Dame.

Growing up, Mac's sons were ball boys and on the sidelines at home games. When the Pios traveled, Christine and the other wives went with them, packing the kids into a rented fifteen-passenger van.

"This place is so special, it's hard to leave," Mac said. "The families here have the same mentality I have—that blue-collar work ethic."

Cook was the quarterback coach at the University of Southwestern Louisiana (USL, now University of Louisiana at Lafayette, or ULL) when he met Mac. They chatted and Cook invited him to sit in on meetings with Jake Delhomme and other USL quarterbacks. "I thought he was a walk-on quarterback," Delhomme said.

He soon found out Mac was an aspiring coach. "Jimmy Mac became a part of us," Delhomme added. "He was in our meeting room every day."

Mac filmed practices and then games from the end zone. He was put on scholarship and traveled with the team. When it was time to do his student teaching, he rejoined Cook at Notre Dame in 1998. They've been together ever since.

"It's not so much what Coach has done, it's what he has done it with and how he has done it with integrity, character, and love," Mac said. "He's the definition of character. If you looked up the word *character* in the dictionary, you'd see his name right next to it. He believes in just doing right and good things will happen. They do more times than not."

The Pios have won ten or more games in twenty of their twenty-five years together, gone undefeated four times, won four state titles, and finished runner-up six times. Their worst record was 8–4 in 2011.

"The biggest thing I'm proud of with Coach is to be at the level we've been at consistently," Mac said. "It starts in the weight room. He believes in the weight room as being a major factor in everything we do."

Mac oversees the strength and conditioning program and the defense.

Cook has the pick of the lot for the quarterback and tailback positions; he lets Mac take the best of the rest for defense, the bedrock of the Pios' consistency.

The epitome of Notre Dame's defensive prowess was the 2015 team, which posted eight shutouts and allowed its fourteen foes only fifty-two points, an average of 3.7 points per game, and a mere sixty first downs, slightly more than four per game.

"Best defense I ever coached," Mac said. "Very aggressive. Very physical. Kind of mean. Extremely disciplined. Made great in-game adjustments. We crushed people in practice."

Practices at Notre Dame are business-like with a laser focus on details. "We treat it like a college atmosphere," Mac said.

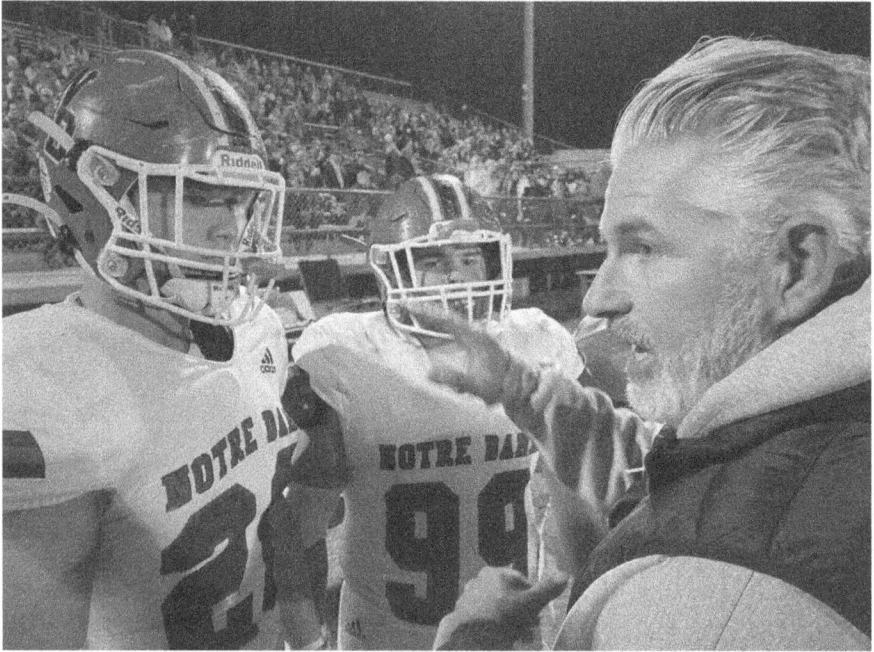

Defensive coordinator Jimmy McCleary huddled on the sidelines with end Alex Stevens, *left*, and tackle Karson Broussard, the Pios' top defenders in 2021 with seventy-two and sixty-four tackles, respectively. "Never had a defensive lineman that was a leading tackler, let alone two of them," McCleary said. Stevens had nine sacks and Broussard five to rank one-two in that category. *Photo by author.*

The offense works on one side of the field, the defense on the other. Within these two practices, coaches instruct each position group.

"Everybody has ownership in this operation," Cook said. "It's all part of the process of trying to develop the team and the coaches where everybody is accountable."

There's no finger pointing or excuses after a loss or poor performance.

"We're always analyzing it and trying to figure out what was our responsibility in it," Mac said. "Where's my ownership in it as a coach? What do we need to do to get better?"

Every time Mac is approached about a head coaching job, he insists the school get permission from Cook first. Then he and Cook discuss the pros and cons of the offer. "For me, it was never about money," Mac said. "It was about growing in my profession and being a quality person. Under him you're going to get both."

Mac summed up Cook this way: "He's a servant leader. If there's a bunch of food on that table and all the kids come in here, he's going to be the last one to eat. He makes sure everybody is taken care of first."

Like his dad, Lew Cook coaches with the mindset of a servant. He wears so many hats he could open a haberdashery shop. From working with the varsity running backs and the freshman team offense to lining up the scout team defense to managing the equipment and the jersey numbers to raising funds for the football program, he's involved in almost everything. When someone doesn't know the answer to something, they holler, "Hey, Lew!"

"Lew is a servant," Cook said. "He's here to serve, and he serves people well."

Lew is selfless, tireless, and relentless in his quest to lighten the load for his father.

"I'm confident in what I can do and my abilities, so it doesn't really bother me if one person knows it, a thousand people, or no one," Lew said. "I can't imagine myself doing anything else. I get to spend time with my dad and help the kids. It's kind of the best of both worlds."

Every Sunday afternoon during the football season, Lew sits in his father's office at Notre Dame, and they analyze the previous game and plan for the next one. "We don't talk a whole lot about winning; we talk more about being successful," Lew said.

"Where he's really separated himself from everybody else is that before most people recognize what the problem is, he's already formulating the solution," Lew pointed out. "He has always been so far ahead of the curve, and he tries to encourage us all to be that way."

At one summer workout, Lew was yelling at a player when his father pulled him aside and said, "Don't fuss! Teach!"

Lew got the message. "In coaching, you're communicating a lot with the kids. You don't want to be whining. You don't want to be fussing. You want to be teaching."

The elder Cook has been known to throw his cap in frustration, pick up some grass and chew it, or mutter, "Kiss ol' Spot's ass." But usually he's as calm, cool, and collected on the sidelines as the moniker "Cool Hand Louie" suggests.

"I never slammed headsets," Louie explained, "because we never had a wide-open budget to where I could do it. If I broke it, I'd probably have to pay for it out of my own pocket."

As a young coach at Rayne High, he often reminded himself: "They need a coach today. They don't need a yeller and screamer."

Lew sees that.

"He's figured out, and it's his personality already, that the calmer he stays during the game, the better the kids are," Lew said. "He wants the refs to ref, the kids to play, the coaches to coach."

"I always say teams take on the personality of the coach—how they think, how they act," Cook added. "I'm not a big rah-rah guy. Our team is not that way either. You don't hear a lot of noise."

You don't hear Cook fussing or cussing either.

"Twenty-five years after I met him was the first time I heard him curse," said Wes Jacob. "Can you believe that? A coach that has been coaching as long as he has, and you don't hear him curse."

Wes played four years for Cook at Crowley High, coached with him there in 1996, and rejoined him at Notre Dame in 2012.

"It was at practice, and somebody messed up and he just let one fly," Wes recalled.

Wes looked at Mac and Gray and they gave him the same shocked look.

"What?" Wes exclaimed. "Did he just curse?"

Wes heard and saw it all growing up in West Crowley. His dad died when he was five years old, and by the time he got to Crowley High he had the kind of reputation that prompted a junior-high coach to send a hurricane-type warning, advising Cook not to let Wes near his football program.

Cook made up his own mind, inviting Wes to join the team. It was a defining moment. No man, Black or white, had ever talked to him like he was a human being.

Wes became a high school All-American receiver his senior season and started four years at LSU. He returned to Crowley High in 2008 to coach football and track. At track meets he joked with Mac and Gray, "I'm going to be the first Black coach at Notre Dame."

Four years later he was about to take a coaching job in New Orleans when Cook said: "It's time; come over here."

"You sure they'll let my Black ass over there?" Wes asked.

"It's not anything like that," Cook said. "Come on, you'll be all right."

Wes is now part of the Notre Dame family. "Coach Cook, I call Pop; Miss Faye [Cook's wife], I call Momma; his sons are my little brothers; his brothers are my uncles."

If the highly competitive Wes and Mac have a disagreement, Wes goes by Mac's office and says, "I love ya."

"I believe that everybody, everything has a purpose and a place," Wes said. "God already has my book written. He already knows everything. This is where I'm supposed to be."

Kevin Magee feels the same way. He was at Crowley High all eight years Cook coached there, and they've been together at Notre Dame since he retired as a public school teacher in 2015. He commutes thirty-five miles each way from his home in Lafayette. "I wouldn't make that drive for anybody else," he said.

Magee was one of the coaches at Crowley that Cook's predecessor recommended he dump. "I was looking at doing something else until he came in and asked me to stay on with him," Magee said. "He saw something in me that I guess maybe I didn't think I had."

Magee was a head coach for twelve years at three different high schools, including Crowley. "The biggest challenge in being a head coach is I was always searching for what we had at Crowley—that chemistry of coaches," he said. "We all were on the same page. We all wanted the same things. We didn't mind the work. Not a lot of egos. To me, that's the big reason for a lot of Louie's success is he has been able to hire good, quality coaches to help him."

At Notre Dame, Magee coaches the sons of players he tutored at Crowley. "They were green-and-gold to the core and now those parents are wearing red-and-white," he said of their switch in school colors and loyalty. "That's the kind of legacy and confidence the kids that Louie has coached want their kids to be around."

Donald James Cormier III goes by Trey or "Gus," short for humongous. He tipped the scales at 330 pounds when he arrived at Notre Dame in 2007 and about 310 his senior season when he started at guard. On graduating in 2011, he became an offensive line coach.

"Coaching the offensive line is about details, especially at Notre Dame because we don't have the biggest and baddest," Gus said. "We have very average kids that work really hard. You must do the little things right to make the big picture pretty. The smallest little things we need to correct as fast as we can so we're playing the last game of the season."

Gus has made it to the "last game," the state finals at the Superdome in New Orleans, six times, twice as a player and four times as a coach. "There are some coaches that are in the Hall of Fame that have never been once, so I understand how lucky I am to be in the position I'm in to be here at the right time for all that to happen."

One of Gus's teammates on the 2008 and 2009 Dome teams was Jake Molbert, a defensive end who went on to play at Louisiana at Lafayette. He became a disciple in 2021.

Jake was such a tenacious defender that Cook had him stand next to him during one practice so the offense could run a few plays. "He was disruptive," Cook said. "He was so quick off the line of scrimmage."

After college Jake worked on offshore oil rigs for four years—thirty days on, thirty days off—hoping to strike it rich. "I never wanted to coach," he said. "I always thought coaches were players who sucked and loved the game."

He changed his mind one day sitting offshore and thinking to himself: "Man, I need to do something I love and get back in shape."

He ended up coaching football at Rayne High and in 2021 became the linebacker coach at Notre Dame. "I love it," he said. "I haven't worked a day since I've been here. That's a great feeling. Most people don't get to do that."

At Rayne High, Cook coached Jake's father, Paul, in football and his mother, Michelle, in basketball. "What he preaches is what he lives by," Jake said. "He's a very faith-filled guy. The reason why he's so good is because of that. He knows where it all starts."

Coaching for Cook is just like playing for him, according to Jake. "You're always working towards making sure things are done the right way, and on time. You're motivated to keep pushing every single day. That's the beauty about all the coaches here. No one is complacent."

The 2022 season marked the twenty-ninth for Chris Stevens in coaching and ninth at Notre Dame. He coaches the safeties on defense and the punt return team and is also the head baseball coach, guiding the school to state titles in 2018 and 2021.

"People say we don't have any Division 1 athletes, we don't have this, we don't have that," Chris said. "But we have a lot of good kids and good high school football players and they're all working toward one goal. That's what makes them even better."

His two sons are proof of that. Thomas earned All-State honors twice in both football and baseball and Alex was selected to the 2021 All-Acadiana defensive team in football.

"All these kids know is Notre Dame—putting on that red helmet or the Pios baseball uniform," Chris said. "They dream of playing Notre Dame football, so when they get that shot, they make the most of it."

Cook is everywhere, attending all school sporting events, from baseball to girls' volleyball and softball games. Going into the 2023 season, the Lady Pios had won four straight state softball titles and set a national record for most home runs by a team in a single season—ninety-five in 2021.

"It's awesome how he goes about his day-to-day business," Chris said. "He knows every kid at this school. He's probably taught or been around their parents, grandparents, aunts, uncles, brothers, or sisters. He makes everybody feel like a friend."

Ben Boulet, a five-foot-seven, 170-pound defensive end, was one of the undersized and underrated players Notre Dame is known for producing.

"I was always a lot smaller than the other guys, so I knew at a very young age that I had to focus on technique," Ben explained. "I had coaches that all they taught was technique, technique, technique. I focused on that and got very good at it."

A serious back injury before his junior year ended his playing career.

"Ben, do you want to wear your jersey on the sideline, or do you want me to get you a coaching shirt?" Cook asked.

Ben opted for the coaching shirt and helped coach the defensive line during his senior season in 2015.

"He had genuine influence while still a student," teammate Adam Berken said. "He had to watch from the sidelines, but he was still contributing because Coach Cook saw his value."

Ben combines coaching the defensive line with running a retail crawfish business. "I get the best of both worlds—a job that pays the bills, and another job that I love to do."

Dustin Albaugh calls himself "fresh meat" because he's originally from Iowa, attending the University of Northern Iowa and working as a strength and conditioning coach at several colleges before landing at Notre Dame in 2021. "Jumped out of the college world, met Coach Cook, and said, 'Let's do it.'"

Dustin coaches the running backs and manages the weight training program.

"I felt like I had known him for years," Dustin said of his initial meeting with Cook. "With all these guys, I've never felt like an outsider. I almost feel like I played here."

"That's what we've said about him—he's one of us just from his work ethic," Jake Molbert added.

Chad Broussard is another newbie, starting as a defensive back coach in 2021 and switching to the offensive line for the 2022 season.

"I've been hearing about the legend of Coach Cook since I was walking around in diapers," Chad said. "He's got all the wisdom in the world. You can go to him for anything. He's got a story about it. He's done it before."

"The island of misfit toys" is an apt description of the Notre Dame coaching staff.

"Everybody brings something different to the table," Chad said. "It makes for a big melting pot of culture that's different and unreal."

Counting himself, Cook is limited to six faculty coaches: Jimmy Mac, Lew, Stevens, Molbert, and Broussard. The rest are considered nonfaculty coaches.

"We've got some good guys," Cook said. "We're blessed—really blessed."

So blessed that he has attracted others with the same servant mentality.

Joe Swank is a retired coach and Billy Hargroder is a para-professional at a French immersion elementary school in Lafayette. Joe worked with the freshman team until he decided to hang it up at the end of the 2022 season; Billy helps with the varsity and is Cook's Man Friday. They wash and dry uniforms after games.

Joe coached at the same middle school where Wes Jacob wreaked havoc as a student. "I kicked him in the ass with my Spot-Bilts," Joe said, referring to the brand of tennis shoes he wore at the time. "He was acting like a jackass."

Billy has been at Cook's side for two decades. "I've been on the Dome floor with him nine times," Billy said. "Whatever he needs, I'm there."

For home games, Fern Hebert makes sure the Pios' stadium is ready and Earl "Butch" John, Cook's former next-door neighbor, drives from his home in Houston, Texas, to handle concessions. Albert John, Butch's half-brother, videotapes all the games and on special occasions barbecues steaks (unseasoned) for the coaches.

Donald Adams no longer coaches football and basketball as he did for Cook at Crowley High, but he's still a disciple. "Whatever Coach Cook needs me to do, I'll do it. If he'd tell me to go to the moon, I'm going to start building a rocket ship and try my best to get up there for Louie Cook."

At games, Adams patrols the sideline, making sure onlookers don't cross the line they're supposed to stay behind and periodically waves the red towel that he takes with him everywhere but church. "You know what the towel is for?" he asked. "Three things: blood, sweat, and tears."

Sometimes Coach A shows up at practice, hollering at Cook, "Chief!"

That's their nickname for each other.

"Chief," Cook replied, "you must be lost."

Asked how he feels, Coach A, an African American, said with a drawl: "Feel like a fly in a bowl of milk."

Coach A greeted Glenn Hunter Jr., a defensive lineman and one of three Black players on the 2021 varsity roster. "Glenn is a good kid, one of the best you could ask for."

He joked with the other players: "All you white boys look the same."

Coach A got into a conversation with a visitor about Notre Dame football.

"There's no cussing, no fussing, no jealousy," he explained. "It's all one word: together. That's what makes them such a good team. They pick one another up. They pat one another on the back. They're not very big kids, but they've got a lot of heart, a lot of discipline, and they execute. They give you all they got."

He asked a question and then answered it himself: "You know the most important thing about Coach Cook? Everybody wants to coach with him, and everybody wants to play for him—Black or white. He's one of a kind, one of a kind."

Before becoming the athletic trainer at Notre Dame in 2006, Jim Dorotics was a trainer at McNeese State University in Lake Charles, Louisiana, for sixteen years.

When he migrated to Louisiana from a small Pennsylvania mountain town in 1979, a friend predicted he'd be miserable "in the God-forsaken heat and humidity" at first, but if he hung in there, he'd never leave. That's what happened.

"I love this place," Dorotics said of Notre Dame, quoting Marv Levy, the coach who guided the Buffalo Bills to an unprecedented four straight Super Bowls: "Where would you rather be than right here right now?"

"It all goes back to Coach Cook," Wes Jacob explained. "He's not just a great coach, he's a great man. He's got his head screwed on right. He's going to do the right thing and treat you like you deserve to be treated."

It's like Jimmy Mac said: "Coach Cook plays an infinite game, not a finite game. It's long term."

15

🏈

The Black Hole

L ouie Cook was on his way to the office one Sunday afternoon in 2021. "See you in a little bit," he said to Faye, his wife for nearly fifty years. "Don't lie!" she said.

Louie's office at Notre Dame is known as "the black hole," and his fate there is unpredictable because so many people pop in to hang out and shoot the breeze.

"Sometimes I'll call, and it sounds like the room is full—and it is," Faye said. "He names who's there. So, they talk and talk and talk and talk and talk. In the meantime, he's not getting his work done. And he's not going to leave until it's done."

Inevitably, he gets home late.

"Black hole got you again," Faye greets him.

One frequent visitor is Bryan "Buck" Leonards, a self-professed "super-duper lurker," who boasts that he has been on the field for all of Notre Dame's thirteen state championship games dating back to 1973. For the last ten, he wrangled a press pass from Louie. "They can't stand lurkers on the sidelines," he said.

Lurker is the term used to describe some of the more colorful black hole regulars. They are essentially groupies that Cook treats like family in his office.

Cool Hugh was a lurker who was ushered off the field at one game. "He'd follow the chain-gang guys and talk to them," Buck said.

Gervis and Potu (the late Gervis Mire and Hilton "Potu" Nero) were old-timers from Louie's hometown of Rayne. They loved football at Notre

Dame almost as much as at Rayne High, but they went to the Pios home games because Louie let them in for free.

"Why y'all don't go watch Rayne High?" asked Todd Gray, then the Pios offensive line coach.

"We ain't watching Rayne," Gervis said. "They lose too much."

"Russell the Love Muscle" was another lurker. He requested a Notre Dame jersey for his daughter, so Louie gave him an older one with the no. 10 that Russell wound up wearing to every game. Hayden McCleary, son of defensive coordinator Jimmy McCleary, wore the same number. The other coaches needled Mac about being Russell's biological father.

The biggest lurkers were two jumbo-sized brothers dubbed Kabuki and Kamala after pro wrestlers with the same names.

Kabuki and Kamala were big Crowley High fans who followed Louie to Notre Dame where they were fixtures at varsity football practices and games because Kamala's son, a bulky offensive lineman, played some as a sophomore. "He wasn't ready to play, but he had a big body, and he was smart," Louie said. "If we got in a bind, I could put him in to take up some space and he'd at least know where to go."

When Louie changed the offense at a midseason practice, Kabuki noticed his nephew didn't see any action. He phoned Kamala, who immediately called Louie: "Cook, what's going on?"

Louie explained the situation, adding: "When the boy is ready to play, he's going to play."

As soon as Louie hung up, Gray called. "Man, Coach, Kabuki and Kamala came turning in here on two wheels like Hawaii Five-O, looking for you."

Louie called Kamala. "Y'all looking for me?"

"Well, Coach, we just hope we made the right decision."

Whenever the brothers had a gripe, they hinted Kamala's son might be better off at Crowley High.

"Y'all both can come by tomorrow morning at about eight o'clock," Louie said. "That will give me time to get the paperwork ready."

"What paperwork?" Kamala asked.

"The transfer papers," Louie said. "Y'all need to transfer him to Crowley."

"Well, Coach, he loves it over there [Notre Dame]."

"Then leave him alone," Louie said. "Quit worrying about him. He's going to be fine. When he's ready, he's going to play a lot."

The next morning Louie found cracklings and boudin on his office desk. Kamala's son ended up starting his junior and senior years.

"The office and all the people who have been through here you could turn into a sitcom," Buck said.

"It's not unusual for guys to float in and out all day long," Louie said.

One day Ron Guidry, three-time twenty-game winner with the New York Yankees, appeared in his office. Guidry was a teammate the year Cook played baseball at USL.

His sister, Josette Cook Surratt, calls Louie's followers a family. "Louie makes the family at Notre Dame."

Louie has so many followers that his brother Robert Cook estimates that two short buses are now needed to carry them all to games. "They're like an entourage," he said. "They follow him through thick and thin."

Boo Schexnayder, a sports performance consultant, said, "Louie is going to heaven, all the people he's taken care of."

Added Louie's son Jeff: "He's given a lot of people a lot of purpose. He's in his third generation of kids, mentoring and changing lives. He makes time for everybody. His door is open, he's accessible."

Duke Daigle is a businessman who heads Notre Dame's basketball team as a nonfaculty coach. "A lot of people would keep that door shut, but it's open and Louie enjoys it when his former players walk in," he said. "That's his life. It makes him happy."

You could see the joy the day three of his protégés visited—Gerald "Big G" Broussard, Kade Comeaux, and Lane Anzalone.

Big G, a six-foot-four, 260-something pounder, played for Louie and then served as his offensive line coach at the University of Southwestern Louisiana (USL). Kade was an offensive lineman on Louie's first three teams at Notre Dame, and Lane was the starting quarterback on the 2006 club.

Big G and Kade now work for an oilfield equipment company and arrived together. "I see a couple guys walk by the window and Big Kade is like an eclipse," Louie said.

Kade was a kid phenom—a six-foot-six, 300-pounder who wowed LSU football coaches at a summer camp by running the forty-yard dash in five seconds flat. The feat was so remarkable that LSU head coach Gerry DiNardo offered him a scholarship on the spot.

"I was sixteen," Kade said. "They're looking at me, waiting for an answer. What do you say? I was stunned."

He talked to Cook about whether to commit with two seasons still to play at Notre Dame. "You're going to get a lot of phone calls from a lot of different people the next two years," the coach warned. "If you commit, you'll save yourself some grief."

That sounded good to Kade. "I didn't like the spotlight. I tried to stay humble the whole time because I knew as good as I was in high school, I was probably going to be average when I got to the next level."

Kade's career at LSU was cut short by Crohn's disease—chronic swelling and irritation of the gastrointestinal tract.

"If he didn't have Crohn's disease, he would've been in the NFL," Louie said. "He could roll over, put his toes behind his head, and lay there for ten minutes. He was so flexible."

Cook encouraged Kade to visit the University of Florida for the experience, but he didn't go, saying he was content at home and not interested in what head coach Steve Spurrier had to say.

This reminded Big G of the 61–14 shellacking USL got at Florida in 1993, when Louie was offensive coordinator for the Ragin' Cajuns and Jake Delhomme was his prized freshman quarterback.

"The biggest mistake Coach Cook ever made was letting Jake get on the plane to go play Florida," Big G said.

The Cajuns had a 6–2 win-loss record at the time and playing for the Big West Conference title the next week.

"They were going to crush us," Big G said. "We knew that. We were telling each other, 'We ain't got a shot, Brim.' We were telling Stokley [head coach Nelson Stokley], 'We need to leave Jake home.' He told us, 'You're stupid. I ought to fire your ass.' We told him, 'They're going to fire you.' We played and, oh, Lord."

The Cajuns were down 40–7 at the half when Jake was mercifully removed from the game. His replacement was from Gainesville, where the game was played. "I put him in because all his family was there," Cook said.

"He goes to hand the ball to the tailback and there's no tailback," Big G said.

"What's he doing?" another coach asked as he hand-signaled teammates at the line of scrimmage.

"I don't know but it looks good," Louie said. "Let him go."

Shortly after Big G and Kade departed, Lane Anzalone showed up.

"Coach has had a lot of successful people learn to grow up and be a man through his program," Lane said. "The most impressive thing is we are such a dominant program but there's not a lot of college athletes that come out of here. Coach takes athletically average kids and makes them successful because he teaches morals and virtues that carry over into life."

Cook returned the compliment. "I've had three quarterbacks that I didn't worry about what play I called. The first one was Jeff [Jeff Cook], who grew up in my house so shame on me if I had to worry about it. The second one was Lane. Now we know why he went on to be a doctor. And Ryan Leonards was the other one."

Jeff guided the Pios to the state title in 2000 and Ryan did it in 2009.

Lane lived out of state for a decade, preparing to return to Louisiana as an ear, nose, and throat surgeon. He has an office across the street from Notre Dame.

Over the years, Lane has wondered why other coaches haven't been able to replicate the success Cook has had at Notre Dame. After all, he's an open book, welcoming them to practices and passing on information that most coaches wouldn't dare share.

"I remember asking years ago why it's not replicable and I got a very humble answer," Lane said. "I still have the same question: Why is it not replicable by others and yet Coach replicates it every year with subpar talent?"

With Lane the signal caller in 2006, the Pios made it to the semifinals before losing to Lutcher, 20–14.

Cook mentioned a comment Lutcher coach Tim Detillier made after the game to Charles Baglio, another high school football coach and one of Louie's best friends: "Well, we're finally even with Notre Dame."

"Tim," Baglio replied, "with what you've got to play with and what Louie's got to play with, it'll never be even. You should be way ahead."

Lane laughed and then seemed to have an epiphany.

"If I was going to be a coach, I know what I would do," he said. "I'd come over here, have Coach Cook write it down, go to Lutcher, and find some better athletes [more naturally gifted athletes], do the same thing, and never lose a football game."

Cook's office has two doors, one adjoining the office of his secretary and the other to the coaches' locker room.

Karen Berken was Cook's secretary for sixteen years and had a front-row seat for the parade of people entering and leaving his office.

"It's affirming to know that people who just live good lives, do the right thing, are appreciated by all the lives that they've touched," she said. "The loyalty to him is unbelievable. It's not because he's a do-it-my-way type coach. It's because he molds you into the best person you can be and puts you into a position that you'll be at your best."

A good example is Karen's son David, a six-foot-three, 230-pounder his senior season at Notre Dame in 2003. "He went from big and slow to big and fast," she said.

David played four years at Rice University, starting forty-eight of forty-nine games at offensive guard.

Cook has never held tryouts, and he doesn't cut anyone from the team. Do what you're expected to do, and you can suit up. "Coach will always find a spot for these young men," Karen said. "They may never be starters. But they will play somewhere, enough to make them feel that they contributed."

Michael Goss Jr. didn't play football in middle school, but he represented the state of Louisiana three times in the Scripps National Spelling Bee in Washington, DC, correctly spelling *oxyacetylene* and other words foreign to most people. His father played football at Notre Dame, so he followed in his footsteps.

"The kid might be the president of the United States one day," Cook said going into Michael's senior season in 2021. "We've got to take care of him."

Cook scrutinized the schedule, looking for the best opportunity to get his six-foot-one, 145-pound wide receiver into a varsity game. "He'll never play when the game is on the line," Cook said. "He knows it."

With the Pios leading 27–0 in the third quarter of the next-to-last game of the 2021 season, Michael caught the only pass of his career, a thirteen-yard reception. "He got a standing ovation," Cook said. "The crowd roared. Everybody was fired up. I was happy he caught it."

Cook doesn't pick a team captain or hand out game balls as a reward for doing a good job. "Winning the game is your reward," Jimmy Mac said. "We're trying to say 'we' as much as possible. There's enough 'you' and 'me' in the world."

"The prima donnas aren't going to make it here because you're not treated like a prima donna," Karen said. "Everybody's equal."

There are no individual awards for best this or that. "We recognize all the seniors and give them a plaque that has all their accomplishments," Cook said. "It has a picture of them as well as the team."

The team's red helmets aren't covered with skulls and crossbones or anything else setting one player apart from another.

The only thing noteworthy about the helmets is how neatly they are lined up before a game. "Each young man who comes to Notre Dame knows that when you step on the field to warm up, you line up your helmets on the sideline," Karen said. "They've seen this since they were little boys. They're not taught to do it. It's tradition."

You won't see the Pios in fancy uniforms or running onto the field through fake fog with rock-and-roll music blaring over the loudspeakers.

"We ain't going to have the flashiest uniforms and do all that look-at-me, dress-like-a-fool stuff," Cook said.

"We always walk onto the field," Mac added. "Everybody else runs, hollers, and screams. The only thing you hear that's loud is when we yell, Pios! That's it. You're coming to watch Notre Dame because you're coming to watch your kids. It's family."

Everything about Notre Dame is low-key and understated—just like Cook.

In a preseason scrimmage against Redemptorist High, David Berken was roughed up by an opposing lineman; he punched back, drawing a fifteen-yard personal foul penalty. The Pios huddled around Cook for the next play. "Berken," he said, "you call the play because I don't have one for third-and-twenty-five."

A tradition at Notre Dame is for players to neatly line up their helmets during pregame warmups. "They've seen this since they were little boys," said Karen Berken, Coach Louie Cook's longtime secretary. "They're not taught to do it. It's tradition." *Photo by author.*

Greg "Crusty" Gilder, an offensive lineman, never got into a game for the Pios, but he was involved in a memorable exchange of one-liners after he missed a block in a practice scrimmage.

"Crusty, you've got to go inside on that block," Cook said.

"Coach, I tried but I got caught up in traffic."

"Crusty, tune in to 98.1 to get the traffic report in the afternoon. Maybe there's a short-cut you can take next time."

A player called Deck (Patrick Dequeant) came up with another classic line when the opposing team scored on the first play of a junior varsity game.

"Coach!" Deck hollered. "We lost the momentum."

Cook laughed in recalling the story. "We'd just started the game. Who had the momentum?"

"He makes it fun," Dave Cook said of his brother. "Some coaches work the kids hard, but they don't have any fun. You've got to keep the fun in the game. And Louie knows how to do that."

He also knows how to deal with parents unhappy because their son isn't playing as much as they want.

"They would come in and pass through my office and their faces were just set in stone," Karen said. "Coach would close the door and talk with them. Pretty soon I'd hear laughter. They would leave smiling. Most of the time he hadn't changed his position on anything. He just has a way of listening."

Karen had a little plaque in her office that read: "Prepare your child for the path, not the path for your child."

"Coach does that," she said. "He doesn't make things easier for a kid, but he shows them strength of character and that hard work pays off. We may not always be state champions but we sure as heck come close most of the time. Winning is never really the issue. It's building these young men—and women—because he has a lot of impact on all the kids at the school."

On game days Cook walks around the practice field and says a rosary. He spends time fine-tuning his play script in his hideout, a dark, cubby-hole of a room in the rear of the school chapel.

"They're not worried about third-and-one," he said of the people gathered in his office. "They're bull-shittin' around and having fun before the game. And I'm worried to death about the game."

"He's got to get out of the office," Faye said.

He either takes refuge in the chapel or he meets Dale Trahan for lunch at a local restaurant.

"It gets both of us away from our black hole and allows us to think and talk about other things outside of the black hole, even though sometimes we talk about things that are happening inside the black hole," Dale explained.

Dale is the owner of three Piggly Wiggly stores in the area. He and Louie met at a reception in the Superdome after the Pios won the state championship in 2000.

"He didn't know me from Adam," Dale said. "I walked up to him and said, 'Coach, you deserve every single bit of the accolades you get.'"

They tease each other about their workaholic tendencies.

Dale calls Louie on a Saturday or Sunday from his Piggly Wiggly office and asks, "Where you at?"

He knows the answer to his question.

"Coach, who else is there?"

Everybody's gone except Louie.

"I've always looked at our friendship as more of a sounding board for both of us," Dale said. "We hardly ever talk about football. We talk about our families. We talk about our faith. We talk about life in general—the good, the bad, the ugly."

The conversations give Dale a perspective unfiltered by football.

"His faith is always his center," Dale said. "He's as regimented about his faith as he's about the way he lives his life and his coaching. His coaching life mirrors his faith life."

Louie's empathy for people stems from his faith. "He's way more than a football coach," Dale said. "Coaching is a vessel that enables him to connect with all these different people."

The only problem with meeting at restaurants is that somebody is always stopping at their table to chat with Louie. They might as well be in the black hole or what Buck Leonards refers to as Louie's Camp. "This is a man-camp," he said.

Whatever, it's a gathering place where Louie can talk or watch television with his coaches and friends. His favorite TV show is *Blue Bloods*, with actor Tom Selleck playing the role of New York City police commissioner Frank Reagan.

The show airs while the Pios are playing on Friday nights so during the football season Louie videotapes it to watch when he gets home. "The wisdom is unbelievable," he said.

Louie quoted one of Reagan's lines: "We do what we can with what we have with where we are."[1]

He turned to Jimmy Mac and said, "That's us."

Mac countered with one of his favorites: "At some point in life you went up the mountain and came back down with your own set of tablets for what is and what is not the right thing to do written in stone, which allows for certainty but not always wisdom."[2]

"That was Gary telling Reagan that," Louie said. (Gary Heller is a former New York City Police Department officer in the show.)

Cook searched his cell phone for another Reagan quote he saved. "Here it is: 'Something is not proper simply because it is permissible, nor is it ethical because it's legal. You have to be held to a higher standard.'"[3]

He tweaked the last line to read: "Coaches have to be held to a higher standard."

On arriving at his office one evening, Louie recognized a car in the parking lot. "Albert's home," he said with a chuckle.

Albert John is Louie's "film guy," capturing every Notre Dame game on film or videotape since he became head coach in 1997.

"His water line at home is broken and he doesn't have cable TV, so he comes over here to shower and watch television," Louie said.

One time Louie was returning to his office from the chapel when he saw Albert sitting on a rail outside. "I can't take it anymore," Albert said.

Louie knew how he felt. "There were so many people and chatter in the office, even Albert looked for a hideout," he said, smiling. "They were wearing him out. The black hole got to Albert."

16

$\diamond$

Worthy Adversary

Brent Indest was deep in conversation about his former coaching rival, Louie Cook, when it hit him. "My first and last wins as a head football coach were against Louie," he said incredulously. "I just figured that out. Wow!"

At the time, Indest's last victory was in 2019, when his Catholic High of New Iberia (Catholic-NI) Panthers beat Cook's Notre Dame Pioneers in the quarterfinals of the Louisiana high school playoffs. After a heart-breaking 43–42 double overtime loss to St. Charles Catholic of LaPlace, Louisiana, the following week, he told reporters, "When we beat Notre Dame, I gave my wife a big hug and said, 'This is God's way of telling me it's time.'"[1]

Indest retired with a twenty-three-year record of 187–86, including four state championship appearances and one state title earned in 2017 with another win over Cook and Notre Dame.

"I owe it to Louie that one of the greatest things I've got going for me is the perception of my ability to beat some of his teams," he said.

Indest came out of retirement in 2022 to coach at Lakeshore High in Mandeville, Louisiana, a Division 4 school directly across Lake Pontchartrain from New Orleans.

"The only thing that makes me think I can still coach is remembering that Notre Dame game, because every game since I lost," he said after dropping his first game at Lakeshore. "Louie played such a huge part of my career because he was the gold standard. No matter where I went, I couldn't avoid the guy."

In leading Lakeshore to the quarterfinals and a 10–3 record in 2022 he didn't have to worry about facing Cook because Notre Dame is in a different division and another part of the state.

Indest's first win as a head coach was in 1996 when his Abbeville team beat Cook's Crowley Gents, 30–15. The Gents got even for their coach on their way to the state championship game in the Superdome, topping Abbeville 40–18 in the first round of playoffs.

Cook was at Notre Dame for all future contests against Indest teams at Crowley, Kaplan, and Catholic-NI. Overall, their teams played each other eighteen times, Cook winning twelve of the showdowns. "It's a testament to his coaching ability because I'm battin' .333 against him," Indest said. "That's good in baseball but not football. He got me way more than I got him."

Before announcing his 2019 retirement publicly, Indest informed Cook privately.

"A lot of people probably perceived that over the years you develop some animosity when you're constantly going against somebody," Indest said. "But my admiration for him just grew and grew and grew. We had evolved into a couple of old warhorses, and I didn't want him to hear the news from anybody else but me."

Indest continued to wear a headset, hosting a sports talk show on a radio station in New Iberia while starting several business ventures. In his new role, he could talk about his favorite pro wrestler as a kid growing up in New Iberia—Dusty Rhodes, the self-proclaimed "American Dream." Dusty endeared himself to young Brent with a classic speech titled "Hard Times."

"My belly is just a little big, my heinie is just a little big, but, brother, I'm bad," Dusty told his blue-collar fans.

"Hard times," he bellowed, "are when a man has worked at a job thirty years and they give him a watch, kick him in the butt, and say, 'Hey, a computer took your place, Daddy.'"[2]

"Dusty Rhodes was my guy," Indest said, grinning. "I was a rambunctious son-of-a-gun."

The youngest of seven kids, he got his butt whipped regularly by his three older brothers. His mother didn't stop them inside the house. Instead, she yelled, "Just take him outside."

On the sidelines, Indest can sometimes be mistaken for Dusty.

In the championship game against Notre Dame in 2017, the television cameras feeding the Superdome's giant video screen caught him storming toward defensive coordinator Craig Brodie, grabbing the headset around his neck, and forcibly putting it on his ears. Craig couldn't hear Brent tell him to match the short-yardage personnel Cook had just put in the game.

"We had to call time out," Brent said, "because Louie, the crafty, evil genius that he is, was messing with our heads."

There's no disputing what was seen on the video screen, but Brent wants folks to know what provoked the outburst and that he ended up hugging Craig. After all, Craig is his brother-in-law.

"Notre Dame fans love to spread this stuff—tell everybody what a jackass I am," Indest said. "Little do they know I love it."

The story goes that a Catholic-NI coach was asked how a game went and he replied: "Indest only fired me twice. That's not too bad."

Indest is fifteen years younger than Cook. They didn't play football in college even though both starred as quarterbacks in high school.

Cook is a grinder who is usually working at 5:30 in the morning. "That 5:30 stuff is for the birds," Indest said.

When Indest wakes up, he would rather head to the golf course than the practice field. "I'm a golfer. I find time to play golf. I don't hide from that."

Their coaching styles are polar opposites. "I'm more the Nick Saban-type and he's more like Tom Landry," Indest said. "Louie is far more stoic. I'm that fiery guy."

Landry was the head coach of the Dallas Cowboys for their first twenty-nine seasons and often was referred to as stoic. Cook shows emotion and tosses his cap every now and then, but he's an altar boy compared to Indest, whose antics include kicking a garbage can across the locker room during halftime of the 2017 championship game at the Dome.

Catholic-NI had a comfortable 19–3 lead over the Pioneers, but he wasn't satisfied. "We had the opportunity to be up big," he said.

At Abbeville for his first four years, Indest assisted a coach slightly more animated than Cook. "Every time I did something, I said, 'What would Gerald Laughlin do?' He was a helluva coach. I was so uncomfortable in my skin. It took me about half a year to say, 'Dude, you've got to be you. Go with your instincts.'"

And his instincts are to be a fiery guy and highly quotable like Dusty Rhodes.

After demolishing archrival Loreauville, 51–0, he was asked about the key to the game. "We were just better than them," Indest said bluntly.

"Louie would never say something like that," he acknowledged. "And I respect him for that because that's Louie. And Louie has always stayed true to who he is. Louie is not going to give you anything in the newspaper to get excited about."

Cook doesn't like personalizing the rivalry with Indest. "Why are we playing this up?" he asked one sportswriter. "I'm not playing Brent. We're playing Catholic High."

Yet talking about the rivalry intensifies Cook's natural competitiveness.

He once broke his leg playing softball, trying to tag up and score from second base on a long fly ball. A year later he was invited to play on a team with some accountants and lawyers.

"You sure you want to do that?" asked his wife, Faye.

"They play just for fun," Louie said.

"You don't do nothin' for fun," she said. "You've got to win all the time."

"No, no, no," Louie protested.

In his first at-bat, he hit a ball in a gap between two outfielders. "Next thing I know I'm diving headfirst into second. I got up and, just by coincidence, made eye contact with Faye, and she's sitting there shaking her head. I realized I'm a dumbass. So, from that point on I said, 'Calm down.'"

Staying calm wasn't going to be easy when Indest came riding into Crowley like a gunslinger into Dodge City, looking to add more notches on his belt.

Indest moved to Crowley High in 2004, putting him four miles away from Notre Dame and in the same district. Another coach welcomed him: "Well, Indest, as long as you realize we're all playing for second, you're going to be fine in this district."

Later, Indest told his coaching staff at Crowley: "It's going to be easy here. We've got a lot of slappies just playing for second place. We ain't playing for second."

Those were brave words for the coach of a team that didn't win a single game the year before and was outscored by a whopping 103–19 in three previous losses to Notre Dame.

"I knew who Louie was, and I knew the level that I had to coach," Indest said. "All year long when I was playing somebody that I knew we could beat, I was game planning for Louie Cook. If you can get to where you can beat him, you can beat everybody else."

Notre Dame and Crowley never played until they were placed in the same district in 2001. The Pios wound up winning nine of the eleven games.

Cook always downplayed the game. "I still have a soft spot for Crowley High," he said. "I had eight really good years there, and I loved the kids."

For Cook, the crosstown rivalry served no purpose. "Life is a lot better in Crowley if we don't have to play each other. It separates the community by creating a little bit of animosity. You want to bring everybody together, not split the town."

Notre Dame has always played its home games at Crowley High's Gardiner Memorial Stadium. When the schools played each other, they took turns as the host and sat on the home side of the field.

Crowley's Brent Indest, left, and Notre Dame's Louie Cook shook hands after their first meeting as head coaches of the two schools in 2004. Cook's Pios romped 41–6 but Indest's Gents would win two of their next three games. From 1996 through 2019, the coaches faced each other eighteen times, Indest's teams winning six of the battles— a .333 percentage. "That's good in baseball but not football," Indest said. *Photo by Dwayne Petry.*

Notre Dame was the home team in Indest's first season at Crowley in 2004, forcing the Gents to the visitors' side of their own stadium. This bothered Indest as much as the 41–6 loss to the Pios. "I don't care who technically is the home team, I'll be damned if my team was going to ever again sit on the other side," he vowed afterward.

"I just felt like it was a huge slap in the face," he said. "You're already dealing with kids that don't have a life. All due respect to Louie, it was a big point in my career when I said, 'I'm going to do what I think is right for my team regardless of who I'm dealing with.'"

Cook pointed out that the first time the Pios played the Gents in 2001, they sat on the visitor's side even though they were the home team. "It never was a big deal to me," he said. "I didn't care whether we sat on the home side or not."

He moved future home games against Crowley to Rayne High School. "It wasn't to our advantage to play Crowley High in Crowley when it was our home game."

The best was yet to come. With each meeting, the rivalry intensified like the buildup to a rematch between two great boxers.

"To be who you are sometimes, you've got to have that person who pushes you," Indest said, citing boxing greats Muhammad Ali, Joe Frazier, Thomas Hearns, and "Marvelous" Marvin Hagler. "Ali needed Frazier. Hearns needed Hagler."

The truth is, Indest needed Cook and a big upset victory over the Pios. He got it the last game of the regular season in 2005, nipping the Pios 8–7 without scoring a touchdown on offense.

The Pios were unbeaten (9–0) and heavily favored over the Gents, who entered the game with a 6–3 record. "I'm a big-time realist," Indest said. "There are games where I know I've got a shot. I felt we had a shot that night but not a real good shot."

The Gents take a bus to games at Gardiner Memorial Stadium as Crowley High is located on the outskirts of town, about three miles away.

A block from the stadium, the Gents passed the home of Russell Zaunbrecher, a Crowley attorney-politician married to one of Brent's cousins. For several years he had a sign in front of his house reading "Go Gents" on one side and "Go Pios" on the other. Zaunbrecher was now out of politics, and his son, Rick, was an All-State tailback at Notre Dame the year before, so only "Go Pios" remained.

Indest stood up on the bus and announced, "After we beat these guys' ass, I'm going to knock down that sign."

He sat down next to his defensive coordinator, Trace Sutton, and chuckled, "We both know that probably ain't going to happen."

At halftime, the Gents trailed, 7–0. "I couldn't believe we were playing them that close," Indest said. "I don't think we had a first down the whole first half. My punter punted more in that game than he had all year."

The offense and defense went to separate areas. He told the offense the adjustments they were making and how they were going to move the ball. He had a completely different message for the defense: "We've got to score on defense because we can't move the ball. These guys are stoning us at every turn. I got nothing left in my back pocket. We've got to score."

Kyron Benoit, who became Crowley High's first African American head coach in 2021, was at both meetings.

"I was the quarterback," Kyron said. "He's going off on me and everybody on the offense and it's like, 'Get it together!'"

Kyron also started at defensive back and heard Indest tell the defense it had to score because the offense couldn't do anything. "My heart fell to my feet and it's like, 'Coach, what's going on?' I'm the quarterback and I'm thinking, 'I guess we've got to win it on defense.'"

Early in the third quarter, a pass by Pios quarterback Andre Robichaux was batted into the air and grabbed by the Gents' fastest defender, Geremy Pilate, who sprinted fifty yards for a touchdown. "I'm not stupid," Indest said. "I'm not going for two. We're going to tie it right there."

The snap from center to Jamal Broussard, the holder on the extra-point attempt, was high so he jumped to his feet and ran the ball into the end zone for the two points that won the game, 8–7.

"We played lights-out defense that night," Indest said. The Gents forced six turnovers and limited the Pios to 179 yards, picking up the slack for the offense that totaled a mere seventy-seven yards and seven first downs.

"It was probably the biggest upset of my career," Indest said.

The win gave the Gents a share of the district title with the Pios and Cecilia High and denied Cook his two-hundredth career win. The loss was the Pios' first in district play in seven years.

At the end of the game, Indest spotted Russell Zaunbrecher walking across the field to congratulate him. "My heart just sunk in my stomach," he said.

"Russell, I need a huge favor," Brent said. "I promised the kids I was going to knock down that sign in your front yard when I left here."

"Go for it!" Russell said.

As the Gents' bus left the stadium escorted by the police, the players were quiet, waiting to see what would happen when they came to the house with the "Go Pios" sign. Indest stopped the bus, jumped up, and said, "Y'all ready?"

He rushed from the bus to the sign and drop-kicked it. "The kids went nuts. They didn't think I would do it, but, of course, I had permission. I might've slightly separated my shoulder in doing it but, oh my God, it was worth it."

In their euphoria over the win, Crowley High fans celebrated by wearing T-shirts reading: "8–7—Enough Said."

Around the same time, Indest was golfing and drinking beer with some buddies who in joking around goaded him to say, "There's a new sheriff in town."

The comment spread like gossip around town. "They loved to take things that I said and vilify me," Indest said of his detractors.

Both teams won their first-round playoff games, setting up a rematch hosted by the Pios in Rayne. This led to Cook and Indest meeting in the Crowley High parking lot at midnight after the games to exchange film.

"Louie, y'all take it easy on us," Brent joked. "I know you're going to kill us."

"I don't know," Louie said. "There's a new sheriff in town."

They chatted briefly, Louie's parting words were food for thought: "You know, Brent, it's not bad to be humbled sometimes."

Looking back, Cook said, "That would've been my two-hundredth win that night. Don't get me wrong, I never wanted to lose to them. But I'm glad it worked out that Crowley was not my two-hundredth win. Crowley High people have had to endure a lot."

Two weeks later, the Pios pummeled Crowley 36–0 to give Cook his 201st win and making the Gents' new T-shirts obsolete. "Nobody wanted them," Cook said.

Meeting Notre Dame in the second round of the playoffs was "the worst thing in the world that could ever happen," according to Indest. "We couldn't even enjoy it for over two weeks until they got us back."

The Pios had thirteen points before their offense went on the field, scoring on two punt returns. The defense scored again on an intercepted pass to make it 20–0. "We played two times in three weeks, and they haven't scored yet on offense," Cook noted.

Pios tailback Scotty Francis rushed for 110 yards, two less than the Gents offense totaled overall. Francis didn't play in the first game because of a knee injury. "I held him out to get ready for the playoffs," Cook said. "I didn't want to lose to Crowley, but five weeks after one of the most humbling losses you can have, we're playing for the state championship. That's the mentality we try to develop."

The rivals also tangled in the last regular-season game in 2006. Both teams had 9–0 records, the Pios rated no. 2 and the Gents no. 3.

"I've got almost my whole team back and basically Louie is putting his former junior varsity team against my returning starters," Indest said. "It took one of the best calls I ever made to win."

Trailing 21–17 with less than a minute to play, the Gents faced a fourth-and-three situation at the Pios' seven-yard line. Indest called timeout. "I literally drew up the play in the dirt."

Figuring the Pios would smother his primary receivers, he came up with a pass play to Mitchell Faulk, a six-foot-six, 270-pound tight end who had only four catches the entire season. "He told me the way we were going to run the play that I was going to be wide open and to just make sure I caught the ball," Faulk said.[3]

"Nobody was close to him," said Jimmy McCleary, the Pios' defensive coordinator. "We were expecting Benoit to keep the ball."

Instead, Benoit lobbed a pass to Faulk for the go-ahead touchdown. A few seconds later the Gents intercepted a desperation pass to score again for a 30–21 victory that gave them the district title and their first undefeated season in forty-two years.

McCleary insists a blown call by the officials cost Notre Dame the game. Leading 21–17, the Pios attempted a twenty-four-yard field goal about three minutes earlier. "It went right down the middle," he said.

The kick was ruled wide left.

"In fact, you can see on the film the Crowley High kids turn around and they all put their heads down as they walk off the field," Cook added. "And then the guy goes, 'No good.'"

"That would've sealed the game for us," Mac said.

Before the showdown, Indest told a sportswriter: "One thing for certain that the losing coach will have going for him is that the loser of this game last year ended up in the state finals."[4]

He was close to being right. The Pios made it to the semifinals while his Gents were knocked out in the second round of the playoffs for the second straight year.

"Most of the times we beat Notre Dame, it was on a big stage," Indest said. "There's no bigger win than a playoff win, but those two regular-season wins over Notre Dame shaped my career more than anything else. It gave me and my players confidence. Wherever I went after that, I was known as the guy that had a team that beat Coach Cook's team two years in a row. It was a helluva thing on my résumé—people knew I could get it done against the absolute best."

Indest was the Louisiana High School Athletic Association's Coach of the Year in 2006. He's the only coach to win the honor at three different schools—Crowley, Kaplan (2008), and Catholic-NI (2014).

To be selected Coach of the Year at the state level, you must be voted tops in your district. Crowley High was the district champ, so Indest should've qualified automatically. But one coach lobbied to wait and see what happened in the playoffs. Cook objected, saying Brent deserved the award.

"That's the kind of guy Louie Cook is," Indest said. "When it was all said and done, I always felt we had each other's back."

The wins and accolades earned Indest a shot as the running backs coach at Louisiana Tech. "Louie was the first person I called for advice on going to Tech," he said.

Cook cautioned Brent on the pitfalls of college coaching. "I hated it," Indest said. "In one way, it was the worst decision I ever made in my life because I left a gold mine at Crowley High. But I would've always questioned it if I wouldn't have tried."

Brent lasted one year at Tech and then returned to high school coaching to stay. He coached at Kaplan (2008–09), at Carencro (2010–12), and at his alma mater, Catholic-NI (2013–19). His teams played Notre Dame ten more times, losing at Kaplan in 2008 before winning three of nine games at Catholic-NI.

"There were many times Louie's teams slobber-knocked my teams," Brent said. "I only had one game where my team just beat the snot out of Louie."

That was in 2014, when Catholic-NI clobbered Notre Dame, 56–28, averaging eleven yards per play on offense, scoring on six runs of 35 yards or more, and recovering two onside kicks.

The Pios were missing five starters that game. They were suspended for going to a party that turned into a brawl at 3:30 in the morning. One player broke his hand, another had the rear window of his pickup truck shot out as he sped away from the melee. A team rule prohibits parties during the season unless there's parental supervision.

The mothers of the players met with Cook along with the school's priest-chancellor and a prominent local businessman.

"Coach, you couldn't suspend them next week?" pleaded the mom who organized the meeting. "Catholic High is a big game."

"I wish you were playing," Cook replied. "You recognize it's a big game. You probably would've gone home at midnight. But these kids must not think it's a big game because they chose to break the rule and they're out until 3:30 getting shot at. We're lucky we're not at a funeral right now."

Midway through the meeting, the businessman spoke up. "Coach, I thank God every night you're our coach. I appreciate everything you've done for our kids, and I always will. If you need me for anything, you can call me any time. I'll see you later."

The mother who wanted the suspension delayed a week when the Pios played a weaker opponent announced she wasn't leaving until Cook changed his mind.

"I'm fixin' to go to the chapel and sit in my little office to do my practice plan," he said. "You're welcome to come sit with me but you're going to be there a long time because I'm not changing my mind. They're not playing."

The story illustrates that doing the right thing is far more important to Cook than winning or avoiding an ass-kicking by a powerful Indest-coached team that reached the Class 2A state finals before losing a game.

"It was the right decision," said Bobby Hanks, chief executive officer and owner of Supreme Rice in Crowley. "The punishment fit the crime."

Hanks's son, Matt, was a starting linebacker on the team, so he knows the players involved. "All the boys learned from it. If you talked to them today, they would say nothing but glowing things about Coach Cook."

One of the times Indest got slobber-knocked by Cook was in a 2018 game halted by lightning with eight minutes to play and the Pios leading, 49–0.

"Lightning started popping and the officials are talking," Indest said. "Me and Louie walk out. And the officials go: 'We're going to shut it down for at least a half hour unless y'all just want to call if off.' I said, 'Let's get out of here!'"

The archrivals ended the 2018 season by playing for the Class 2A crown at the Superdome.

Catholic-NI's Trey Amos scored on an eighty-three-yard run to begin the game. After a trick play that gained big yardage, Indest turned to Craig Brodie, his defensive coordinator and brother-in-law, and said: "I'm out of tricks. We've got to beat 'em straight up now." The Pios won, 42–21.

The following day Louie's brother Dave saw Brodie and needled, "You're not palling around with your brother-in-law. What's the matter?"

"He jumped my ass about that tight-end reverse," Brodie said.

The Pios ran the play twice, tight end Thomas Bellard gaining forty yards the first time and thirty-five yards later in the game. "How many times are you going to let Louie run that frickin' reverse for forty yards?" Brent yelled at Brodie.

"I don't know," Brodie said, "but as often as he calls it, he's going to get forty yards."

Early in the 2017 season, Notre Dame pounded Catholic-NI, 37–0.

"When I knew Louie had me, we shut it down," Indest admitted. "I just wanted to get out of there with my dignity."

Catholic-NI punted eight times, managing only six first downs and 123 yards on offense. Indest milked the clock, running the ball on all but nineteen plays. "I didn't want to show him anything because I knew there was a good chance I was going to play him again," Indest said.

The hunch proved right. They played again for the state championship in the Dome.

Indest reminded his players of the blowout in their week-four meeting: "Nobody got eaten. Sure, we got our tails whipped, but nobody got hurt. We just didn't execute well enough."[5]

"It is kind of tricky," Cook said of rematches. "You kind of think, 'Do we get away from some of the things that got us here?'"[6]

Indest counted on Cook following the same script. "What I always tried to do with Notre Dame was take advantage of their coaching," he said. "They were very predictable defensively in what they did at that time. They ended up changing because they had to evolve just like I evolved. They were very predictable because great teams usually are predictable."

He changed the blocking schemes to take advantage of the discipline of Notre Dame defensive ends, enabling runs around them.

On the opening play of the game Catholic-NI's JaDan Stokes raced forty-one yards to Notre Dame's thirty-seven-yard line. That's as far as the Panthers got in the first game. By halftime, they reeled off seven plays gaining ten yards or more.

"When you can make a kid question what he's coached to do, you got 'em," Indest said. "And that night we made their defense question what they were coached to do."

Catholic-NI rolled to a 33–16 victory, giving Indest his only state title.

Ironically, his last win over Notre Dame in 2019 was at Crowley's Gardiner Memorial Stadium and he sat on the visitor's side, where he swore he'd never sit again. Of course, this time he was at Catholic-NI, not Crowley High.

"Going into that game, we had very little confidence," Indest said. "But one thing I did have, I had the best player on the field—Trey Amos."

The heart of the Pios offense, tailback C. J. Thibodeaux and tackle Ben Robichaux, were sidelined with injuries, so Amos hogged the spotlight, rushing for 157 yards and two touchdowns, including the 45-yard scoring run that won the game, 24–21.

"We had a great rivalry," Cook said. "It was always a good game. Brent is a good coach. Nobody gets more out of their kids than he does, and he knows the game as well as anybody."

Shortly before Indest retired, Cook sent him a book titled, *LEAD . . . for God's Sake!* It's a parable about a high school coach who learns to lead from the heart.

He has seen other young, talented coaches wear down and burn out. "Brent was intense—a really good competitor," Cook said. "He was tough. He was hard. A different approach than what I have but he got a lot of good results."

When Louie learned Brent was retiring, he told his longtime nemesis, "I'm going to miss the games we had."

He added: "They helped me as a coach. They made me challenge and push myself a little harder."

Just like Frazier was to Muhammad Ali and Hagler to Hearns, Indest was a worthy adversary.

17

🏈

Forty-Two

The number 42 is synonymous with Jackie Robinson, who broke Major League Baseball's color barrier. But the number also is closely linked to Orlando Thomas, a hard-hitting free safety for the Minnesota Vikings from 1995 to 2001 who got his start in football at Crowley High School playing for Louie Cook.

Orlando wore jersey number 42 at the University of Southwestern Louisiana (USL) where he earned All-American honors during his junior and senior years. He was the forty-second overall pick in the 1995 NFL draft and wore no. 42 his last five seasons with the Vikings. He died in 2014 after a decade-long battle with Lou Gehrig's disease—amyotrophic lateral sclerosis (ALS). Thomas was forty-two, the same age his father died.

Orlando wanted to be like his boyhood idol, Ronnie Lott, a rock 'em, sock 'em All-Pro safety for the San Francisco 49ers in the 1980s, who made 42 one of the most feared numbers in NFL history.

Ironically, Orlando's number at Crowley was 13. That was his age at the start of his freshman year in 1986 when he was a bean pole barely wide enough for double digits on his back. He couldn't bench press the bar, so he used a broom with weights secured on the end.

"I only weighed 90 pounds, wasn't very fast, and looked as if I'd break in two if someone hit me," Orlando acknowledged. "Only Coach Cook thought I could play."[1]

"He's out there fightin' his heart out," Cook recalled, "but he's not standing out like some of the ninth graders that were fifteen years old."

Orlando Thomas wanted to wear no. 42 like his boyhood hero, Ronnie Lott, an NFL Hall of Fame safety who played for the San Francisco 49ers in the 1980s. Orlando wore the number at the University of Southwestern Louisiana as shown here and later with the Minnesota Vikings in the NFL. Ironically, he was the forty-second overall pick in the 1995 NFL draft. He also died at age forty-two, the same as his father, Michael Wayne Clement, whose initials, MWC, are on Orlando's jersey. Clement died in 1993. *Photo by Brad Kemp.*

Shane Garrett, who played for Texas A&M and the Cincinnati Bengals after starring at Crowley, remembers his cousin Orlando as a scrawny kid with big feet. "He wasn't very athletic, but he was always tough."

Orlando didn't play in a single varsity game his first two years and yet at the end of his sophomore season, he proclaimed he was going to play in the NFL.

"You don't think I can do it, Coach?" Orlando asked.

"Are you doing everything that you can to give yourself a chance?" Cook replied.

"What do you mean, Coach?"

"I don't see you out there with the track team."

Orlando was lifting weights regularly, but he wasn't on the track team.

"You don't need to get faster?" Cook asked. "The weights will help strengthen you, but you've got to be able to run as fast as possible."

Orlando was running track the next day.

"Football is all about running," Cook said. "You don't have long runs but there are a lot of bursts. If you go out for track, you're going to do a lot more running that will help you get faster."

Garrett kept tabs on Orlando as he progressed through high school and college. "He got bigger, stronger, and he had that heart," Shane said. "He wasn't the best athlete on the field, but nobody had a bigger heart. He worked hard. That was the dream. He was like me. We're going to play professional football."

Orlando and Cook were also alike.

"He reminded me of myself," Cook said. "I lived in a fraternity house for three years and I wasn't going to drink. I was going to do what I was going to do. And Orlando was the same way. He was driven."

Orlando cracked the starting lineup at cornerback his junior year. In practice, he faced Wes Jacob, a high school All-American wide receiver who went on to star at LSU. "He'd come up so hard from free safety he'd knock himself out half the time," Wes said. "He gave it his all, all the time."

By Orlando's senior year in 1989, he was a sculpted, six-foot-two, 180-pound ball-hawking safety who sometimes played wide receiver. During the regular season, he racked up thirty tackles, twenty-one assists, and seven interceptions on defense. Playing part-time on offense, he caught twenty-six passes for 508 yards and a touchdown.

Crowley was waving the Class 3A state championship banner four years after snapping a twenty-two-game losing streak. "Orlando was the motivating factor," Cook said. "He was the spiritual leader. He had such a strong will to succeed that he willed us to the state title."

The signing date for the nation's best college football prospects came and went in February without Orlando getting a nibble. He doubled up on his track workouts, going to school an hour earlier so he could run in the morning and afternoon and make it home in time to babysit for his two brothers.

The extra work paid off at the state track championships. He clocked an impressive 49.70 seconds in the 400-meters and was the anchorman on Crowley's winning 1,600-meter relay team. Meanwhile, he lowered his time in football's speed barometer, forty-yard dash, to 4.4 seconds.

Suddenly, the phone calls started coming in—USL, Nicholls State, and McNeese State in Louisiana and Mississippi State. Tennessee offered a track scholarship. LSU invited him to try out as a walk-on. "He's not a super athlete," Cook told one reporter, "but I'll take a dozen of him."[2]

Cook didn't have to convince Gerald Broussard, his former coaching sidekick at USL. But Broussard had to sell his boss, head coach Nelson Stokley.

"Stokley's big deal was: 'Will he hit anybody?'" Broussard said.

Doubts about Orlando's toughness were planted by another USL assistant who concluded he wasn't worthy of a scholarship.

Stokley also questioned Broussard's objectivity. "Gerald," he said, "you're just trying to sign one of Louie's kids."

Broussard got USL's track coach Charles Lancon to back him up on Orlando's speed.

"We signed Orlanda Thomas, but he finished as Orlando Thomas," Broussard said.

The ending of his first name was misspelled with an "a" on his birth certificate and legally changed to "o" while he was at USL. His nickname growing up in Crowley was "Poosie" but in college he became known as "Crowley High" because he always had a Crowley Gents T-shirt under his USL jersey.

A newspaper headline going into Orlando's junior season in 1993 summed up his first two years at USL: "No Doubting This Thomas."[3]

As a redshirt freshman in 1991, he had eighty-five tackles (fifty-five solos) and two interceptions, prompting Stokely to rave, "If there's a better freshman safety in the country, I'd like to see him."[4]

In 1992, he accounted for sixty-four stops (forty-one solos) and one interception.

By 1993, he had bulked up to 193 pounds, running the forty-yard dash in 4.27 seconds, bench pressing 350 pounds, and squat lifting 450. "Oh, he was a stud," Broussard said.

"He was brutal," added Mike Doherty, USL's secondary coach. "He was the toughest football player I ever coached. He had an unbelievable knack for playing that centerfielder, as much versus the run as the pass. The other team knew exactly where he was because if he found them, they were going to see the side of his helmet."

As good as he was, Orlando was relatively unknown outside of Louisiana and the Big West Conference until 1993, when he led the nation's Division 1-A colleges with nine interceptions and made ninety-six tackles to set a career record for USL defensive backs. This earned him various second- and third-team All-American honors and had some greedy agents clamoring for him to enter the NFL draft instead of playing another year at USL.

Cook returned to USL in 1992 as offensive coordinator, so he and Orlando were together again.

Orlando was part of an army of players, Black and white, who streamed into Cook's office regularly to chat. At the end of the '93 season, he walked in for his daily afternoon meeting, closed the door, and asked, "Coach, do you think I should declare for the draft?"

"I've got no idea," Cook said, "but I'm going to find out."

Through an agent he knew in Chicago, Cook learned that Orlando was projected to be selected in the fifth round of the 1994 NFL draft. He also was informed that Orlando could get insurance to protect himself if he was injured during his last season at USL. Nowadays, colleges insure their athletes, but it wasn't done regularly at that time.

"Orlando, I don't think it's smart to come out," Cook said. "But we can get you a million dollars' worth of insurance coverage. If you trip over a dog or are injured playing football and disqualified from the draft, you're going to have a million dollars."

Orlando agreed and Cook got the insurance policy. "It cost $10,000 but he was going to sign a multimillion-dollar contract. It was worth it."

Despite opposing teams keeping the ball away from him, Orlando intercepted six passes to give him a four-year total of eighteen, third best in USL history. His 347 career tackles were 129 more than any other defensive back to play at USL. He was selected as the Big West Conference's Defensive Player of the Year and garnered more All-American honors.

"I'm glad I stayed," Orlando said. "I've gotten a little more physical and I've gotten more good coaching. It's given me a chance to still be like a kid."[5]

His market value was higher, and more agents wanted a piece of the action.

One day Cook got a call from a so-called sportswriter wanting to do a story on Orlando. He arranged for the telephone interview to be done in his office. Orlando hung up the phone in thirty seconds.

"That ain't going to be much of a story," Cook said.

"Coach, that was an agent," Orlando said. "He lied to you."

Approximately fifty agents contacted Orlando.

"Let's do this," Cook told Orlando. "I'm going to write down my three favorites and you write your top three. And then, we'll go visit."

Mark Bartelstein, the Chicago agent who helped them earlier, was on both lists, so they set up a trip to meet him.

"You got a heavy coat?" Cook asked.

"No, Coach."

"It's going to be cold and snowing up there."

Cook outfitted Orlando with a warm coat and off to the Windy City they went with his mother, Rosa Marie Clement, and Ron Prejean, a long-time Cook pal who is a highly respected Lafayette accountant.

"When they're choosing someone to represent them, their life's work, all their dreams and goals are being put on your shoulders, so they have to believe how much you care," Bartelstein explained.

Orlando picked Bartelstein to share his dream of starring in the NFL.

Back in Louisiana, Cook helped Orlando buy a suit for festivities around the Blue-Gray Bowl he was to play in on Christmas Day, get his driver's license, and lease a car. "Here's a first-team AP (Associated Press) All-American football player, and he doesn't have a driver's license," Cook said, chuckling.

Orlando used Cook's Mercury Sable for the driving test. "Man," Cook said, "I hope they don't take you through West Crowley because the brothers will be laughing at you for driving that old car."

Cook was at Orlando's house in West Crowley when the Vikings drafted him in the second round, the forty-second player picked. "We got the guy we wanted," exulted Vikings head coach Dennis Green.[6]

Orlando got the contract he wanted—a four-year, $2 million deal, plus a $600,000 signing bonus.

"Orlando was kind of like a young stallion just getting his legs underneath him, trying to figure out how to go through life," Bartelstein said. "Coach Cook was incredible in Orlando's development. He was everything to him—a father figure, first and foremost; a coach obviously; and a mentor. All those things Orlando accomplished don't happen without Coach Cook."

Orlando topped the NFL with nine interceptions in 1995 and added six in 1996, including the playoffs, to total fifteen picks altogether, more than anybody else during that two-year period. But the playoff heist against the Dallas Cowboys was costly, as he tore both the anterior cruciate ligament (ACL) and lateral collateral ligament (LCL) in his left knee while being tackled on the return by the Cowboys' Herschel Walker.

Orlando cried as he was carted off the field and again in the locker room. "As soon as I got hurt, I knew just that quick that I blew my knee out and my career could be over with," he said.[7]

The reckless abandon that Orlando displayed on the field carried over to the off-season, when he hung out with his buddies at "The Gambling Shack" in West Crowley, drinking and playing Bourrè (*Boo-Ray*), a popular gambling card game in the Acadiana region of Louisiana.

The Vikings' Green didn't want Orlando to get near Crowley let alone Wil Turner's Lounge, the Shack's official name.

But Orlando was treated like royalty there. He had his own cook, a guy named Pop, who made sure Orlando ate first. If he was there on a Sunday, people traveled from Texas and other towns in the surrounding area to get a piece of the sizeable pots. He ended up becoming co-owner of the place, which has since been refurbished by his brother, Michael, and renamed OT's Hall.

West Crowley was hopping when Orlando was in town, putting local police on the hot seat because the potential for trouble kicked up a notch. That's what happened twice one Sunday in early July 1997.

At three o'clock in the morning, police responded to a so-called "disturbance" at a closed lounge. The large crowd outside refused to leave, throwing bottles at police officers. Orlando was arrested.

Later that Sunday, around midnight, a second incident in front of another bar brought police back to the area. They tried to break up a fight and make arrests when Orlando allegedly interfered. He was arrested again and jailed for inciting a riot (a felony), disturbing the peace with profanity, and not being in possession of a driver's license.[8]

Orlando went to see Cook.

"Coach," he explained, "I wasn't trying to hurt nobody, but I wasn't going to let them come in here and bully those guys like that. It wasn't right."

"I know how you are," Cook said, "but you just got to make sure you do it in the right way."

It was a page out of the handbook of another no. 42, Jackie Robinson, renowned for his fighting spirit and standing up for what's right.

"Orlando didn't care who it was," Cook said. "If it's right, it's right. If it's wrong, it's wrong. That's how he lived."

Orlando ended up pleading no contest to a misdemeanor. He paid a $100 fine, was put on unsupervised probation for ninety days, and performed fifty hours of community service for his role in the altercations.[9]

The 1997 season was a struggle for Orlando, nagged by right hamstring problems resulting from overcompensating for his ailing left knee. He had only two interceptions and finished the season as a backup to rookie Torrian Gray. "So, if you're not healthy and you're not making plays, what's the purpose of being out there?" he asked.[10]

He rebounded to start all sixteen games in 1998 and received a four-year, $11 million contract, including a $2.75 million signing bonus, most of it deferred with incentive money intended to improve his workout habits and health. "I really thought I was going to be an ex-Viking," a surprised Orlando said.[11]

"I told him it's like winning the lottery, everybody is going to be hitting you up," Cook recalled, cautioning Orlando: "Choose wisely but don't think it's going to last forever. Don't go giving money away."

Cook returned to Crowley High in 1996. During his last four years at USL (1992–95), the athletic department at Crowley piled up $40,000 in debt, which Orlando helped reduce with a $10,000 donation and $20,000 loan.

When Cook was offered the job at Notre Dame in 1997, Orlando encouraged him to take it despite pleas from other Blacks in the community to get him to stay at Crowley. Orlando wanted what was best for Cook and his family because he considered himself part of it.

Faye Cook baked chocolate goodies for Orlando and quarterback Jake Delhomme when they were at USL. Finally, Orlando said, "Miss Faye, I don't want to hurt your feelings, but I really don't like chocolate."

She switched to cherry, strawberry, and lemon sweets.

"He was an extremely kind, polite, caring, and loving young man," she said.

One day a Mercedes Benz pulled into the carport at the Cooks' house. It was Orlando wanting to show his beloved coach and wife the car he had just bought.

"Louie was gone so I get in the car and started singing like Janis Joplin: 'Oh, Lord, won't you buy me a Mercedes Benz?'" Faye said.

Orlando had a blank look on his face because he didn't know the song that was a hit in 1971, the year before he was born. "That's old school, Miss Faye."

Orlando was at a Notre Dame–Port Allen game during the Vikings' bye week in 2000 and noticed a weakness in Port Allen's defense that could be exploited for a big gain. He mentioned it to Faye, sitting nearby in the stands.

"Go tell Louie," she said.

He was reluctant to give his former coach advice.

"You'd better tell him," Faye repeated several times.

Just before the second half started, Cook felt someone come up from behind and grab him around the neck. It was Orlando.

"Looks like I'm going to have to take over the offense, Coach."

Notre Dame was trailing, 13–0.

"Go ahead, you got 'em," Cook said.

"Where's Jeff?" Orlando asked, referring to Cook's son Jeff, the team's outstanding quarterback.

"He's not playing," Cook replied.

"You can keep it, Coach."

"Oh, that's how it works," Cook laughed. "You only want to coach when we've got the good players."

"Coach, the post route is open," Orlando said, referring to a pass play that Cook has used effectively over the years.

"Orlando, if I can get Jeff in the game, we can try it."

Jeff was suited up but was under doctor's orders not to play because of a hamstring injury that hindered his mobility.

With less than a minute to play, Port Allen had the ball, leading 13–9. "They kneel on it three times, the game's over," Cook said.

The Port Allen quarterback took a knee twice. Instead of kneeling a third time, however, he spiked the ball, stopping the clock immediately and forcing a Port Allen punt that went only ten yards. There were twenty-two seconds still to play and the Pios had the ball on Port Allen's thirty-three-yard line.

Jeff walked onto the field and on the game's last play lofted a touchdown pass to wide receiver Luke Guidry running the post route Orlando suggested. The Pios prevailed 16–13 and ended up going undefeated (15–0) and winning the Class 3A state title. "We snatched victory from the jaws of defeat that night," Louie said.

Orlando spent his last five years with the Vikings trying to recapture the magic of his first two years. He broke both shoulder blades toward the end of his career and continued to battle hamstring and knee problems, limiting him to eight interceptions those five years, one less than he had as a rookie.

"When I came in, I was young, and I felt I was one of the best," Orlando reflected. "Then you get hurt, and you feel like all of a sudden, you're the last man on the totem pole."[12]

The Vikings released him in early 2002, shortly after firing Dennis Green.

When Green was named head coach of the Arizona Cardinals in 2004, he invited Orlando to tutor the team's defensive backs that spring as an intern. Meanwhile, Cook helped him get a coaching job at Comeaux High School near Youngsville, on the outskirts of Lafayette, where Orlando and his wife, Demetra, had bought a two-story, four-bedroom house.

Orlando started having muscle spasms, his shoulders twitching and jumping. "My shoulder is dislocated," he said to Demetra at one point.

He went to see Cook at Notre Dame the day before Thanksgiving 2004. "Coach, I've been diagnosed with Lou Gehrig's disease. My momma, nobody knows. I'm going to tell 'em this weekend."

Orlando told Demetra: "Some people were born to climb mountains. Some were born to move them."

He was up against ALS, an immovable mountain that destroys the nerve cells in the brain and spinal cord, ultimately making it impossible to walk, sit, talk, eat normally, or breathe without a ventilator. Eventually, he would be fed through a tube and his throat cleared regularly by a suctioning device.

"Going through ALS is like going through a hurricane every day of your life," Demetra said. "When it's life and death, you don't have time to look at the tree that's coming through the window or the roof that's caving in. You learn how to be more disciplined in your mind and your heart, so you're not distracted from whatever it is that God has you doing."

Orlando was far more than a client to Bartelstein.

"He was such an important person in my life and so inspiring to me and so many others," the agent said. "His career was inspiring, but the way he lived his life after contracting this horrific disease was even more inspiring. It was hard for everybody in Orlando's life to watch what happened to a guy that was almost indestructible. He was an incredible athlete, strong as can be, and such a vibrant personality, and to see that stripped away day by day was really tough."

ALS shortened the lives of baseball greats Lou Gehrig and Jim "Catfish" Hunter, former heavyweight boxing champ Ezzard Charles, and Dwight Clark, a tight end famous for "The Catch" that lifted the 49ers over the Cowboys in the National Football Conference championship game in 1982.

A 2021 study of nineteen thousand former and current NFL players found that they are over three times more likely to be diagnosed and die from ALS than the general male population in the United States.[13]

Gehrig was nicknamed "The Iron Horse" and considered invincible when the disease halted his then-record streak of playing in 2,130 consecutive games. In his farewell address at Yankee Stadium on July 4, 1939, Gehrig told the capacity crowd: "Today I consider myself the luckiest man on the face of the earth."[14]

The last line of Gehrig's famous speech expressed how Orlando viewed ALS: "I might've been given a bad break, but I have an awful lot to live for."[15]

Orlando never stopped saying his signature phrase at Crowley High: "Every day is a holiday."

"I've had the life of ten people," he told Demetra.

"We never thought about death because Orlando was all about life," she said. "He never focused on anything that was happening to his body. He ran this house the way he always ran this house."

"I could sense the authority in him," added Orlando Jr., who was seven years old when his father was confined to his bed.

His mind remained sharp, his spirits high, his faith unwavering.

Inscribed on the wall facing the bed he laid in the last seven years of his life are the words: "Every day holds a possibility of a miracle."

"We never stopped living life," Demetra said. "We weren't focused on ALS. Once Orlando lost his voice, we just started communicating with his eyebrows. I never missed his voice because he was still so vocal, and his energy was so present and strong. You knew when he was mad. You knew when he was about to say something."

She told one interviewer: "ALS is a disease that takes, takes, takes, and takes. But we've been able to take more from it than ALS has taken from us. ALS was a vehicle to bring Orlando and me unbelievably close."

Orlando and Demetra met in September 1997 at a hand car wash called Cheese in North Minneapolis, on the opposite side of town from the Vikings' training facility in Eden Prairie.

It was a popular place with Black athletes and women who wanted to meet them. But Demetra didn't know that Orlando played for the Vikings, and she wasn't particularly fond of athletes. "I always felt like they were arrogant," she said. "I had no interest in ever wanting to get to know one."

Demetra was a nurse living in the area and knew the co-owner of the car wash. That's how she wound up in the owner's office with Orlando sitting behind his desk, resting his big feet on top of it. "Orlando started this full-fledged conversation, and it was very, very interesting and personal."

At one point, Orlando said: "Man, one day I got up, I looked in the mirror, and I didn't like the man I saw."

Still hanging over Orlando's head was a felony charge for the riot he was accused of inciting that summer in Crowley. It would be reduced to a misdemeanor later.

Demetra was in a relationship that was going nowhere, but she was guarded.

"I gave my life to Christ, and I'm telling you, I've had so much peace ever since," Orlando said.

Demetra had attended church her entire life and knew what Orlando meant, but she wasn't singing from the same hymn book yet. "I'm not going to play with God," she told friends. "When God is ready for me, He'll get me."

Besides, she was at a car wash talking to this guy in a white T-shirt and red shorts. She didn't know he was a star for the Vikings until someone asked for his autograph.

Orlando kept talking: "I got injured on my job. And it humbled me."

Demetra was selling natural health and nutritional products at the time. "I have an herb," she said. "It's 100-percent guaranteed, your money back. It'll help your recovery."

She made an appointment to meet him again at the car wash and give him a bottle of the herb. "God definitely used Orlando," she said. "I knew he was going to have this special place in my heart."

At their third meeting, Orlando announced, "You're going to be my wife."

Demetra heard a different voice: "It must be done right."

She laughed. "I had never heard God speak before. But I knew what he meant. I'm a believer. Whatever is supposed to be, it will be."

Orlando met Demetra on September 12, he proposed to her on December 18, and they were married on February 27, the birth date of Orlando's late father, Michael Wayne Clement.

One of the questions Orlando asked Demetra was, "Would you live down South?"

The question had a greater significance that Demetra didn't understand until she relocated to Louisiana. "Orlando never left Crowley," she said.

Even after the Vikings warned him not to go to Crowley, he went back. The joke was: "Man, Orlando going to find the hood."

His sense of community not only included his family in Crowley, but also his Gambling Shack friends whom he gambled with as they drank and chanted: "Up to it; down to it; we do it because we're used to it; forget those who don't do it; so, let's drink, drink, drink." An expletive was added to the last line for emphasis.

"I didn't understand the man I married because I didn't understand community and [the] 'you never forget where you come from' concept," Demetra said. "I was thinking, 'Why does that even matter? Who's responsible for their siblings? Who's indebted to their parents forever?' No, you grow up, become an adult, and live your own life. That's how I grew up. So, I didn't understand."

Louisiana is one of the least transient states in the country. Most people never leave and if they do, they usually come back because of their families.

"This place is like no other place because they operate so differently," Demetra said. "It was so different I'd go back to Minnesota even when we were married."

And then a hurricane named ALS turned their lives upside down and inside out. "We knew God put us together," Demetra said. "We just didn't know that God had a plan that would unfold through ALS."

Orlando had always feared that he would wind up back in Crowley on a bike—broke. "ALS taught us that life is way beyond money and material things," Demetra said. "God has sustained this family on faith."

Demetra found herself in what she calls "a high spiritual place," like an angel assigned to take care of Orlando and the five children in their blended family.

They were inseparable. When Orlando was bedridden and could no longer speak, she sat beside him on the bed and became his voice. The high-technology machine they were provided to communicate with wound up in the attic, and they came up with their own system. Demetra would go through the alphabet and stop at the letter Orlando wanted when he raised his eyebrows. "He was a country boy and that was what he wanted to do," she said.

"It bonded us and allowed me to experience his relationships, which taught me how to have relationships," Demetra said. "Prior to that, my relationships were based on needs or something vain. But it wasn't about the person."

She watched and learned about Orlando from the people who passed through the bedroom that was his world.

Except for the ventilator, suction machine, and oxygen tank that was his life support system, the room hasn't changed much since he died. The same bed is there as well as the sixty-inch television atop a large armoire dresser. The TV shows and movies recorded for him to watch again and again remain neatly organized—the *Andy Griffith Show, Gunsmoke, Dallas, Dynasty, The Jamie Foxx Show, Godfather,* and *Scarface,* to name a few. The inscription about the "possibility of a miracle" is still on the wall next to the dresser.

Visitors would come and go, some saying very little and others a lot.

"No matter who came, he would always inquire about their kids," Demetra said.

"How's Miss Faye?" Orlando asked Cook.

"That's always the first question," Cook recalled. "Then it was, 'How's the boys?' Every time."

The visits by Coach Cook gave Demetra a window into their relationship. "It was like old times," she said. "They would go down memory lane and just enjoy each other."

She got to see their love for each other. "Coach Cook not only helped Orlando's dreams come true but bigger than that, he was an amazing role model and someone that truly loved him."

On one visit they watched a highlight film of Orlando playing for the Vikings, picking off passes and making crushing tackles. Cook was reminded of Orlando at USL, hitting a Miami of Ohio player so violently that he had to be taken to the hospital.

The guy pummeling people in the film was in the bed next to him, about seventy pounds under his last playing weight of 225, unable to move a muscle. The contrast was startling and saddening.

"Orlando knew the condition he was in was because of football," Demetra said. "He verbalized that quite often."

For a while, he quit watching football on TV because he hadn't received the compensation money he was due. "Orlando," Demetra said, "if it's God's will, a check will show up in the mail." Eventually it did.

The last time Cook visited Orlando was in early 2014. The University of Louisiana at Lafayette (ULL), which used to be USL, had just initiated the Orlando Thomas Courage Award and the first recipient was Orlando. Jake Delhomme presented the award, and Cook accepted it on Orlando's behalf and was now taking it to him.

Stu Cook accompanied his father. He was a student at ULL, majoring in kinesiology and trying to decide what to do with his life. He was thinking about following his dad into coaching.

"It's just a game but part of why I wanted to teach and coach to continue his legacy," Stu said. "It's kind of like if your parents owned a successful grocery store and you want to take it over and continue the tradition. Me and Dad talked about it one night."

Coach Cook pulled out a big box full of letters from former players. Stu shuffled through them, reading as many as possible.

"I just want to tell you how much I appreciate having you as a coach at USL back in 1983," a player named Dan Childress wrote in 2010. "Though I was there a short time, you have always been a big influence on me as a person and a coach."

Coach Cook and Stu took the Courage Award to Orlando. Growing up, Stu collected Vikings memorabilia given to him by Orlando.

"What's that big-time van I see parked in the driveway?" Coach asked Orlando, lying in bed, only his head visible. "It's yours?"

Mark Bartelstein, the agent they both favored, purchased out of his own pocket a new van fully equipped for transporting Orlando wherever he needed to go.

"I hear Mark got that for you," Cook added. "I guess we picked the right guy."

There were tears in Orlando's eyes.

"I look at Dad," Stu said. "He's crying. Tears rolling down his face. First time I'd ever seen my dad really cry."

Stu made up his mind that day to be a high school football coach. "I hope I can make an impact on somebody's life like that," he thought to himself.

The 2022 season was Stu's seventh coaching, all as an assistant at Southwest Louisiana high schools. "Sometimes if I lose sight of why I got into coaching, it's nice to revert back to that day," he said.

Stu remembers his dad telling him: "Nobody is going to know what years we won championships. They're not going to know how many games we won. But they're going to know how we made them feel."

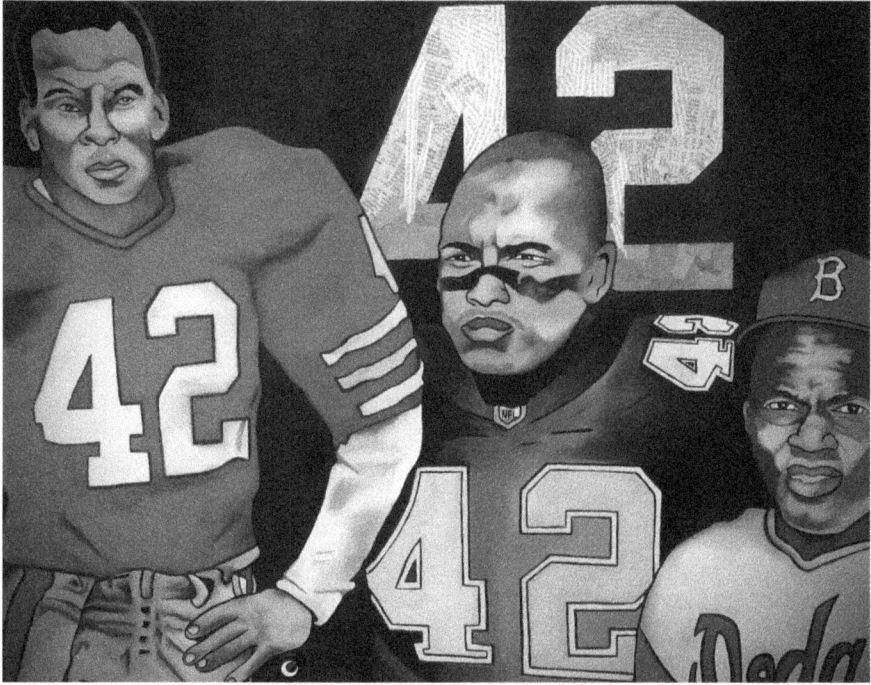

From Jackie Robinson, *far right*, to hard-hitting NFL safeties Ronnie Lott and Orlando
Thomas, *far left and center*, the number 42 has come to symbolize excellence, courage,
and perseverance as celebrated in this bold, compelling painting by Sydnei SmithJordan,
a Black artist who lives in Cape May, New Jersey. *Courtesy of Sydnei SmithJordan.*

Coach Cook helped Orlando feel like every day was a holiday, that he
could play in the NFL, and even move mountains.

Orlando didn't conquer ALS, but he battled the disease for a decade,
well beyond the two-to-five years most people survive.

When he was forty-one, Orlando was hospitalized with a cracked rib
that damaged his lungs. A catheter bag was used to pump fluid from
the lungs. His body began to shut down, one organ at a time. He looked
pasty, almost like he wasn't there.

"We had situations like that before where I walked out of his room and
then back in and they pronounced him dead," Demetra said.

"He's not dead," she would tell the doctor, pleading, "just clear his
airway."

This time Demetra asked for the catheter bag to be removed.

"I learned a lot about the body as I was caring for Orlando," she said.
"One organ will overcompensate for another. If you deny an organ its
purpose, it will fail to function."

Demetra even talked to his organs: "Come on, you can work, come on."

One of the nurses said, "Orlando thinks he's forty-two."

So, Demetra whispered in his ear: 'Orlando, you're not forty-two, you're forty-one."

His organs started working again and his color came back.

"He was drafted forty-second, he wore number 42, and his dad died at forty-two," Cook said. "He pushed himself to make sure he turned forty-two before he died."

Orlando died on November 9, 2014—19 days after his forty-second birthday.

Perseverance is the one word that Demetra singles out to describe her husband. The same word applies to another courageous man who wore no. 42—Jackie Robinson.

18

🏈

Nothing Good Happens
after Midnight

Louie Cook uses stories to teach.

The lessons usually take place after practice. The players gather around Cook, kneeling on the grass. Sometimes the talks last fifteen to twenty minutes, causing the players to joke about the permanent grass stains on their knees.

At Crowley High, one player complained to Joe Cook, an assistant coach and Louie's cousin, "Cuz, every time he clears his throat, it's another ten minutes."

Every story has a point, whether it's perseverance, fortitude, gratitude, humility, or accountability. He has stories about the dangers of smoking, drinking, and staying out till the wee hours of the morning. The message behind one story originated with his father, Lewis Cook Sr. He always told Louie, "Nothing good happens after midnight."

The only time Louie was out past midnight growing up was when his father dispatched him to look for his youngest brothers, Dave and Robert. But Louie has faithfully passed that message along to future generations.

"My dad told me that; I told my kids that; I tell the team that," he said. "I've said it year after year."

Garrison Gautreaux, a member of the Notre Dame football and baseball teams, was sitting behind the steering wheel of his pickup truck parked behind "The Crossing at Mervine Kahn," a historic department store in downtown Rayne converted into a reception hall for social events. A wedding party was winding down as Garrison waited for friends to arrive and stay the rest of the night at a house nearby.

The details of what happened next have yet to be disclosed publicly but it's known that just past midnight Sunday, May 16, 2021, he was shot to death by two strangers.

"Who would want to kill a seventeen-year-old kid?" asked Captain Tony Olinger, assistant chief of police in Rayne. "He had his whole life ahead of him. And it got snuffed out and nobody knows why."

The two forty-one-year-old men arrested and charged with second-degree murder aren't talking. "We really don't know why it happened," said Capt. Olinger. "We know it happened and we made two arrests. But we haven't been able to pinpoint why yet. And sometimes you never know."

Why?

Louie Cook was asking that question after getting a text message from Capt. Olinger: "Just to let you know we found Garrison Gautreaux shot dead in his truck behind The Crossing around one this morning. He was at a party at K. Broussard's house."

Karson Broussard was a star linebacker for the Pios in 2021 and the starting catcher on the baseball team that had just won the Class 2A state baseball championship. Garrison, a pitcher–first baseman, sat out the season with a stress fracture in his back. The teammates celebrated the next afternoon (Saturday) with a crawfish boil at Broussard's place, a farm on the outskirts of Rayne that has a pond large enough to water ski and kneeboard.

"Garrison was the funniest dude you would have ever met," said Hudson LeBlanc, a teammate and best friend. "We hunted, fished, wrecked four-wheelers—anything that high schoolers do."

Grady Faulk played tight end and Garrison defensive end, so they were pitted against each other in practice as well as 4-H projects where they showcased the livestock raised on their family farms.

"He was my closest friend," Faulk said. "He was the guy I used to go to about everything. He was my big brother that I never had and to lose him, I kind of felt like I lost everything."

The six-foot-three, 210-pound Garrison was having his way with offensive linemen in spring practice.

"You must be feeling pretty good," Cook said to him as they were walking off the practice field. "We can't block you."

"Yeah, I'm feeling good," Garrison said.

"Well, you're doing good," Cook replied.

That was the last conversation they had.

Why?

Almost everybody in the Acadia Parish communities of Rayne, Crowley, Church Point, Iota, and Mire was asking that question in the wake of Garrison's murder.

"That's the main question: Why?" LeBlanc said. "It was pointless. Made no sense."

"He was a light for a lot of people and once he left that light was gone," added Faulk, who questioned his faith. "In Catholic schools you're taught your whole life that Jesus loves you and then he takes away your big brother—the guy closest to you."

Karson Broussard didn't know how to act or feel. "You don't want to do anything," he said. "You don't think about football. You don't think about anything except him and what you could've done to not let that happen."

"The entire community was hurting," said Karen Berken, Cook's secretary who retired at the end of the 2021 school year. "It was like losing a member of your family."

Many of the mourners at St. Michael's Church in Crowley for the rosary didn't know Garrison, but they still wept openly because they knew that could've easily been their own son.

"Out of all that pain comes such a feeling of community and family," Karen said. "It's a strong bond because everybody is in the same boat."

St. Joseph Church in Rayne was also packed for the funeral. Except for a small section reserved for the Gautreaux family, all of the approximately eight hundred seats were occupied forty minutes before the service began. People continued to pour in, lining the walls of the church. Half of them were teenagers.

Several pallbearers were teammates and wore their Notre Dame jerseys as they carried Garrison's casket into the church followed by an honor guard of more jersey-clad players. It was a poignant sight that captured the school's proud football tradition. "I saw guys that graduated ten to fifteen years ago showing up in support of Garrison and Notre Dame," Cook said.

Many of the Notre Dame students come from rural areas and don't know each other before starting school there. "The friends you make last a lifetime," Karen said. "It really is a pride coming from a sound education, sound faith, and sound mentality of working your tail off to achieve what you want."

Karen lived on a farm in Thornwell, forty miles from Crowley, before moving to town. "Farming is a hard life," she said. "A lot of these farmers have a slew of kids, and those kids grow up working on the farm. It's a good place. Not a perfect place but a really good place."

The tragedy occurred just before the start of final exams.

"Finals didn't matter to my son, Alex," said Chris Stevens, the Pios head baseball coach. "He was a pallbearer and just buried his friend. So, math, English, science didn't matter to him at the time."

Grady Faulk didn't go out of his house for a while. When he finally did, he went to Garrison's grave so he could talk to him. "He was always there for me," Faulk said. "That's what I missed most."

Cook canceled the last week of spring practice and gathered his players in the Notre Dame chapel.

"This is where we really get our faith tested," he said. "You know how we always talk about trying to achieve the ultimate goal of getting to heaven? Garrison just got there early. Hopefully, he's achieved his goal. When you want to doubt or blame someone or wonder why this happened, offer a prayer for Garrison and his family."

Why?

Cook was asking that question, too. He pointed out that everybody grieves differently. Crying isn't a sign of weakness any more than silence is strength. "Your faith is being tested right now. Hang together. Be there for one another."

"My dad knew the kids were trying to figure out how to act," said his son, Lew. "He did a great job of setting expectations, basically putting stuff out there and letting the kids process and handle on their own. He took away the pressure of being judged by how you react."

He was a buffer for the students with others who weren't as sensitive to the situation as they should be. "To me," Lew said, "we had this hurricane hit, and my dad was the eye where everything was calm. He kind of expanded that eye and pushed the craziness out."

A sticker with a cross and Garrison's initials, GCG, was placed on the Pios' red helmets in honor of his memory. Cook mentioned him a couple of times during the 2021 season, but there was no "Win one for the Gipper," the famous line Knute Rockne, the legendary Notre Dame University head coach, once uttered in a half-time pep talk.

"We've got a chance to honor Garrison," Cook said before the Pios played in the 2021 Kiwanis Jamboree at Cajun Field in Lafayette, a preseason dress rehearsal with abbreviated twenty-four-minute games used as a tune-up for the regular season. "I'm not going to bring it up every week, but I know he means a lot to you guys. I spoke about him today because he would've been in that uniform with you guys and rarin' to go. You know how he would've done. It was his turn. He would've played his ass off. Let's go do that!"

"The biggest thing is we had each other to get through it," said Karson Broussard. "And just knowing that he [Garrison] was up there, watching us and helping us, it was a good feeling."

Cook has an uncanny ability to read people and situations. He's low-key and steady as a rock, just what was needed by kids who had to deal with all the issues around the COVID pandemic before and after Garrison's death.

In honor of their late teammate, Garrison Gautreaux, Notre Dame seniors Nicholas Swacker (2), Hudson LeBlanc (54), Alex Stevens (26), and Zach Lamm (80) took his jersey no. 45 to midfield prior to a home game in 2021. Five months earlier, two strangers shot Garrison to death in downtown Rayne, Louisiana. *Photo by Jason Faul.*

In the beginning, when COVID shut down everything, defensive coordinator Jimmy McCleary asked, "Coach, what are you going to do?"

"The first thing I'm going to do," Cook said, "is go home and smear some lamb's blood over my door so when the plague comes, it will pass my house like in the *Ten Commandments*."

Whatever the circumstances, Cook keeps his sense of humor.

"I think we're going to stay home today," he joked with the organizer of the Jamboree.

The Pios were up against Acadiana High, 5A state champs the previous two years. Up to 2022, high schools in Louisiana were classified 1A through 5A based on the number of students. With approximately 1,700 students, Acadiana was 5A, Notre Dame 2A. Schools are now organized by divisions with Division I the largest schools and Division IV the smallest. Notre Dame is in Division III.

"Main focus is to survive," Cook confided to an observer. "If we all get on the bus, I'll feel it was a good night."

Acadiana scored a touchdown early and made it a significant one at the end with a goal-line stand to win 7–0. "Go toe-to-toe with the best team in the state and all we got was an ice bag on the shoulder," Cook said.

He had a good laugh over a comment during the game by sophomore guard Matt Brown. "Coach, I took your advice," Matt said. "If you don't know what you're doing, hit somebody."

The Pios had no starters returning on offense and only five on defense. With so many newcomers, it was going to be challenging for the 2021 team to meet the expectations set by their predecessors. One day Jimmy McCleary was lamenting the difficulties ahead.

"Mac, you can't stop preaching," Cook said. "You can't stop fighting the fight. Look what Jesus Christ faced. And he was trying to get everybody to go his way. At least he could do a miracle to get his point across. We can't, Mac. We have no miracles to perform."

"I've got to write that down," Mac said.

He called Cook later that day. "Coach, tell me that again. I didn't write it down."

Hurricane Ida threatened to wipe out the season opener against Southside. Ida veered east of Lafayette, where the game was played but the start was still delayed by a lightning storm.

"The beauty about coaching the Pios the last twenty-four years," Cook began his pregame speech, "is that it didn't matter what the circumstances were—cold, hot, wet, dry, delayed, whatever—the Pios always showed up. And they always played their ass off and pounded the opponents as best as they could. You know what we've got to do. Play every play—forty-eight minutes."

The players ran onto the field as Cook slowly followed, memories of playing championship games in the Superdome top of mind.

"I always stay behind," he said. "The first time we played in the Dome, I ran all the way to the forty-yard line."

Cook stopped and asked himself: "What am I doing?"

He was asking the same question shortly before kickoff when lightning forced the players to take shelter for two hours. Cook made a brief visit, sitting on the mats with them. Hardly a sound was made as quarterback Nicholas Swacker and tailback Lucas Simon reviewed the play call script.

Swacker wound up completing thirteen of nineteen passes for 183 yards and two touchdowns and Simon rushed 118 yards for two scores to pace the Pios to a 26–14 victory.

Afterward, Cook met with the team in the end zone, some of the players forming a line for him to walk through.

"My time is running down," he told them. "So, I'm trying to enjoy every moment watching you guys fly around and have some fun. Looked like y'all had a good time out there tonight. Got after their ass and stuffed them. We made some plays. I'm really, really proud of you guys. Great job. Let's get our prayer, get on the bus, and get our tails home."

The players knelt in a circle with their coach, arms around each other, as they recited the Lord's Prayer. It was a touching moment, their love and caring for each other glowing like a lighthouse.

"He has a great gentleness about him, and he doesn't come off as 'I know more than you,' even though he does know more than you," said Kevin Foote, a sportswriter and sports talk show host. "He's the greatest coach in the history of our area but he never acts that way. Everyone loves him."

COVID reared its ugly head over the next two weeks.

Sulphur High had one player test positive for COVID, requiring the school to forfeit the game.

The Pios played their homecoming game against Comeaux as planned, but none of the players attended the dance that followed because of the risk of getting COVID and being quarantined for ten days.

"Do what you think is best," Cook told the players.

They voted unanimously to sit out the dance. "We've worked too hard the past four years to throw it away," Karson Broussard explained. "There were bigger things ahead of us that we were thinking about."

In beating Comeaux, another 5A school, the Pios discovered a new tailback to back up Simon—Jake Brouillette.

"Brouillette was a nice surprise," Cook admitted after the converted cornerback rushed for eighty-three yards on seventeen carries in his first game at the position. "He looked like he'd been doing it a long time."

The Pios' schedule is front-loaded with bigger schools, providing stiffer competition while accumulating team points for "playing up," ensuring a higher seed for the post-season playoffs.

Up next was Teurlings Catholic, a 4A school in Lafayette, where Cook's older sister, Josette Cook Surratt, is a speech teacher and a coach with more state and national titles than he's won. "You're not the Cook with the most championships," Louie is reminded when the archrivals meet.

Louie and Josette played along with Scott Brazda of KATC-TV in Lafayette, who wanted to have fun with the rivalry for a story he was doing.

"Say you get lucky and win this game," Brazda said. "Are you going to call Josette the next day and talk about the game or will you call her and talk about everything but?"

"I'd probably be more inclined to call her if we don't win," Louie said. "Although she bleeds Cook blood, there's a lot of Teurlings' blood in there."

"Louie, just say these few words: I love my sister."

"I love my sister."

"But I wouldn't mind getting one more point than she has," Brazda prompted.

"I wouldn't mind turning up that Teurlings' blood in her system a little bit with a win," he ad-libbed.

Later, Cook tallied up his record against Teurlings—19–5. "We beat 'em the last six times, which should never happen 'cause they are three times the size school we are, but we've been able to get on them a little bit. They're going to be ready to play 'cause obviously they're tired of us beating 'em."

Sonny Charpentier was the head coach at Teurlings for twenty-two years. He retired in 2016, saying: "The wins didn't add up to the losses."

Cook was quoting Sonny after the Pios were handed their first loss of the season, a sound 34–21 whipping.

"They got a few easy ones," Cook said, referring to a seventy-nine-yard touchdown pass and a pair of sixty-three-yarders that led to scores. "I didn't figure it would be quite that easy."

"We've got a tough, hard-working group of kids," Mac said. "Everything that we practiced, everything that we saw, we did well. Anything that looked different, it was Katy bar the door."

Cook and Mac have coached together for twenty-five years—longer than most people are married these days. Over a long season that begins with workouts in January, they often find solace in reciting lines from their favorite movies.

"We sit here and laugh and laugh," Mac said. "Half of it is probably because we're worn-out tired."

"What has happened here?" Cook asked, mimicking Rev. LaSalle in *The Life and Times of Judge Roy Bean*. "They are a stench and an abomination. I got a shovel if you don't."

"They were some bad men," Mac quoted Judge Bean, quickly adding Rev. LaSalle's response, "Vengeance is mine, sayeth the Lord!"

In unison, they repeat Judge Bean: "It was."

Mac's favorite exchange in the film is when Judge Bean asked outlaw Big Bart Jackson, "What kind of talk is that for a man of strong moral fiber?" Big Bart replied: "I've slowly come unraveled, Judge."[1]

Mac may have felt that way after the Teurlings' aerial assault on the Pios' defense for 423 yards, but they regrouped to hold Cecilia, another 4A school, to thirty-seven yards of total offense in a 13–3 victory.

The Pios sailed past Welsh, 47–7, the next week in their district opener, setting up a showdown with Lafayette Christian Academy (LCA), a dominant force in Louisiana high school football with four straight state championships.

LCA was in a 2A district with a 4A-caliber team that included at least three players headed to NCAA Division 1 football programs. That was too much talent for the Pios to overcome in a 24–10 loss.

The *Acadiana Advocate* story on the game had an unusual twist as it focused on the coaches' admiration for each other instead of the contest itself.

"Everybody wants to talk about their good players and all the talent they have, but they never get the credit for how well they're coached," Cook said of LCA head coach Trev Faulk, a former linebacker at LSU who played two years in the NFL with the St. Louis Cardinals.

Faulk reciprocated: "Coach Cook is a legend in our state. I personally have spent a lot of time with him over the years. He has helped me become the coach I am, and he has a blueprint for what a program should look like and how to run a program."[2]

This mutual respect has its roots in the 2016 season when Tyler Shelvin, a Black NFL-sized defensive tackle with potential to match, played for Notre Dame.

Faulk, who's also Black, coached Shelvin at Northside, a high school in Lafayette with discipline problems at the time that caused Faulk to resign and Shelvin to transfer to Notre Dame. Faulk eventually ended up at LCA.

Faulk steered his five-star college prospect to Notre Dame as he believed Cook was best suited to pick up where he left off. So did Tyler's grandmother, Deborah Silas.

"I knew he was an excellent coach and that Notre Dame's football team had won state, but I had never met him," Deborah said. "Once I did, oh, my God. He's the best. He cares for his students."

How much he cares was apparent on her first visit with Tyler to Notre Dame.

"I know his daddy, momma, and you want him over here, but what about Tyler?" Cook asked Deborah. "I'm going to find out."

Cook and Tyler met by the weight room. "I talked to everybody else who wants you over here. What do you want to do?"

"Coach, I'd like to come."

"You sure?"

Cook explained what was required to wear Notre Dame's red helmet.

Tyler agreed, and Cook got him a customized helmet and pads because of his size.

"He talked to me every day, made sure I was comfortable, made sure I was straight," Tyler said. "You have to grind when you're playing for Coach Cook. He's going to make sure the job is complete and is done the right way."

Tyler, at six-foot-three, weighed about 360 pounds when he got to Notre Dame for his senior season in 2016. He was down to 340 by the end of the Pios summer workouts.

Tyler's father, Germole, observed one of the early morning sessions and said to Cook, "He's done more today than he did the whole time he was at Northside. I wish I'd had him here as a freshman."

"That wouldn't have been good," Cook replied.

"What do you mean?" Germole asked.

"If he would've been over here working for four years like our guys, it'd be criminal," Cook deadpanned. "And then, they'd get him for manslaughter."

Tyler didn't always look like the state's top college recruit. "But when he cut it loose, he was way better than anybody else," Cook said.

"Coach Cook doesn't care what color you are, how much money you got, he just doesn't care," Deborah said. "It's just about the game and making the child comfortable with the surroundings of football and all the accolades that come with it. He's a very unique individual when it comes to coaching."

Tyler played on LSU's 2019 national championship team and was selected by the Cincinnati Bengals in the fourth round of the 2021 NFL draft. He's the first player coached by Cook at Notre Dame to make it to the NFL.

"Tyler had already been offered a full scholarship at LSU, so he knew what he needed to do to keep that promise to Coach Orgeron [Ed Orgeron, LSU's head football coach at the time]," Deborah said. "He fought tooth-and-nail. Tyler was ready."

Tyler was prepared because of the close relationship between Faulk and Cook and their willingness to work together on his behalf.

That closeness was obvious when they embraced at midfield after LCA beat Notre Dame in 2021. "I have nothing but love and respect for you, Coach," Faulk said. "Let's do it again in New Orleans."

While Cook liked Faulk's idea of going to New Orleans for the state championship game, he wasn't too keen about playing LCA again. "First downs were victories for us," he said. "It was an uphill climb all the way."

The Pios rebounded to blank Catholic High of New Iberia 41–0, prompting Cook to recall the time he told the team if the bus gets to the game, they were going to win. The situation was the same for the last two regular-season games in 2021. The Pios' buses arrived safely, and they coasted to 55–0 and 41–6 victories.

The Pios earned the number 2 seed in the divisional playoffs behind LCA and a first-round bye. This had Cook yearning for the Good Old Days when teams had to win four or five straight weeks to be state champs. They needed three wins this time around.

"It's a shame to say, it's the haves and the have-nots," he said. "There's no in-between anymore. Everybody is getting into the playoffs."

Slightly more than two-thirds of the football-playing high schools in Louisiana made the playoffs in 2021, leading Ken Trahan of the website, CrescentCitySport.com, to conclude: "The days of playing well, fighting and earning a playoff spot are long gone, barring any significant change in the future and there is certainly no confidence, at least from our perspective, that this will ever occur."[3]

"The satisfaction of a win is not what it used to be," Cook lamented. "Maybe it's because we're supposed to win all our games."

The Pios were heavily favored to beat St. Thomas Aquinas in the quarterfinals, and they did, 42–7. But the win came at a steep price—season-ending injuries to tailback Lucas Simon and backup quarterback Aidan Mouton.

Simon was the team's leading rusher with 821 yards on 116 carries and fifteen touchdowns. He was a decoy on a screen pass play when he fractured his right foot. "Felt like a rubber band popped in the bottom of my foot," he said.

The injury to Simon was particularly costly because he also was a reliable placekicker and punter, consistently booming the ball into the end zone on kickoffs. Mouton suffered a concussion late in the game.

"If Swack gets hurt, we're done," Cook said of quarterback Nicholas Swacker going into the Pios' semifinal game against the St. Charles Catholic Comets.

Swack resembled "The Leaning Tower of Pisa," the top of his lean, six-foot-three frame tilted forward by a sixty-degree curvature of his spine called spondylolisthesis. He had surgery to straighten it after the season.

Cook considered retiring prior to the 2021 season. "He was one of the reasons I came back. I wanted to coach Swack."

Nicholas's father, David, played briefly for Cook at Crowley High and coached with him both at Crowley and Notre Dame. Cook even helped David get a job writing sports at a Lafayette newspaper.

Young Swack put in extra time preparing for his turn at quarterback. "I'd be leaving school and go by the practice field and there would be Swack throwing the ball," Cook said. "I thought Swack could do a good job. So, I wanted to stick around and help him."

After reviewing the videotape of the St. Charles offense, Jimmy Mac commented, "It's like playing yourself."

The Comets entered the game with a 9–0 record and seven shutouts, including four straight. "St. Charles is good," Cook said. "It's going to be a war."

In his pregame speech to the players, Cook repeated a story he'd told before other big games. "There was a gentleman who was faced with

Nicholas Swacker was one of the reasons why Louie Cook decided to continue coaching after the COVID pandemic. "I wanted to coach Swack," he said of the quarterback who had to wait until his senior season in 2021 to start. Nicholas's father, David, played for Cook at Crowley High and coached with him at Notre Dame. Nicholas guided the Pios to a 9–3 record and the state playoff semifinals, completing 57.5 percent of his passes for 1,448 yards and ten touchdowns. *Photo by Christell Faul.*

fightin' for his life—life or death situation—in a hospital, who was told the only time to get up out of bed was to go to the bathroom if he had to.

"His doctor walked in and said, 'Going to do this surgery on you tomorrow. If you want to shower and get cleaned up, you can go ahead and do that.' The man said: 'Doc, I fought in World War II and every time we got ready to go into battle, we just went how we were. And we cleaned up after the fight.'

"He was fighting for his life. I know it to be a true story. I was standing in the room next to the guy. It was a long time ago when my dad faced his second open-heart surgery."

Cook paused for a moment: "We fight for another week. We fight for our football lives tonight. We're going to make plays for God's glory and for your teammates. We'll cover kicks as best we can. We'll run kicks back as best we can. We'll block best we can. We'll tackle best we can because that's what we're trained to do for each other.

"And we're going to do it for forty-eight minutes and not worry about what's on the board or anything other than getting our job done. Play with everything you have from your heart, your soul, and your mind to make the plays that have to be made. Play as hard as you can play, as long as you can play. Do that for one another."

St. Charles returned the opening kickoff seventy-three yards to set up its first touchdown less than three minutes into the game.

The Pios were without their starting tailback, fullback, and one of their offensive linemen. "We need some wrinkles because they're going to be on our ass," Cook told offensive line coach Gus Cormier.

He pulled a double pass out of his bag of wrinkles. Tailback Jake Brouillette lined up for a direct snap with Swacker split out wide. Brouillette tossed the ball to Swacker, who launched a missile to wide receiver Zach Lamm for a seventy-four-yard gain. Two plays later Swacker ran it in from the three-yard line.

The Comets tacked on seven points to take a 14–7 lead into intermission. "Need a few more tricks," Cook said to his wife, Faye, as he headed to the locker room.

"Keep fighting the fight, we'll get something going and get back in this thing," Cook encouraged the team. "It ain't over yet. We'll find out a little bit more about ourselves right here."

The Pios used another wrinkle, a direct snap formation featuring slashing runs by Brouillette, to get the offense rolling in the second half, eventually scoring on Swacker's eight-yard touchdown pass to Joe Frank. The point-after-touchdown kick failed, allowing the Comets to stay on top, 14–13.

St. Charles responded with a field goal to make it 17–13 and then staved off the Pios' comeback attempts, which were hampered by a concussion that Brouillette suffered in the fourth quarter. "We just wanted one more week," Cook said to Faye after the game.

Brouillette, the cornerback-turned-tailback, finished the season rushing for 725 yards on ninety-seven carries, a 7.5-yard average. Swacker completed 57.5 percent of his passes for 1,448 yards and ten touchdowns.

It's a tradition at Notre Dame for the players to gather around a statue of Mary in front of the school and recite the Lord's Prayer.

Swacker addressed his teammates before they prayed: "I know this isn't how we thought it would go down but it's not how everybody else thought it would go down either. Going into the season we were doubted like crazy—too small, too young, too inexperienced. Regardless of the score, this was the most fun, and we seniors thank you all. I know Garrison is looking down and smiling because that's all he wanted was for us, to have fun and play hard, and that's what we did."

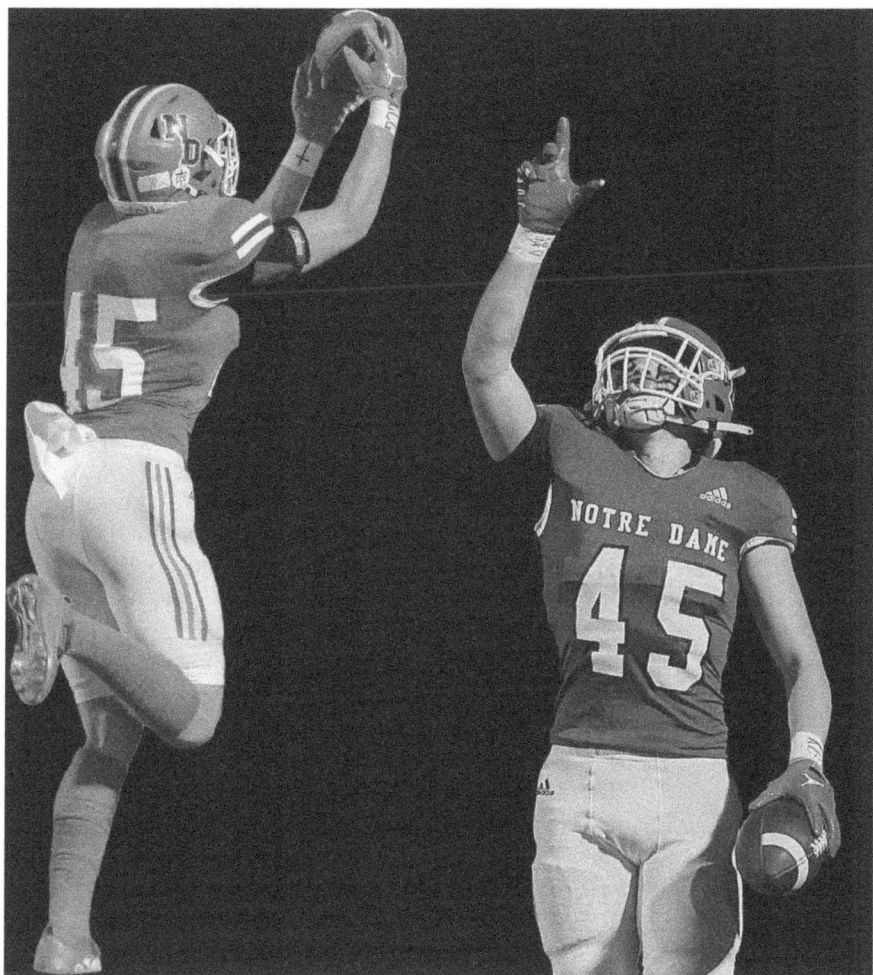

On senior night in 2022, Notre Dame tight end Grady Faulk paid tribute to his former teammate, Garrison Gautreaux, by wearing his jersey no. 45 and initials, GCG, on his helmet and taped wrists. Grady did his late pal proud, scoring on a thirty-yard pass from quarterback Aidan Mouton to start the game and then pointing toward the sky. Grady ended up with five catches for ninety-seven yards as Notre Dame whipped previously unbeaten Welsh High, 56–28, to win the District 5-2A title. *Photos, left to right, by Jason Faul and J. C. Orillion.*

Fast forward to the last regular-season game in 2022. Grady Faulk wanted to honor his friend, Garrison, on senior night by wearing his no. 45 jersey. "I wanted him to be remembered—put him back into everybody's head."

Garrison Gautreaux "meant a lot to me and a lot of other people," said Glenn Hunter Jr., a friend and fellow defensive end on the Notre Dame High football team. After Garrison's tragic death on May 16, 2021, Hunter did this drawing of Garrison to keep his memory alive. *Courtesy of Glenn Hunter Jr.*

Only a handful of people knew what Faulk was doing. Garrison's parents were aware as they granted their permission, but Grady's mom and dad expected their son to be wearing his usual no. 6. "I wanted to surprise them by wearing his number because he was close to the family," Faulk said.

The passage of time since Garrison's death caused Faulk to make some changes in his life, including taking his Catholic faith more seriously. "There's a plan," he said. "God didn't take him for no reason."

Faulk taped his wrists, printing the initials of a cousin, Kennedy Brooke Thompson, on his left wrist and GCG for Garrison Cole Gautreaux on his right. Kennedy had died Grady's freshman year.

On the Pios' first play of the game, the six-foot-four Faulk caught a perfectly thrown pass from quarterback Aidan Mouton for a thirty-yard touchdown.

Faulk tapped his chest two times, once each for Kennedy and Garrison. He kissed his right fist and then looked up and pointed skyward. "I had two angels on top watching my every move," he said.

It was an emotional moment for Faulk, who shed a few tears after making the catch. He did what he set out to do—keep the memory of his best friend alive.

Epilogue

It was the perfect ending. The 2022 Louisiana High School Athletic Association (LHSAA) football playoff brackets were set up for it to happen.

Top-seeded Isidore Newman High School of New Orleans would play third-seeded Notre Dame of Acadia Parish in the Select Division III championship game at the Superdome.

Arch Manning, the most famous high school quarterback on the planet, would face Coach Louie Cook's undersized, overachieving sons of crawfish farmers, the most successful prep team in Louisiana from 2013 through 2021, winning 93 percent of its regular-season games.[1]

It was the kind of match-up a Hollywood scriptwriter might imagine.

Arch was the nation's most prized high-school football recruit of the 2023 class and the latest and greatest from America's first family of quarterbacks. His grandfather, Archie, and uncles, Peyton and Eli, are NFL legends.

By comparison, the Notre Dame Pios are a bunch of unknown, gritty kids right out of *Rudy*, the movie about a boy who fulfilled his dream of playing in a game for Notre Dame University. There was even a title for the script: *Rudy II*.

The only person thinking about all this was another dreamer—me.

Cook and his defensive wizard, Jimmy (Mac) McCleary, had more important things to do in preparing for the Pios' first playoff game against Lake Charles College Prep (LCCP), a Class 3A public charter school loaded with Division 1 college prospects.

"When the brackets came out, I knew we were in trouble," Mac said.

Never mind the Trailblazers' 6–6 mark and 19th seed. They were bigger, faster, and more athletic than the Pios. "They're LCA all over," Mac noted, referring to powerful Lafayette Christian Academy, which moved up two classifications in 2022 and still finished runner-up in its division.

The Pios had a first-round bye so Cook and Mac went to see the Trailblazers stomp their opponent by nineteen points.

"We knew we had an uphill battle," Cook said. "We don't match up well."

The Pios entered the playoffs with an 8–2 record, both early-season losses to bigger schools.

The Trailblazers were as good as Cook feared, jumping to a 13–0 first-quarter lead. "They're running up and down the yard on us," he admitted. "We've got no answers."

At half-time, they were ahead, 20–7. "I started thinking about washing my car the next week and wondering where all the stuff is at my house," Cook quipped later.

Thanksgiving Day was coming soon. In twenty-six years at Notre Dame, Cook's teams played the day after Thanksgiving twenty-one times. "Dumbass coaches work their ass off so they can work on their days off," he joked.

It looked like he was going to have plenty of time to wash his new Hyundai Santa Cruz. And then, it started raining—touchdowns. Altogether, there were six in the second half, four by the Pios and two by the Trailblazers. By the time the downpour ended, the score was tied 34–34, forcing overtime.

"It has been so long since we've played an overtime game, I forgot how it went," Mac said.

"It's been twenty-two years since we played one," Cook added.

In overtime, each team gets the ball on the ten-yard line. Whoever scores the most points in an overtime period wins.

The Trailblazers scored a touchdown on their third play to go ahead 40–34. With two missed extra-point kicks in regulation, they went for two points and failed.

The Pios needed a TD and successful extra-point kick to win. On third down from the 10, quarterback Aidan Mouton rolled to the left and back to the right before tight end Grady Faulk got open in the end zone. "I was hoping he'd turn around and look at me," Faulk said.

Mouton fired a strike that Faulk crouched down to catch. Kicker Cameron Fuselier split the uprights to seal the win.

"What was the score?" Cook asked his son, Jeff.

"41–40," Jeff replied. "There were some big-time plays."

One was the only score by the Pios in the first half, a thirty-one-yard touchdown pass from Mouton to wide receiver Teddy Menard.

Notre Dame players form an arch of honor for their beloved coach, Louie Cook, as he joined them in the end zone after a game to recite the Lord's Prayer together. Cook turned the tables on his players following their come-from-behind overtime 41–40 victory over Lake Charles College Prep in the second round of the 2022 state playoffs. "I'm going to do the bowing tonight," he said. "You guys are awesome." *Photo by J. C. Orillion.*

Tailback Jake Brouillette scored three times in the Pios' second-half comeback, including a forty-one-yard run to give the Pios their first lead, 27–26, about four minutes into the fourth quarter. One minute later safety Kade Cooley intercepted a pass and returned it forty-four yards for another touchdown, making it 34–26. It took the Trailblazers just eighty-one seconds to even the score.

"They gave us their best shot and we took every bullet," Mac said.

The Trailblazers totaled 592 yards on offense compared to 307 for the Pios.

"They outplayed us everywhere but on the scoreboard," Cook said. "It was a mismatch. The only thing they couldn't match is the heart that our guys got. You can't block that; you can't tackle that."

David Berken, a senior on the 2003 Notre Dame team that went to the Dome, immediately sent Cook a text: "Pios found a way to win."

Cook shared the message with the players. "Not many teams could've done what you guys did," he said. "You just kept battling, finding ways to make plays."

Seth Lewis, a sports reporter for KATC television in Lafayette, wasn't surprised. "No coincidence that Louie Cook's club weathered the storm," he told viewers.

In the quarterfinals the next week, the Pios cruised past the Episcopal School of Baton Rouge, 47–0, with Brouillette running wild for 211 yards and three touchdowns on only eleven carries. "In the next round, surprise, surprise: St. Charles," Seth Lewis announced.

"Death, taxes, and Notre Dame versus St. Charles Catholic in the LHSAA high school football semifinals," wrote Matt Sims of CrescentCitySports.com. "The three guarantees in life."[2]

The schools are virtually clones of each other, playing smash-mouth defense and grinding foes down on offense.

The first time they tangled in the semis in 2016, St. Charles scored on a fake field goal, a blocked punt, and a stripped fumble return to prevail, 21–10. The Comets nipped the Pios 24–22 in 2020 and 17–13 in 2021.

Cook reminded his players of the Pios' 27–7 victory over the Comets in the second round of the 2012 playoffs. "We went over to their place and beat 'em. They were the defending champs."

The Comets were again the defending champs, and the game was on their home field in LaPlace, Louisiana, thirty miles from New Orleans.

"It's our time!" Cook rallied the team.

"The teams are pretty evenly matched," he said later. "Last year [2021] we had a first down at the seventeen-yard line, and we couldn't finish it off. Two years ago [2020] we had a chance to tie on a two-point play. We didn't get it done."

He confided to a friend: "Have to admit the last couple of years we played them in the semis, it stung. But not as much because we would've played LCA again. Hate to play those guys."

Injuries had the Pios limping to the finish line in 2021. "The Good Lord, He knows what He's doing," Cook said.

In 2022, the Pios came up short again, 17–10, managing only a field goal and a touchdown on a fifty-nine-yard blocked punt return by linebacker Johann Hensgens with slightly more than three minutes left in the game.

The Comets limited the Pios to 195 yards total offense—83 rushing and 112 passing. The closest the Pios got to the end zone was the seven-yard line. The Pios were almost as good on defense, holding the Comets to 260 yards, but their touchdowns came on a 32-yard run and 40-yard pass play.

"Both defenses played lights out," Cook said. "Offensively, we weren't good enough. They got the edge on us right now. Can't seem to get that step on 'em. Maybe one day we'll get back on 'em."

St. Charles went to the Dome and won the state title for the second straight year.

Meanwhile, Arch Manning and his Newman High mates didn't fare any better than the Pios. In fact, they were eliminated in the quarterfinals.

The morning after the loss to St. Charles, Cook was in his office. "I've come to realize that I hate losing more than I enjoy winning," he said wistfully.

Cook was feeling badly but not for himself. "This is the first senior class that didn't go to the Dome," he lamented.

The following Monday Cook addressed the team in the school's chapel.

He talked about coaching in the 2008 US Army All-American Bowl, an all-star game in San Antonio, Texas, featuring the best high school football players in the country.

One of the players was quarterback Andrew Luck, who became a two-time All-American at Stanford University and star in the NFL for the Indianapolis Colts.

While coaching the all-stars Cook noticed that few of them were vastly superior to some of the players he coached at Crowley and Notre Dame high schools. "The difference was what we do at five-foot-ten, 175 pounds, those guys were doing at six-foot-three, 210," he said.

The receivers in the All-American Bowl were bigger and faster. But Cook didn't think they were a "whole lot better" or played any harder.

"That's the beauty of high school football," he said. "There's an innocence. You can be five-foot-six and 150 pounds and still be a helluva high school football player."

Cook mentioned a defensive end for the Pios (Steven Bruner) who had two arms but couldn't use one of them because of injuries sustained in a car accident. He taped the damaged arm to his chest, put his shoulder pads over it, and started every game as a senior in 2002.

"That's what I love about coaching high school football," Cook said. "I had my chances in college. Where did I end up? I ended up here. I've got no regrets."

He motioned toward his assistant coaches in the back of the chapel. "All these coaches are the same. They could get other jobs and make more money than they can make here. This is where we want to be . . . with you guys."

The 2022 team added to the school's football legacy, finishing with a 10–3 record.

Jake Brouillette, who switched from cornerback to tailback the year before, rushed for 1,258 yards and twenty-five of his twenty-seven touchdowns.

Quarterback Aidan Mouton passed for 1,097 yards and thirteen touchdowns despite breaking a bone in his throwing hand in the season opener and missing five games.

Wide receiver Teddy Menard caught forty-six passes for 702 yards and thirteen touchdowns while tight end Grady Faulk had forty-one catches for 721 yards and six scores.

Linebackers Jackson Casanova and Johann Hensgens paced the defense with seventy-nine and sixty-seven tackles, respectively. Safety Kade Cooley had six pass interceptions and cornerback Tripp Mixon five.

Cameron Fuselier, the team's hard-working placekicker and punter, went from erratic to highly reliable, the kind of progress kids often make under Cook's tutelage.

Going into the 2023 season, his fiftieth in coaching, Cook will be seventy-two years old. With 392 career wins, he will likely hit the 400 mark by the end of the year.

"Hope you coach to 100," Nick Gossen urged him one day. Nick was a member of the first Notre Dame team in 1967.

Cook's three sons want him to keep going. "If he's healthy and feels good, he needs to be out there," Jeff said, citing the milestones of fifty years coaching and four hundred wins.

Faye Cook is on board no matter what her husband does. "From the get-go, it's whatever makes him happy. If he wants to do it, go for it. If he's had enough, I'm good."

The two-hour bus ride back to Crowley from LaPlace gave Cook time to ponder his future and the St. Charles game, but that wasn't top of mind in his comments to the team in the Notre Dame gym around midnight.

"No one in here is defined who they are by a football game," Cook began. "When I said class and character always wins out, I wasn't necessarily talking about the scoreboard."

Most of the players were sprawled around him on the floor.

"Life is not always going to give you everything you want," he continued. "You faced a lot of adversity tonight. Some of y'all handled it perfectly. Some of you got a little flustered. You've got to learn to deal with adversity because the adversity you faced tonight is nothing compared to what you might face down the line when it's more important than whether you won or lost a football game."

Cook thanked the players for their dedication and hard work. "I feel really good about what's going to happen to you guys. That's what it's all about."

He ended by saying: "Love you guys."

Now, that's the perfect ending.

Appendix

Lewis Cook Jr.
Career Coaching Record

Year	School	Wins	Losses
1977	Rayne	2	8
1978	Rayne	6	4
1979	Rayne	7	4
1980	Rayne	6	5
1981–84	Assistant coach–USL		
1985	Crowley	6	5
1986	Crowley	10	2
1987	Crowley	9	3
1988	Crowley	10	2
1989*	Crowley	13	2
1990	Crowley	8	3
1991#	Crowley	11	4
1992–95	Assistant coach–USL		
1996#	Crowley	12	3
1997	Notre Dame	10	3
1998	Notre Dame	9	3
1999	Notre Dame	10	3
2000*	Notre Dame	15	0
2001	Notre Dame	11	3
2002	Notre Dame	11	2
2003#	Notre Dame	14	1
2004#	Notre Dame	12	3
2005#	Notre Dame	11	2
2006	Notre Dame	12	2
2007	Notre Dame	11	1
2008#	Notre Dame	13	1

Year	School	Wins	Losses
2009*	Notre Dame	15	0
2010	Notre Dame	13	1
2011	Notre Dame	8	4
2012#	Notre Dame	12	2
2013	Notre Dame	11	1
2014	Notre Dame	9	3
2015*	Notre Dame	14	0
2016	Notre Dame	12	1
2017#	Notre Dame	11	1
2018*	Notre Dame	13	0
2019	Notre Dame	8	2
2020	Notre Dame	8	2
2021	Notre Dame	9	3
2022	Notre Dame	10	3

TOTALS			
Rayne	4 years	21	21
Crowley	8 years	79	24
Notre Dame	26 years	292	47
Overall	**38 years**	**392**	**92**

*State champs
#State runner-up
Note: USL stands for University of Southwestern Louisiana (now University of Louisiana at Lafayette)

Notes

INTRODUCTION

1. *Los Angeles Times*, January 19, 1986, Part III, 21.

CHAPTER 1

1. *The Daily Advertiser* (Lafayette, LA), September 2, 2012, 8D.

CHAPTER 2

1. Link to *Andy Griffith Show* quote: https://www.quotes.net/mquote/881818.
2. *Crowley (LA) Post-Signal*, November 17, 1967, 6.
3. *Crowley Signal*, March 17, 1921, 1.
4. Ken Trahan, "Bloated, Flawed State Football Playoffs Begin with 40 Losing Teams," *Crescent City Sports*, November 9, 2021, https://crescentcitysports.com/bloated-flawed-state-football-playoffs-begin-with-40-losing-teams/.

CHAPTER 3

1. C. S. Lewis, *The Screwtape Letters* (New York: HarperOne, 1996), 61.

CHAPTER 4

1. *Rayne (LA) Acadian-Tribune*, February 16, 1967, 7.
2. *Rayne Acadian-Tribune*, September 21, 1967, 4.
3. *Rayne Acadian-Tribune*, October 8, 1970, 7.

CHAPTER 6

1. *Lafayette (LA) Daily Advertiser*, November 16, 1981, 8.
2. *Lafayette Daily Advertiser*, November 10, 1981, 13.
3. *Lafayette Daily Advertiser*, November 10, 1981, 13.
4. *Lafayette Daily Advertiser*, October 25, 1981, 49.
5. *Lafayette Daily Advertiser*, September 11, 1983, 35.

CHAPTER 7

1. *Crowley (LA) Post-Signal*, September 8, 1985, 11.
2. *Crowley Post-Signal*, September 29, 1985, 15.
3. *Crowley Post-Signal*, November 15, 1985, 11.
4. *Lafayette (LA) Daily Advertiser*, November 22, 1986, 10.
5. *A Cannon Streaks across the Field*, https://youtu.be/KNImBsO4DrA.
6. *Lafayette Daily Advertiser*, November 27, 1986, 41.
7. *Lafayette Daily Advertiser*, February 11, 1987, 25.
8. *Crowley Post-Signal*, December 3, 1989, 12.
9. *Crowley Post-Signal*, December 3, 1989, 12.
10. *Lafayette Daily Advertiser*, December 10, 1989, 25.
11. *Lafayette Daily Advertiser*, December 15, 1991, 36.
12. *Lafayette Daily Advertiser*, December 15, 1991, 36.
13. *Lafayette Daily Advertiser*, December 15, 1991, 31.
14. *Lafayette Daily Advertiser*, December 15, 1991, 36.

CHAPTER 8

1. *Lafayette (LA) Daily Advertiser*, October 18, 1992, 17.
2. *Lafayette Daily Advertiser*, October 18, 1992, 18.
3. *Lafayette Daily Advertiser*, October 18, 1992, 18.
4. *Lafayette Daily Advertiser*, October 13, 1992, 17.
5. *Lafayette Daily Advertiser*, October 25, 1992, 17.
6. *Lafayette Daily Advertiser*, August 8, 1993, 31.
7. *Lafayette Daily Advertiser*, September 12, 1993, 21.

CHAPTER 9

1. *Crowley (LA) Post-Signal*, March 2, 1993, 1.
2. *Crowley Post-Signal*, February 18, 1996, 11.
3. *Lafayette (LA) Daily Advertiser*, September 7, 1996, 33.

CHAPTER 10

1. *Lafayette (LA) Daily Advertiser*, December 12, 2008, 34.

CHAPTER 11

1. *Lafayette (LA) Daily Advertiser*, November 27, 1999, 22.

CHAPTER 12

1. *Crowley (LA) Post-Signal*, December 12, 2004, 1.
2. *Lafayette (LA) Daily Advertiser*, December 2, 2000, 7.
3. *Lafayette Daily Advertiser*, December 8, 2000, 21.
4. *Lafayette Daily Advertiser*, December 9, 2000, 20.
5. *Lafayette Daily Advertiser*, December 9, 2000, 20.
6. *Lafayette Daily Advertiser*, December 6, 2008, 27.
7. *Lafayette Daily Advertiser*, December 6, 2008, 30.
8. *Lafayette Daily Advertiser*, December 14, 2008, 36.
9. *Crowley Post-Signal*, December 6, 2009, 12A.

CHAPTER 13

1. *Lafayette (LA) Daily Advertiser,* December 12, 2009, 31.
2. *Crowley (LA) Post-Signal*, November 24, 1967, 5.
3. *Sports Illustrated*, September 13, 1971, 66.
4. *Lafayette Daily Advertiser,* December 12, 2003, 14.
5. *Lafayette Daily Advertiser,* December 13, 2009, 42.

CHAPTER 15

1. Slight variation of quote widely attributed to Theodore Roosevelt, although in his autobiography he credits it to Squire Bill Widener of Widener's Valley, Virginia: TR Center—TR Quotes: Do what you can with what you've got where you are (theodore rooseveltcenter.org).

2. *Blue Bloods*, Season 4, Episode 17: "Knockout Game." https://www.tvfanatic.com/quotes/shows/blue-bloods/episodes/knockout-game/.

3. *Blue Bloods*, Season 5. https://www.cbs.com/recommended/photos/1004084/15-powerful-frank-reagan-quotes-from-season-5/4/.

CHAPTER 16

1. *The Daily Advertiser* (Lafayette, LA), December 19, 2019, B5.
2. Dusty Rhodes, "Hard Times" speech. YouTube: https://youtu.be/9py4aMK3aIU
3. *Crowley (LA) Post-Signal*, November 5, 2006, 1B.
4. *Crowley Post-Signal*, November 3, 2006, 9A.
5. *The Daily Advertiser*, December 7, 2017, C3.
6. *The Daily Advertiser*, December 7, 2017, C3.

CHAPTER 17

1. *The Daily Advertiser* (Lafayette, LA), December 8, 1989, 16.
2. *The Daily Advertiser*, May 19, 1990, B2.
3. *The Daily Advertiser*, August 26, 1993, 39.
4. *The Daily Advertiser*, September 24, 1991, 18.
5. *The Daily Advertiser*, November 20, 1994, 21.
6. *The Daily Advertiser*, April 23, 1995, 39.
7. *Minneapolis (MN) Star Tribune*, September 4, 1997, 34.
8. *The Daily Advertiser*, July 2, 1997, 6; *Crowley (LA) Post-Signal*, July 2, 1997, 1.
9. *The Daily Advertiser*, May 16, 1998, 4.
10. *Minneapolis Star Tribune*, December 19, 1997, 52.
11. *Minneapolis Star Tribune*, February 25, 1999, 30.
12. *Minneapolis Star Tribune*, August 26, 1998, 37.
13. *MedPageToday*, December 16, 2021, https://www.medpagetoday.com/neurology/generalneurology/96234.
14. "Gehrig Delivers His Famous Speech at Yankee Stadium," YouTube, https://youtu.be/nNLKPaThYkE.
15. "Gehrig delivers his famous speech."

CHAPTER 18

1. Quotes from *The Life and Times of Judge Roy Bean*. See https://www.imdb.com/title/tt0068853/.
2. *TheAdvocate.com (Acadiana Advocate)*, October 15, 2021, https://www.theadvocate.com/acadiana/sports/high_schools/lca-knights-pull-away-from-notre-dame-behind-more-big-plays-on-defense/article_426d83ea-2ddf-11ec-b126-2b48f388fe84.html

3. *CrescentCitySports.com*, November 9, 2021, https://crescentcitysports.com/ bloated-flawed-state-football-playoffs-begin-with-40-losing-teams/.

EPILOGUE

1. In 2013, the LHSAA designated private schools as select and public schools non-select and divided its football playoffs accordingly. Notre Dame and Isidore Newman were Class 2A/Select Division III schools in 2022.

2. *Crescent City Sports*, December 3, 2022, https://crescentcitysports.com/st-charles -catholic-earns-opportunity-for-repeat-by-downing-notre-dame-17-10/.

Index

About the Author

Gaylon H. White is the author of four books, *The Best Little Baseball Town in the World* (2021), *Left on Base in the Bush Leagues* (2019), *Singles and Smiles* (2018), *The Bilko Athletic Club* (2014), and coauthor with Ransom Jackson Jr. of *Handsome Ransom Jackson: Accidental Big Leaguer* (2016). All five books were published by Rowman & Littlefield.

Called "one of the best sports books of 2014" by Bruce Miles of the *Chicago Daily Herald*, *The Bilko Athletic Club* is a blast from the past revolving around beer-loving, home run–hitting Steve Bilko and the 1956 Los Angeles Angels of the old Pacific Coast League.

Accidental Big Leaguer covers the career of Ransom Jackson Jr., a two-time National League All-Star in the 1950s and the last Brooklyn Dodger to hit a home run. The book was a grand slam with Allen Berra of the *Chicago Tribune*, who wrote: "We can only hope that among today's players there's someone as sharp and funny as Handsome Ransom Jackson to remember them."

Singles and Smiles received the Negro Leagues Research Committee's Robert Peterson Recognition Award named after the author of the trailblazing book on Black baseball, *Only the Ball Was White*. *Singles and Smiles* traces the life of Artie Wilson, the greatest shortstop nobody heard of, from Birmingham, Alabama, where he was born in 1920 to Portland, Oregon, where he lived fifty-five years until his death in 2010 at the age of ninety.

"Meticulously researched and compellingly presented, *Left on Base in the Bush Leagues* is the best book on 1950s minor league baseball ever, a milestone worthy of sharing the same bookshelf with *The Glory of Their*

Times," according to Jim McConnell, author of the critically acclaimed biography *Bobo Newsom: Baseball's Traveling Man.*

The Best Little Baseball Town in the World prompted Kevin Kernan of the website *Ballnine*, to write: "The timing is perfect for this book considering what's happening currently with the minors. White can be the voice for baseball in small town America."

The Los Angeles–born White graduated in 1967 from the University of Oklahoma with a bachelor's degree in journalism-broadcasting. He was a sportswriter for the *Denver Post*, *Arizona Republic*, and *Oklahoma Journal* before working nearly forty years for such varied companies as Hallmark Cards, Inc., Goodyear Tire and Rubber Company, Control Data Corporation, and Eastman Chemical Company.

At Eastman, White worked closely with industrial designers and in 2015 the Industrial Designers Society of America selected him as one of its fifty most notable members from the past half-century

He and his wife, Mary, live in Kingsport, Tennessee. They have three children and seven grandchildren.

www.ingramcontent.com/pod-product-compliance
Lightning Source LLC
Chambersburg PA
CBHW030259100426
42812CB00002B/500